AFRICAN CHRISTIAN
MARRIAGE

African Christian Marriage

Benezeri Kisembo
Laurenti Magesa
and
Aylward Shorter

Geoffrey Chapman
London and Dublin

A Geoffrey Chapman book published by
Cassell & Collier Macmillan Publishers Ltd.,
35 Red Lion Square, London WC1R 4SG
and at Sydney, Auckland, Toronto, Johannesburg,
an affiliate of
Macmillan Publishing Co., Inc.,
New York

ISBN 0 225 66181 0

Printed in Great Britain by
The Camelot Press Ltd, Southampton

Contents

The Authors

Benezeri Kisembo

Born in 1944 in the Toro District of Uganda, Benezeri Kisembo read for a B.A. in Religious Studies, Sociology and Education at Makerere University, Kampala, from 1967 to 1970. Until 1971 he worked as Youth and Student Secretary of the (Anglican) Church of Uganda, Rwanda and Boga-Zaïre. In that year he commenced work for an M.A. in Religious Studies and was appointed Lecturer in Biblical Studies at Makerere University two years later. He continues to lecture in the Department of Religious Studies and Philosophy at Makerere. He also serves on the provincial Youth Committee and a number of other committees of the Church of Uganda. His wife, Lovey Baghaya, comes from a different ethnic group, the Basoga of Uganda. They were married in 1971 and have two children. Benezeri Kisembo has contributed to the *Occasional Research Papers in African Religions and Philosophies*, published by his University Department.

Laurenti Magesa

Laurenti Magesa was born in 1946 in the Musoma Region of Tanzania. He carried out his philosophical and theological studies at Ntungamo and Kipalapala Seminaries in Tanzania, and obtained the Diploma in Theology from Makerere University, Uganda. He was ordained a priest for the Roman Catholic Diocese of Musoma in 1974 and spent a year doing parish work there. In 1976 he was appointed lecturer in Dogmatic Theology at Kipalapala Seminary where he is still working. He has contributed a number of articles on theological subjects to periodicals in Africa and America and contributed a paper on African Liberation Theology to the Conference on Christianity in Independent Africa held at Jos Campus, Nigeria, in 1975. He also participated in the Churches' Research on Marriage in Africa, travelling to meetings in Uganda, Kenya and Malawi.

Aylward Shorter

After serving as an army officer in Kenya and Malaya, Aylward Shorter read Modern History at Queen's College Oxford. He joined the "White Fathers" missionary society in 1955, and was ordained priest in 1962 after studies in Ireland, Holland, Canada and Britain. After a year studying Missiology at the Gregorian University in Rome, he returned to Oxford to take the Diploma in Anthropology. He then did two years of fieldwork among the Kimbu of Tanzania for his doctoral thesis in Social Anthropology, presented to Oxford in 1968. Since then he has been lecturer in African Pastoral Anthropology at the Gaba Pastoral Institute, now situated in Eldoret, Kenya. For some years he was a part-time lecturer in Anthropology and Moderator of the Theology Diploma Examination at Makerere University in Uganda. He is a Consultor of the Vatican Secretariat for Non-Christians and a Member of a Family Research Committee set up by the Unit on Education and Renewal at the World Council of Churches.

Among his previously published books are: *Chiefship in Western Tanzania* (Oxford, 1972); *African Culture and the Christian Church* (Chapman, 1973); *East African Societies* (Routledge and Kegan Paul, 1973); *Prayer in the Religious Traditions of Africa* (O.U.P., Nairobi, 1975); and *African Christian Theology* (Chapman, 1975).

Acknowledgements

In the first place the authors wish to record their gratitude to the late Fr. Killian Flynn, O.F.M. Cap., Secretary-General of AMECEA, who was a driving-force at the start of the CROMIA project and who opened its planning meeting in 1971. They are also grateful to his successor, Bishop Vincent J. McCattley, who has offered continuous support and encouragement throughout the five years of the project. Next they wish to remember gratefully the enthusiasm of Professor Tjaard Hommes of Notre Dame University and the funds he obtained for the start of the project. They are equally grateful to the Right Reverend Desmond Tutu, formerly of the Theological Education Fund, later Dean of Johannesburg and now Bishop of Lesotho; to Mr. Ferdinand Luthiger of the Swiss Catholic Lenten Fund and to Monsignor W. Wissing and Fr. P. W. Fischer of Missio, all of whom helped to make the project financially possible.

Our thanks are due to Rev. Ralph Hatendi, Scripture Distribution Consultant of the United Bible Societies in the Africa Region and CROMIA Chairman; Rev. Canon Trevor D. Verryn of the Ecumenical Research Unit, Pretoria; Rev. George K. Mambo of the AACC, Nairobi; Rev. Dr. David Barrett of the Anglican Consultative Council; Dr. Norman Thomas of Mindolo Ecumenical Centre, and Fr. Adrian Hastings of St. Edmund's House, Cambridge, all of whom helped with the organization and conduct of meetings and research.

We are particularly grateful to Sister Agnes Baldwin of Limbe, the Franciscans of La Verna, Rev. W. P. Chibambo of Chilema and Rev. Christopher Carey of Trinity College, Nairobi, our hosts at various meetings. We are especially in the debt of

Monsignor F. Mkhori of the Malawi Catholic Secretariat for his kindness during our visits to Malawi.

We also record our indebtedness to Archbishop Donald Arden of Central Africa, Archbishop Joseph Fitzgerald of Bloemfontein, Archbishop Robert Selby-Taylor of Cape Town, Bishop Eliewaha Mshana of Pare, Dr. Leslie Clements of the WCC, and the Staff and Students of The Pastoral Institute of Eastern Africa, Gaba, during the years 1971–6, for their interest, help and encouragement. Our thanks are due to those who read the typescript of this report before publication: Archbishop Arden, Dr. Thomas and Canon Verryn, already mentioned, and Rev. Silas Ncozana of Malawi. Finally, a word of thanks to Mr. Francis A. Lubowa, Research Assistant of the AMECEA Research Department, who has seen CROMIA through from start to finish and who typed the manuscript for the publisher.

Foreword

Those of us, black and white, who have the privilege of serving the African Church thank God daily for its vitality, its generosity and its extraordinary power of growth, especially in the decade since independence.

Yet we have also known that there has been a worm in the bud. Adrian Hastings pointed to it when he remarked that the test of vitality of a Church was not the number of baptisms but Christian marriages, their number and their quality. In 1970 the Anglican Archbishops of Africa invited him to study this matter more deeply. *Christian Marriage in Africa* was the result.

The facts this brought into the open were bleak. In few places do more than half the Anglicans or Catholics marry in church, and a third of such marriages are likely to fail or turn polygamous. In parts of East Africa the number of marriages has halved in ten years. In the Anglican Church, between 7 and 23 people are confirmed for every couple married in church. This is one of the themes of this study:

In many places the Church is in a process of excommunicating itself. Does it need to do so? Is it being faithful to the spirit of Christ in doing so?

Most of the mass excommunications of the missionary era have been due to the refusal of the missionaries to recognize the way in which Africans have married from time immemorial. This to them was not marriage but "concubinage" or "customary union", to be replaced as soon as possible by the real thing. It was humbling therefore to learn from Hastings that until the eleventh century the Church's marriage liturgy was seen in Europe as an optional extra. Customary marriage (disguised now as engagement) continued throughout the Middle Ages to be regarded as the core of marriage, after which public opinion permitted intercourse—a pattern which is still normal in rural England.

We owe a great debt to the team which has produced this fascinating study, based on the living experience of hundreds of African married couples. This is what *is*, not what missionaries or theologians would like it to be. For the first time Africa itself speaks about something that lies at the heart of its own culture and of the Christian faith. It is now for the African Church to set a course for the future which will enable Christians to respond in their own way to the challenges of Christ without losing touch with the realities of daily life and without betraying the solid values of their own tradition.

✠ DONALD ARDEN
Archbishop of Central Africa

Introduction

1 *About this book*

This book is the final report of a five-year programme of research into the sociology and theology of marriage with special reference to East, Central and Southern Africa, and general reference to the whole African continent. The programme was known as The Churches' Research on Marriage in Africa (CROMIA), and its steering committee appointed the three co-authors to draw up this report for publication.

The research took place in eight countries of Africa.[1] More than two hundred people were directly involved in the organization and carrying out of the research, and at least 2,500 people were interviewed during the various phases of the project. At least sixteen Christian churches were involved directly or indirectly in the programme.[2] Twelve major research reports were commissioned, thirty-one theological position papers were written, and there were a number of pilot studies and incidental pieces of research from which the programme benefited. Besides the initial planning meeting held in Uganda, there were three theological colloquia in South Africa, Kenya and Malawi and two committee meetings.[3]

It is obviously impossible for a small book like this to represent adequately the whole mass of information and experience accumulated by such a project. The true and lasting results of the research and discussions are probably to be found in the dicoveries made by those who participated in them, rather than on the printed page, and it was a conscious aim of the project from the beginning that this should be so. Nevertheless, we hope that, through this book, we can reach the general reader, particularly the pastor, the religion teacher and the social worker, as well as the various levels of leadership in the churches, and give them some idea of the trends revealed and pursued by CROMIA. It is not the wish of the authors, nor of the committee they represent, to take decisions for anyone or for any church. We try, in this book, to present the facts and the current thinking in contemporary Africa. For too long Africa has been an object of research by outsiders. For too long Christian theology has been written for Africa by outsiders. This book represents an attempt by Africa to do her own socio-religious research and to respond theologically to her own social problems.

It is necessary to say something about the relationship of this report to that made by Adrian Hastings for five Anglican Archbishops of Africa in 1973. (*Christian Marriage in Africa*, London, SPCK). CROMIA was launched at almost the same moment that Hastings set about his survey.[4] Adrian Hastings made a very valuable contribution to the initial planning meeting of the project, and to a great extent determined its shape and scope. It was decided to concentrate on the same geographical area as Hastings and to follow his suggestions for further research. At the same time it was hoped that use could be made of information from other parts of Africa and the subjects of enquiry broadened to include topics which were not in Hastings' brief. In general therefore, Adrian Hastings provided CROMIA with a number of research hypotheses. These have been tested and modified accordingly. On several questions our research and discussions have provided further justification for the positions taken by Hastings. In several cases we have provided a wider range of pastoral options and have been led by the evidence of our research to emphasize a particular aspect among a number of alternatives proposed by Hastings. We have not attempted to improve on Hastings' excellent historical sketch of the theological positions adopted by the churches with regard to various pastoral problems concerning marriage.[5] This book, therefore, is not intended to replace the very important work of Adrian Hastings, but it is intended to carry his discussion a stage further on quite a number of points.

In calling our book *African Christian Marriage*, we do not wish to suggest that marriage is not primarily a universal, human reality. However, we do appreciate that there are concepts and presuppositions about marriage which are particular to the cultures of Africa. We also believe that, in the light of Christian faith, the reality of human marriage can be more fully understood and lived. The title of the research project was the subject of a certain amount of debate at the planning meeting and it was agreed that our interest was not simply in the marriage of Christians, but in the ways in which a Christian understanding of marriage could help to strengthen and develop the institution of marriage in Africa. This idea was reflected in the name we chose: The Churches' Research on Marriage in Africa. It would certainly have been unrealistic to limit our enquiry to the marriages of Christians alone. On the other hand, our aim has been to draw certain, pastoral conclusions from the research concerning Christian marriage ideals and norms in relation to the values, practices and social trends of contemporary Africa. Now that the research is finished and that we are drawing conclusions from the work that has been done, we think it appropriate to describe our concern as being for "African Christian Marriage".

2 *History of the Project*

CROMIA followed in the wake of several initiatives by individual churches concerned about the apparent failure of pastoral policies for marriage. One of these initiatives was the call in 1967 by the Association of Episcopal Conferences in Eastern Africa (AMECEA), a body uniting the seventy Roman Catholic bishops of Kenya, Malawi, Tanzania, Uganda and Zambia, for "an expert study" of customary rites in connection with marriage preparation and the rituals of customary marriage. The bishops directed their request to the social anthropologist at the AMECEA Pastoral Institute, then situated at Gaba, Uganda. They asked for recommendations in several spheres connected with marriage and family life.[6] The social anthropologist did not take up his appointment at Gaba until 1968, and it was two years before the AMECEA Research Department (an integral part of the AMECEA Pastoral Institute) had "cut its teeth" on its first project. At length, Aylward Shorter, the director of the AMECEA Research Department (and "social anthropologist"!) approached Killian Flynn, the Secretary General of AMECEA, with the outline of a project which was approved by the AMECEA Plenary Study Conference at Lusaka, Zambia, in August 1970.

The same AMECEA Plenary Study Conference agreed to release Adrian Hastings to carry out the commission entrusted to him by the Conference of the Anglican Archbishops of Africa at Lusaka in February of that same year. Hastings was asked to study "the problems arising out of African marriage customs, both rural and urban, in relation to full membership of the Church",[7] and he was able to begin work in December 1970. His report was discussed by the Anglican Archbishops again at their Kampala meeting in 1972, and was published in 1973.

A third initiative was taken by the Roman Catholic Bishops of Rhodesia in setting up an Interdiocesan African Marriages Commission in 1967 to "investigate the position on African marriages from the legal and canonical points of view".[8] This commission made a wide impact by sending a short questionnaire on the subject to every Roman Catholic Episcopal Conference in Africa. The Commission's final report was submitted in 1970. Two years later, a second African Marriages Commission was set up to offer more permanent recommendations and to confront a situation that was still deteriorating rapidly. It presented its report at the end of 1973.[9]

AMECEA called the CROMIA Planning Meeting, which was held at Gaba, Uganda, in March 1971. It was attended by twenty-eight delegates from the countries of East, Central and Southern Africa, representing Christian Councils, Catholic Secretariats, University Departments of Religious Studies, Theological Colleges and Seminaries, Ecumenical Institutes and Church Research Institutes. In the group were bishops, priests and pastors, laymen and women, university and college lecturers and a medical doctor. Adrian Hastings was present to speak about his own project, and Kevin Kinnane, Secretary General of the Rhodesian Catholic Bishops' Conference was there to present the work of the Rhodesian African Marriages Commission. Trevor Verryn, Director of the Ecumenical Research Unit in Pretoria, attended as the personal representative of Archbishop Robert Selby-Taylor, Anglican Archbishop of Cape Town, and Bishop Donald Jacobs of the Mennonite · Church represented the East African Religious Education Committee of which he was Chairman. Professor John Mbiti was the most distinguished academic present.

The meeting, which was opened by the AMECEA Secretary General, held a wide-ranging discussion, in both work-groups and in plenary session, on every possible aspect of marriage and family life in Africa. It worked out the broad shape of a three-year programme of sociological and theological research, and it elected an organizing committee from among the participants to set up a structure for the running of the project.

3 Structure and Financing of the Project

The Organizing Committee met at once and chose a nine-member Steering Committee (cf. Appendix I). It also directed the Executive Secretary to invite nine distinguished churchmen and women to constitute a panel of consultors and to head a mailing list of nearly two hundred interested persons (cf. Appendix I).

The programme was due to begin in 1972, but was delayed for a year by the failure to find the necessary funds immediately. Notre Dame University in America kindly financed the Planning Meeting and, through the kind offices of Professor Hommes, made a further grant. Money had also initially been given by AMECEA. Eventually, grants were made by MISSIO, Germany, The Theological Education Fund of the World Council of Churches and the Swiss Catholic Lenten Fund.

During 1972 some initial pilot projects were carried out. Njelu Kasaka made a study of Marriage Patterns in a Rural Re-Settlement Area of Tanzania, and Joseph Ssennyonga studied Christianity as a Factor in African Marriage Patterns in Kampala City, Uganda. These were followed in 1973 by a survey conducted in the Mityana area of Buganda (Uganda), and by another made by Ron Hart in the Nassa area of northern Tanzania.[10] Reports of these studies were issued as circulars, together with other theological and sociological reflections on Marriage in Africa. Altogether thirty-one circulars were issued by the project between 1971–5 (cf. Appendix II).

The Steering Committee met for the first time at Blantyre in Malawi in March 1973. It drew up a detailed plan for three years of research: 1973–6. It had before it the published report of Adrian Hastings, and this was a great help in deciding on the research priorities. As a result of the meeting, ten sociological research studies were commissioned, one each in Kenya, Malawi, Tanzania, Uganda, Rhodesia and Lesotho, and two each in Zambia and South Africa. It also commissioned an expert legal study and an All-African comparative study, and laid plans for a series of theological colloquia. Finally, it asked for a detailed bibliography to be compiled. Trevor Verryn undertook the co-ordination of the research and colloquium in Southern Africa, while Aylward Shorter agreed to handle the co-ordination of the rest of the project (cf. List of Studies commissioned by the project. Appendix III).

The first theological colloquium was held at La Verna Conference Centre, Transvaal, South Africa in September 1974, and thirteen papers were presented and discussed, together with other written comments on some of the papers. The meeting was opened by the Roman Catholic Archbishop of Bloemfontein, Archbishop Joseph Fitzgerald. The second theological colloquium was held at Trinity College, Nairobi, Kenya in November of the same year, and eleven papers were presented. Bishop Eliewaha Mshana of the Lutheran Church kindly took part. The third theological colloquium took place at the United Church Lay Training Centre, Chilema, Malawi in April/May 1975, and five papers were presented. The colloquium was held in conjunction with the final committee meeting of the project. Archbishop Donald Arden, Anglican Archbishop of Central Africa, kindly took part.

Between 1971 and the end of 1975, a great many contacts were made, and a great deal of incidental material was amassed. Some of the material was put at our disposal by visitors to the Pastoral Institute, researchers, university lecturers, etc. Some of it was kindly sent to us by correspondents, engaged in similar research in other parts of Africa. Another important source of material was provided by our participation in conferences organized by other bodies on the subject of marriage and family life. The two most important were the consultation on the Challenges of Family Education in Africa in the 1970s, sponsored by the AACC and held at Yaoundé, Cameroun, in November/December 1972, and the World Assembly "Familia '74", sponsored by the International Confederation of Christian Family Movements and the Family Education Office of the World Council of Churches and held at Dar-es-Salaam in June 1974.

4 Conclusion of the Project

The final Committee Meeting of CROMIA at Chilema considered all the material which had come in, both the reports and papers commissioned by the project and other material at our disposal. Not only did it decide the shape of this book and the detailed contents of each chapter, it also planned a whole series of publications. The research reports and theological papers contributed from Southern Africa have already appeared in an offset volume, for limited circulation, edited by Trevor Verryn and entitled *Church and Marriage in Modern Africa* (Johannesburg, 1975). The committee asked for a companion volume to this, edited by Aylward Shorter, and containing all the research reports and theological papers from East and Central Africa, the Legal Study and the All-Africa Study. The Rhodesian research report being the longest and most ambitious was only partly complete. Two volumes of mimeographed reports were available to the project, but another three volumes still had to be written. Sr. Aquina was asked by the committee to make her own arrangements about the publication of this report in full. The AMECEA Research Department was asked to publish a selection of the approximately 3,000 items of bibliography in mimeographed form. Finally, the Executive Secretary was asked to prepare a small booklet summarizing the conclusions of the project, suitable for translation into African vernaculars.

References: Introduction

1 Kenya, Malawi, Tanzania, Uganda, Zambia, Rhodesia, Lesotho, South Africa.
2 Anglican (five provinces), Church of God, United Church of Zambia, Congregationalist, Dutch Reformed Church, Greek Orthodox, Lesotho Evangelical Church, Lutheran, Mennonite, Methodist, Moravian, Presbyterian, Roman Catholic (seven episcopal conferences), Society of Friends, Vapostori Independent, various Zionist Independent Churches.
3 The first committee meeting was held at Limbe, Blantyre in Malawi; the second at the United Church Lay Training Centre at Chilema, also in Malawi. We are grateful to the authorities in Malawi for allowing us to host our international meetings there. It was the most convenient place for East, Central and South Africans to meet, having regard to the immigration laws obtaining in other countries.
4 Adrian Hastings was commissioned by the Anglican Archbishops in February 1970 and released for the work by AMECEA in August. CROMIA was approved by AMECEA in August 1970.
5 cf. Hastings, 1973, pp. 5–26.
6 AMECEA, 1967, *Pastoral Perspectives in Eastern Africa After Vatican II*, Kisubi, Uganda, pp. 94–9.
7 cf. Hastings, 1973, p. 3.

8 Report of the Inter-diocesan African Marriages Commission, 1973
   (mimeographed), Chap. 1, p. 1.
9 *Ibid.*
10 Ron Hart, 1973, CROMIA/24, was not commissioned by us. The
   author kindly allowed us to make use of his work.

Authors' note

Following the instructions given us by the Committee of the Churches' Research on Marriage in Africa, we have divided each chapter into three sections: a long section, presenting relevant sociological case material, a section devoted to theological reflection, and a final one dealing with models for pastoral action. The presentation of the case material poses few problems, except that there is so much of it that our treatment must inevitably appear selective and fragmentary. We can only urge the interested reader to refer to the full text of the research reports in the offset volumes entitled *Church and Marriage in Modern Africa*. At the time of going to press, only one of these volumes has appeared, that edited by Trevor Verryn. This means, unfortunately, that we have been obliged to refer to the original typescripts of the reports and papers from East and Central Africa, there being no book available.

Obviously, there were theological differences of opinion in the material submitted to the project, and we have tried, as far as possible, to respect these. However, we have also tried to indicate the general opinion or trend of thinking that emerged from the various papers, discussions and meetings. Those who think that we should have referred more frequently to well-known western theologians must be reminded that we are presenting the thought of writers from Africa, and that we are limited by the contributions submitted to us.

We present a variety of models for pastoral action, showing what the various churches are doing, and what other proposals have been made. We are not, of course, taking decisions for anyone, but we do indicate the solutions which we believe were favoured by the participants in our project.

A final word about our method of work: We worked from an

outline based on the resolutions of the Chilema meeting. Each of us drafted a portion of the book, which we reviewed together as a committee, integrating the drafts into a single, coherent report, rather than a symposium of separate essays. Since all three of us come from East Africa, and do not possess specialized knowledge about Central and Southern Africa, we accepted the committee's request that we send copies of the typescript to readers in Malawi, Zambia and South Africa. We remained the final arbiters of the alterations that were proposed, and these were made at proof stage.

AMECEA Pastoral Institute   Benezeri Kisembo
Eldoret, Kenya   Laurenti Magesa
March 1976   Aylward Shorter

Chapter 1

Church Marriage Rates and Contrasting Concepts of Marriage

I Case Material

1 Concept of the Church Marriage Rate

The concept of a church marriage rate, which has been effectively used by Adrian Hastings, derives from that of the general marriage rate.[1] The latter is simply based on the observed fact that in a balanced, normal population, in which divorces and remarriages are not unduly numerous, there are about eight marriages per 1,000 of population each year. Marriage, in this context, means any formal commitment between a man and a woman to cohabit more or less permanently. Roman Catholics and Anglicans require a marriage ceremony in church, and most other Christian churches, even though they may recognize the validity of civil or customary marriage for their adherents, impose certain conditions on them and invite them to ask for the Church's blessing on their marriage. The church marriage rate, therefore, refers to the number of marriages recognized each year by a church per 1,000 of its church population. The churches have various ways of computing the size of their own church population. For Roman Catholics and Anglicans who practise infant, as well as adult, baptism, the church population consists simply of the baptized. In so far as records and estimates are realistic, and in so far as the church is well established in a general population, the church marriage rate should reflect the general marriage rate, as being in normal circumstances eight per 1,000.

Although, as Hastings admits, the church marriage rate is

concerned with a wedding or blessing in church rather than with Christian married life, the churches have regarded a church marriage as a decisive element in determining acceptability for communion. On the churches' own criteria, therefore, a high or a low church marriage rate is extremely important. Francis Murray, for example, interpreted the declining church marriage rate in Tanzania between 1957 and 1967 as a turning away from the Church itself, but this is evidently going too far.[2] It is a very common experience to find Christians in irregular marriage situations in African countries who, despite being barred from the reception of the sacraments, remain fervent and active members of the community. Where the celebration of the Eucharist is relatively infrequent, as it is even in Roman Catholic out-station communities in Africa, excommunication may not be felt as a great hardship. Nevertheless, the question of the availability of the Eucharist apart, it is an abnormal situation for a high proportion, if not a majority, in a local church community to be excluded from its sacramental life. In attempting to determine the causes of a rise or a fall in the church marriage rate in Africa, one is bound also to question the churches' assumption that church marriage possesses the critical importance ascribed to it.

Hastings examined church marriage statistics (mainly Roman Catholic, Anglican and Lutheran) in East, Central and Southern Africa during a single, specified year for which comparable sets of figures could be found. He also studied developments in certain cases over a period of years. Hastings' work was not a complete statistical survey, but rather an attempt to document observed trends in church marriage in the chosen areas. Given the dearth of relevant statistical material in Africa, it is probably not possible to do more than Hastings did. Subsequent statistics have confirmed the trends revealed by Hastings for the 1960s in the area of his study, so also have supplementary studies.[3] Evidence from West Africa also reveals that Hastings' conclusions are even more widely applicable.[4] The figures and the trends revealed by them have simply to be accepted.

Hastings' conclusions were as follows: In general at least half the Christians of East, Central and Southern Africa never marry in church at all. However, there is a considerable difference between countries and even between parts of a country. High marriage rates are found in most of Malawi and the contiguous areas of Zambia and Tanzania, as well as in urban South Africa.

In these places some two-thirds marry in church. Most of the rest of Tanzania, central Kenya, western Uganda and rural South Africa occupy a middle position in which about half of the Christians marry in church at some time in their lives. A third group is that of Zambia and Rhodesia in which a third of the Christians marry in church. Finally, in the area north of Lake Victoria, from Tanzania to Kenya, and including the whole of southern Uganda, a densely populated area, only about one in eight of the Christians marry in church. A final conclusion of Adrian Hastings is that there has been a massive decline in the church marriage rate over the twelve years preceding his study. (His book was published in 1973.)

Statistics from Ghana reveal a comparable trend in West Africa.[5] In that country slightly less than a quarter of all Roman Catholics marry in church and a decline is apparent in all the dioceses save one over the same period of years as that studied by Hastings on the eastern side of the continent.[6]

Identifying the trends is one thing; accounting for them is another. Adrian Hastings offered a number of shrewd hypotheses to account for high and low marriage rates. These hypotheses have now been tested by further research and the conclusions will be outlined in subsequent sections of this chapter. The spadework done by Adrian Hastings has enabled us to carry the enquiry forward with a reasonable degree of certainty.

2   Low and Declining Church Marriage Rates

Four general reasons were offered by Hastings for the declining church marriage rate in Africa: the cultural revolution since political independence which has involved a "re-Africanization" of society, the fact that churches have lost control of the schools and with it the opportunity of preparing youth for Christian marriage, the vast growth in church membership and consequent loss of pastoral efficiency, and finally widespread "social unrest" entailing the loosening of the bonds of the old society. In spite of this final, clear-sighted suggestion, Hastings opined that in eastern Uganda, which has the lowest church marriage rate in the whole area of study, there was a greater stability in customary marriage which not only resisted the introduction of elopement and prostitution, but resisted also the introduction of church marriage.[7] While this is partly true of rural South Africa, as we shall see, it is definitely not the case in eastern Uganda.

3

Hans Boerakker carried out research in eastern Uganda in order to determine the causes of the extremely low church marriage rate.[8] His work was concentrated on the Padhola area, in villages with a high proportion of Christians. Whereas Hastings had assumed that the church marriage rate was never high in eastern Uganda, Boerakker demonstrated that until about 1935 church marriage was readily accepted in the area. In the early years of the century when the mission was just beginning, evangelization was directed mainly at unmarried boys who deferred church marriage until the baptism of their wife had taken place. By the early 1930s the church populations possessed a balanced structure and very high church marriage rates obtained. These began to decline about 1935, and, with the exception of a rise in the early 1950s occasioned by a Roman Catholic campaign for "good marriages", the decline continued until 1974 with one eighth of the Christians marrying in church, and the majority of adults excluded from communion.

Boerakker shows convincingly that fear of indissoluble, monogamous marriage is generated among young Christians by their experience of social instability. This instability is the direct result of the emancipation of the younger generation, an emancipation to which the churches have contributed by their concentration on education and on work among the youth. Consequently, there is a generation-cum-education gap. Young people handle their own affairs and choose their own partners. Practically all marriages begin by elopement and the payment of the so-called "money to speak". Subsequent negotiations are bedevilled by the fact that the choice of marriage partner cannot be separated from the payment of bridewealth. The raising of bridewealth by the bride's parents and the postponement of payment by the young man are interacting factors. Pastors refuse to officiate at a wedding until bridewealth has been paid, and the result is that most marriages go through an uncertain, trial period which, even if it does not end in separation, is seldom rendered definitive by a church marriage.

Obviously, the churches are not solely responsible for the generation-cum-education gap. All the forces of modernization are pointing in the same direction. Not only education but also the development of law favours the unaccustomed instability. The possibility of legal divorce proceedings with the wife as plaintiff is a novelty that threatens a system in which marital stability is guaranteed by males rather than females in the families concerned. The church marriage rate began to decline long before the churches lost control of the schools and long before the "re-Africanization" of independent Africa took place. It began to decline because customary marriage, so far from possessing a greater stability, had begun to decline first. In the early days of the mission there was no difficulty in accepting indissoluble church marriage. The majority of customary marriages were monogamous and all were indissoluble. Fear of indissolubility and monogamy was a direct result of changes in the structures of traditional society and the removal of social pressures that favoured marital stability.

Boerakker provides some evidence for educational and pastoral inefficiency which is directly related to the marriage statistics. Roman Catholic pastors in eastern Uganda have followed a very lax policy regarding infant baptism. The children of non-practising parents have been baptized indiscriminately, resulting in large numbers of "baptized pagans". Such people receive no Christian education, let alone marriage preparation, and their numbers swell the church population, thus forcing down the church marriage rate. Differences between marriage rates in eastern and western Uganda, he contends, may be due in part to differing pastoral policies in regard to baptism.

The mentality of those who postpone church marriage indefinitely is further illustrated by research carried out in an area north of Kampala, Uganda, and in village settlements of Tanzania. In the Mityana area, north of Kampala, a survey conducted in 1972 interviewed 1,483 married members of the Roman Catholic Church and the Church of Uganda.[9] Less than a third of the respondents were married to their actual partners in a church ceremony. For those without a church marriage, a few had been married in church to an earlier partner from whom they were now separated, and this fact prevented the regularization of their present union. A slightly larger number had not married in church because their partner belonged to another church or faith. Nearly half of all the respondents said they were "not ready for church marriage", "did not think church marriage necessary", or "did not want church marriage". Some respondents spoke of bridewealth not being paid yet. As bridewealth is not a financial burden at all in the area, its non-payment by the husband is a sign of his lack of

5

commitment to the marriage. Although "not ready" for church marriage, over 40% of the respondents had been in their present marriage for a period of three to ten years, and a similar proportion had been in their present marriage for a period of eleven to over thirty years. Fear of childlessness may have played a part in premarital experimentation and in the early break-up of a marriage, but it was clearly not important as a cause of postponing church marriage, when marriages were of such long standing and almost unanimously blessed with children.

The Mityana survey revealed a general dislike for church marriage and the idea that respondents had of church marriage was not only inadequate but distorted. In all replies it was the legal consequences of Christian marriage, monogamy and indissolubility, that were emphasized, not the nature of the commitment itself. Christian marriage was "God's law" for Christians and the priest, not the spouses, was the minister of marriage. Such legalistic and clerical attitudes are certainly the consequence of inadequacies in Christian marriage catechesis. Too much has been said about the conditions and consequences of church marriage, and too little about marriage itself. The evidence from eastern and central Uganda is confirmed by research in Tanzania. In an attitudinal survey of fifty-four Roman Catholic catechists in Nassa deanery, northern Tanzania, Ron Hart discovered that the vast majority (89%) thought it no sin for a Christian boy and girl to cohabit after customary engagement.[10] A slightly smaller number (74%) thought it definitely better for them to live together for a time, rather than to get married immediately, in order that they might get to know one another (kwideba). In Tumbi, a rural re-settlement area in central Tanzania, Njelu Kasaka interviewed forty-one married people, of whom more than half were Christians without a church marriage.[11] Of these, nearly half again were not ready for church marriage because they "did not know each other", there was a deliberate "trial", the bridewealth had not been paid or there was opposition from parents.

If there was no initial antagonism in eastern Uganda, as Hastings supposed, between customary and Christian marriage, there certainly has been in parts of rural South Africa which also possesses a low church marriage rate. Patrick Whooley studied three locations in Ciskei, South Africa.[12] In this area all the churches took up an intransigent attitude to customary marriage, particularly to the custom of *thwala* or symbolic capture of the bride, believing that it offended against the bride's freedom of consent. The traditional point of view was that a girl who submitted to capture was likely to remain faithful, whereas one who walked freely into a marriage ceremony might go back equally freely to her own parents. A church marriage without *thwala* is regarded as mere concubinage. The result has been that nearly all married Christians have been excluded from communion at one time or another in their lives, since a very small percentage marry in church in the first instance, and even the percentage of those who fix up their marriage in church afterwards is relatively small. The churches can draw no comfort from the knowledge that the traditional system is now breaking down and that the custom of *thwala* is disappearing. In the two locations which enjoyed a greater degree of urban influence and in which traditional structures had been weakened, a slightly higher proportion of Christians married in church in the first instance, but the growing phenomenon of elopement and concubinage is just as problematical as regular customary marriage.

A very important consideration in South Africa, as well as in other African countries, is the contrast between the statutory and customary concepts of marriage, and the fact that the churches instinctively favour the statutory concept. Brendan Conway, in his masterly survey of marriage laws in East, Central and Southern Africa, illustrates the difference between the two concepts.[13] Statutory marriage is based on the idea of contract and this includes four elements: the contract takes place at a specific moment in time; it involves a formal ceremony or registration; it is concerned with the effect of validity; and it assumes certain Christian conditions, notably the free consent of the partners and monogamy. Customary marriage has an essential pluralism, and the term refers to a large number of differing systems with more or less elements in common. Customary marriage is usually not tied to a specific moment in time or to a single ceremony. It is a process involving a whole series of rituals and exchanges and it is usually potentially polygamous. It is less concerned with the problems of consent and validity than with relationships between persons and groups. Although church Canon Law receives no statutory recognition in African countries (in contrast to Muslim and Hindu law in Kenya and Uganda), the churches looked to the

7

statutory, civil law of the country to safeguard free consent in marriage and to enforce monogamy among married Christians. In most countries church marriage was ideally, if not usually, statutory marriage.

In South Africa statute and custom are kept in two watertight compartments, and while customary marriage is recognized to exist, its validity is not accepted for the purposes of statutory law. Customary marriages are not solemnized in South Africa, but they may be registered. At statute law they are regarded as "conjugal associations" which are automatically dissolved when the parties enter upon a statutory marriage. The material rights of customary wives and widows, however, remain unaffected. Ministers of religion may be designated marriage officers and may solemnize and register marriages under statute law according to their own church formulas. In Natal and Transvaal women, even those who have attained their majority, require an enabling certificate issued by a Bantu Commissioner before they can be married according to statute. This document certifies the women's own consent and that of her father or guardian. The law allows a minister of religion to hold an "unofficial" religious, marriage ceremony, provided that it does not purport to effect a marriage the validity of which is recognized under the law of the land. It is understandable if, in these circumstances, the churches have sided with statutory marriage, and have seen no advantage in ignoring the law. Another aspect of the problem arises from the prohibition by statute of inter-racial marriages; and a minister of religion who decides that it is against his conscience to act as a marriage officer under an unjust law has to weigh this against the support which the law gives to church marriage and his usefulness to Christians who need a marriage certificate.

Rhodesia is another area with a low church marriage rate. Adrian Hastings asserts that the chief cause preventing or delaying marriage in church in Rhodesia "appears to be a legal one".[14] Elsewhere, he concedes that the problem "goes deeper than law".[15] His second intuition is correct. In common with South Africa, Rhodesia's basic, statutory law is Roman–Dutch Law; however, as Conway shows, it has been fairly massively influenced by English Common law and the opinion of Christian missionaries.[16] In fact, in Rhodesia, the bond between missionary and legislator was particularly close. Rhodesian law gives a qualified recognition to customary law and even modifies aspects of it. Customary marriages are invalid unless they are registered by the District Commissioner, but many of the effects of invalid customary marriage are given recognition at law. Before a marriage officer (including a minister of religion appointed as a marriage officer) can solemnize an African marriage under statutory law, an enabling certificate must be obtained from the bride's District Commissioner or District Officer attesting the consent of the girl's parents or guardian.

The procedure of obtaining the enabling certificate certainly creates difficulties and has been abused by District Commissioners for political or tax purposes. However, as Sister Aquina shows, it is a very minor cause of failure to marry in church. Sister Aquina studied three areas in eastern Rhodesia and also the regions of the Nambya and Tonga.[17] She estimates that about 40% of all Christian couples in the eastern region marry in church, but a very much larger percentage register their marriages in order to obtain housing. In Nambya and Tonga the percentages are very much smaller. In Rhodesia statutory marriage is basically felt to be an alien institution and parents are afraid of its indissoluble character. They therefore withhold consent to the enabling certificate until bridewealth has been paid. Once again, as in eastern Uganda, postponement of marriage and rising bridewealth are interacting factors. The difference in Rhodesia, however, is that the law upholds the customary status of women as minors and strengthens the hands of parents who make full payment of bridewealth the condition of an indissoluble marriage. Whereas in eastern Uganda it is the young men who are delaying church marriage, in Rhodesia it is the representatives of a more resilient customary system backed by statutory law who are responsible for the delay. The difference between customary and statutory marriage is dramatically demonstrated, according to Sister Aquina, by the kind of witnesses attending the registration at the District Commissioner's Office and those attending a church marriage. At the District Commissioner's all the traditional witnesses to customary marriage, members of the parental generation, are in attendance. At the church ceremony the witnesses are members of the younger generation who see the churches as agents of change and church marriage as a status symbol that goes with education.

Initially, the churches gave strong support to the marriage laws believing them to offer a safeguard against bigamy. Latterly the churches have had grave misgivings about the enabling certificate, and the Roman Catholic Bishops issued a policy statement in 1969, according to which, if it is impossible to obtain an enabling certificate, and if a genuine customary union exists, a priest, after reference to the diocesan curia, may bless the customary marriage. The bishops made this statement after seeking counsel's opinion that such a course of action would not be contravening the law. The priest must point out, however, to the parties involved that their church marriage has no civil recognition, and the church marriage certificate that he issues should also contain a note that this marriage "does not purport to refer to any civil marriage ceremony". Clearly, priests who follow this course of action do not gain very much. The couple is restored to church communion, but parental pressure to dissolve a union for which full bridewealth has not been paid is still as strong, added to which there are no legal sanctions if the marriage becomes polygamous, which, under law, it has every right to be.

Adrian Hastings placed most of Zambia on a par with Rhodesia where the marriage rate is concerned, with a third of the Christians marrying in church. This is borne out by the study carried out in the Copperbelt town of Kitwe by Norman Thomas and Daniel Chisanga.[18] Most Africans are reluctant to marry according to statutory law (therefore, in church) because of the difficulty or impossibility of obtaining a subsequent divorce. In Kitwe customary marriage is disappearing in its traditional form and self-contracted or so-called "U.D.I. marriages" are increasingly common. Marital instability and fear of an indissoluble, monogamous marriage are characteristics, as they are in the eastern Ugandan model.

Zambia, like Kenya and Uganda, enjoys a basic legal dualism. Both English, statutory law and traditional customary law are recognized, but once again, church marriage falls under the statute. Not only the minister of religion, but also the place of the ceremony, must be licensed and a registrar's certificate, analogous to the Rhodesian enabling certificate, must be obtained before a church marriage can take place. It seems that a church blessing on customary marriage is allowed by the law, but, given the conditions described by Thomas and Chisanga, it is not likely that much would be achieved by it.

We shall discuss the legal systems of Malawi and Tanzania in the next section, and, for the sake of completeness, it would be worth saying a word about Kenya and Uganda here. The picture is again one of two legal systems: English common or statute law (with some Indian modifications) and African customary law. Subsidiary legislation has been passed modifying custom in virtue of certain ordinances derived from statute law. For civil marriage in Kenya, an enabling certificate is required and the place of marriage must be licensed. For Christians, the minister of religion is licensed and acts, himself, as registrar. Widows are also protected by law from the leviratic custom, should this be against their will. There is no provision for the registration of customary marriages in Kenya. In Uganda, however, the recent decree of 1973 requires the registration of customary marriages, and non-Africans can contract a customary marriage. Subsequent monogamous or Mohammedan marriages are void. Ugandans have the same option between customary and civil rites of marriage as in Kenya, with special provision for Hindus and Muslims. Church marriage falls within the scope of civil and statutory law, without any provision being made to simplify procedures for Christians, as in Kenya.

The identification of Christian marriage with statute marriage has certainly had the effect of accentuating the aspects of consent and monogamy. Where the law protects the traditional African view that all women are minors, it offends against Christian ideas. In so far as it enforces the Christian ideal of exclusiveness of marriage, it helps to equate Christian marriage with the bare concept of monogamy in the minds of Africans. In practice, too, since divorce under the statute is not so easy to obtain, it has helped to emphasize the indissoluble character of Christian marriage. It has therefore been partly responsible for a general impoverishment of the concept of Christian marriage, reducing it to certain of its more frightening, and seemingly impossible, effects. The proposition that statutory procedures have been a cause of Christians delaying or refusing church marriage is, in fact, questionable. The main causes of the declining church marriage rate are: contemporary social and marital instability and an impoverished concept of Christian marriage.

3   *High and/or Rising Church Marriage Rates*
Adrian Hastings cites the opinion of Archbishop Arden that the high incidence of church marriage in Malawi is attributable to the country's African Marriage Registration Act.[19] This suggestion must be seriously considered, but before it is, our

11

attention must be focused on another hypothesis which has emerged from the discussion of the study made in Central Malawi by Stephen Kauta Msiska, Harry Welshman and Doris Gastonguay.[20] The findings of this study among 258 married Christians (mostly Presbyterians) confirms the picture of a high church marriage rate, with two-thirds or more marrying in church. However, in most of Malawi, as in most of the contiguous areas of Zambia and Tanzania, the family system is matrilineal. It is a well-known fact that matrilineal marriages, particularly when they are also uxorilocal, tend to be unstable, and a high proportion of the Malawi respondents indicated that the husband resided at the wife's home at the time of marriage. The question of residence is crucial for the stability of the marriage. As long as the husband is economically dependent on his wife's family, it is difficult for him to change his residence, but the introduction of a cash economy helps to erode the rights of the wife's brothers. Free emigration on the part of the men is closely related to this process. At any one time more than 50% of all the married men in Central Malawi are labour migrants in Rhodesia or South Africa. The cash they earn helps to give them a relative economic independence from their wife's family. Church marriage usually occurs at the moment of migration and appears to be the means by which husbands assert their rights over against the wife's family. The indissoluble character of Christian marriage is therefore attractive in this situation and is being used in the gradual erosion of the traditional, matrilineal system. The figures suggest also that church marriage is a stabilizing factor and that Christian marriages tend to be considerably more stable than non-Christian ones.

We must now turn again to the question of law. Malawi is unique in that a special act (The African Marriage (Registration) Act) caters for the church marriage of Africans and registration by any minister of religion authorized by a Christian denomination. This certainly simplifies procedures, since it dispenses with the need to obtain a registrar's certificate and with the requirement of performing the ceremony in a licensed place of worship. Apart from this facility, however, there are no other advantages for the parties concerned. The registration of the church marriage has no legal significance whatsoever, either at statutory or customary law. This legal mitigation, peculiar to Malawi, may be a contributory factor to the high incidence of Church marriages, but it is not the principal one.

By contrast, in Lesotho where there are no such legal provisions, church marriage offers real advantages to the labour migrant. Andrew Spiegel carried out research in Ha Mokgatla, a village in Lesotho, composed of three settlements.[21] His aim was to trace the effects of labour migration on Christian marriage. Spiegel estimated that 55% of the marriages in the village were split at the time of his investigation as a result of the system of labour migration to South Africa. However, church marriage was highly favoured because employers in South Africa are prepared to pay higher wages to a migrant who can produce proof of his marriage, and there are also insurance and compensation benefits. Elopement is encouraged by the labour migration system which demands hasty marriages, but the churches usually will not give a marriage blessing until customary marriage negotiations have, at least, begun. A full church marriage with all the trappings of a "white wedding" is beyond the financial reach of most of the men, but the issue of a marriage certificate offers a considerable attraction. We shall return in a subsequent chapter to the problem of the effects of labour migration on Christian marriage. The causes and effects of the system are very complex and are all part of the modernization experienced by Lesotho. It is difficult to judge whether the churches are aggravating or mitigating an evil system, and it certainly also imposes a note of caution when the popularity of church marriage is being taken as a sign of the health of Christian married life in a given area.

Adrian Hastings noted that urban South Africa was another area of high church marriage rates. He believed the cause to be twofold.[22] On the one hand, there was a greater breakdown of customary ceremonies here than elsewhere, and on the other, a marriage certificate was useful in obtaining basic amenities in town. However, he also noted that housing could be obtained by the mere registration of a customary marriage at a Bantu Commissioner's Office.[23] The burden of the argument, therefore, is that high marriage rates in urban areas are caused by the breakdown of the customary system and the adoption of new attitudes of life in general, and marriage in particular.

We have already noted that the breakdown of customary marriage systems is not necessarily to the advantage of church marriage, and the attraction of church marriage even when it accompanies customary marriage, is often that it "dignifies" the marriage, and, as an "appendage" or "additive", confers greater social prestige. Church marriage in the African town is an expensive affair and is celebrated on a much larger social scale than many marriages in Europe or America. Church marriage is part of the life-style of the urban dweller in Africa. Martin Peskin made a series of case studies in Soweto, Johannesburg, the largest African urban complex in the continent, where about one million Africans live.[24] Peskin found that it was not a question of customary marriage breaking down, nor even of any overt competition between church marriage and customary marriage. Rather, there is a dialectical interchange between a variety of cultural elements, and individuals operate with church marriage, civil marriage and customary marriage systems at different moments, depending upon a given set of interpersonal relationships or a given social context. Geography has remarkably little to do with this dynamic of married life in Soweto, and distance from a rural homeland is not such an important factor.

Peskin presents in detail a case study of an urban church wedding in Soweto. It is the wedding of two university graduates, Stanley and Emily. Stanley and his family were residents of Johannesburg, while Emily's parents had lived there for a time before returning to Pietersburg about 260 miles to the north. Soon after Emily informed her parents of Stanley's intentions, Stanley went with his grandmother, mother's brother and a friend to open negotiations in Pietersburg. Emily's family was represented by her parents, her grandmother, her mother's brother from Johannesburg and other relatives and neighbours. Before the meeting, an initial payment was made by Stanley's family and Emily was subjected to an intimate interrogation by her family. The bridewealth was fixed, and after it had been accepted by Stanley's family, the confrontation between the families took place. The negotiations ended with the ritual slaughter of two goats. Emily then went to Johannesburg where she did some shopping for wedding clothes. An attempt by Stanley and Emily to get married at the Bantu Commissioner's Office in Johannesburg failed because they did not have the necessary documents. However, they were eventually successful in getting a marriage certificate from the Commissioner after their church marriage.

Emily returned to Pietersburg where she was secluded until the wedding day. A diviner was called in to "strengthen" the surroundings and the home, and this was followed by the arrival of the wedding cake welcomed by the songs and praises of neighbouring women. On the wedding day Stanley and his party were made to observe a great many petty customs and to pay a number of fines. The female representative of Stanley's family gave the bride a fairly intimate bodily inspection before she finally dressed in her wedding gown and veil. On leaving the house, the bride had to pass through an arch of branches while the ancestors were invoked. Arrived at the Catholic mission church, Stanley and Emily went through the church ceremony in which the bridegroom placed a ring on the bride's finger. The Roman Catholic Sisters then held a small reception with tea and cake for the newlyweds and wedding gifts were presented. On the way back from the church a thunderstorm broke out and a child in a neighbouring house was struck dead by lightning. Even Stanley who had been sceptical about the protective medicines was now grateful for them. There followed eating and drinking at Emily's parents' home. When the feasting and speeches came to an end, a ritual tug-of-war between the two families took place. The bride and bridegroom then left with Stanley's family for Johannesburg. At Stanley's home another series of rituals took place culminating in the celebration of Emily's pregnancy and the birth of their first child. After the marriage Emily took up a teaching post for a time and Stanley returned to complete another degree course at the University. Such was the wedding of two "westernized", urban-dwelling, university graduates in South Africa!

As we have seen, one of the basic legal problems in African countries is the incompatibility of two different legal systems, each having its own concept of marriage. As Brendan Conway pointed out,[25] attempts at bringing custom into the statute have not proved very successful. The other courses open to the legislator are illustrated by the examples of Malawi and Tanzania. In Malawi the two systems are held apart, as it were, with the minimum of communication or interference between the two. The church, meanwhile, is not tied to either system, or to either concept of marriage. In Tanzania the 1971 law of Marriage Act gives statutory recognition to all the options. Following the recommendations of the Spry Commission in Kenya, recommendations that were never implemented in that country, the Tanzanian law recognizes four marriage forms: civil, Christian, Islamic and customary. Islamic and customary marriages are presumed to be polygamous. Except for

Christian marriages in which the parties remain Christians, a marriage which is presumed to be monogamous may be converted, with the consent of both parties, into a polygamous marriage. Notice must be given of the intention to marry, but no registrar's certificate is required. The marriage must be registered within thirty days of its taking place. All ministers of religion who bless marriages must be licensed, but the place of marriage requires no licensing.

After examining all these developments in the various African countries one is forced to conclude that registration in some form or another is necessary and that some realistic system of unified, public law is ultimately indispensable. The law, as Conway points out, should not determine how people live. Rather it should reflect their way of life and the options that life in their country places before them. If the system of public law in a country is realistic and fair, then it would be folly for the churches to try to stand aside from it.

II   Theological Reflection

1   *Sacramentality and Marriage*
Several lessons can be drawn from the preceding section. The delay or refusal to marry in church stems partly from a fear of indissoluble marriage. This in turn derives from an impoverished understanding of marriage, presented and accepted as a legal contract having certain effects. Such an idea of Christian marriage actually repels young people at a time when the structures of society are changing and when social safeguards for a stable marriage no longer exist. There is need, therefore, for a fresh approach to marriage that will explain its stability and offer an ideal that attracts, rather than repels. Such an approach is outlined by Louis Peters in his discussion of sacramentality in relation to marriage.[26]

Peters is looking for a way of presenting Christian marriage which is not only acceptable, but which, when accepted, will by itself encourage stability. Once it is understood and accepted, legal requirements and social safeguards will again become meaningful in the light of this new approach. This is not, therefore, merely a catechetical proposal, a solution in the sphere of religious education only. It is one that entails the rebuilding of a Christian community in which everyone is

16

convinced of the essential nature of marriage, and undertakes to preserve and promote it. In speaking of the sacramentality of marriage, we are making no judgement about the Biblical institution of marriage as a sacrament and whether Jesus himself determined its matter and form. This is important because the terms "sacrament" and "sacramentality" have for long been a part of Roman Catholic theological vocabulary, and have been viewed with suspicion by Christians of other denominations. We are speaking rather of the effective sign value of marriage as it is understood by Christians. Basically, marriage is called a sacrament because it is part of the created order and the whole of this created order is sacramental. In fact, sacramental thinking is the characteristic form of man's first thinking about reality. Everything is a symbol of a higher reality, a sacrament of God. The sacramental character of the created order is found especially in those human realities which man experiences as central to his whole existence, realities such as birth, death, eating and drinking, marriage. The ceremonies and rituals with which man surrounds these experiences are an expression of the fact that it is in these situations that he experiences the transcendent character of his life, and the divine origin and goal of his existence. It is especially through human relationships that man experiences the communication of God's love. Human values such as friendship, sharing, and fidelity are the ways in which human beings relate to one another in God's infinite love. God's love is sacramentally communicated in every human encounter, whether it be inter-personal, group or inter-group, and man is called to respond to that love through these relationships.[27] These are the so-called "natural sacraments" which become experiences of salvation for mankind.

Marriage, then, is one of these natural sacraments understood according to the general dimension of all human relationships. It is experienced as a communication of salvation, and not merely as an institution for procreation. The sacramental nature of any marriage is expressed in the love between the partners, a love which is not just limited to the other partner, but which is the expression of man's desire to meet the ultimate and unlimited reality which is God. In marriage the partner becomes the sacrament of God who gives himself totally to man and to whom man gives himself totally. God's covenant with man makes the covenant between husband and wife possible, and in so far as each of the partners tries to express

God's love in his or her own love for the other, their marriage becomes an effective sign of grace, of God's covenant love. Man is not free to reject this call when he marries, because the marriage partner is, in God's purposes, a vehicle and expression of God's love itself. Every marriage, then, is meant to be an expression of the totality and fidelity of God's love. A sacrament cannot be reduced to the idea of a bare contract with certain arbitrary effects, such as—in the case of marriage—indissolubility. Marriage is not indissoluble because of a sacramental rite or blessing at its start. On the contrary, it is the indissolubility of the marriage which makes it a sacrament of God's love, and the marriage partners commit themselves to indissolubility as a task which they have to realize. In so far as we are speaking about "natural sacraments" we are not necessarily demanding explicit faith in God. We are talking about love and the quality of love. The true test for the sacramental character of a marriage lies in the quality of the love found in the relationship.

The sacramental character of marriage is further expressed in its fruitfulness, for procreative marriage represents God's creative act and enlightens us further about the sacramental character of creation. As Brian Hearne points out, marriage is considered by some theologians to be the best paradigm of a sacrament, deeply rooted as it is in the human and the concrete, yet taken over and transformed by the love of God.[28] The prophets of the Old Testament also showed a predilection for marriage as a sign of God's faithfulness to man. All sacraments are signs of God's covenant love, but marriage, in particular, teaches us that creation is creation for the covenant.

Yet another sacramental aspect of marriage is its social character. Marriage acts as a healing agent in human society. It brings the community into being, both through procreation and through the alliances it creates. As an expression of God's saving love, this function of marriage is sacramental. Human society, therefore, has a right and a duty to safeguard marriage and to make laws concerning it.

So far we have been dealing with marriage as a "natural sacrament". With the Incarnation of the Word, "*the* Sacrament of God", we are given the fullness of the revelation concerning the goal of creation and the eternal covenant which God establishes with man in Jesus Christ. For those who have faith in Christ, marriage is not only an effective sign of God's love, it is a sign of that love as it has been revealed in the life, death and resurrection of Jesus Christ. In the perspective of the Incarnation marriage acquires its deepest significance, as an expression of God's irrevocable love for man in Jesus Christ. As such it is not only the sacrament of God's covenant with his people, but of Christ's with the Church, the fellowship of all those who will be finally called. In so far as married people express in their union the mystery of Christ's love for his Church, their marriage, their family home, becomes "a domestic church", having a vocation within, and a responsibility to, the wider Church. The marriage of two baptized persons is, therefore, more than a private affair between themselves, it has a sacramental function within the Church at large.

What constitutes marriage, as marriage, is its sacramental character of expressing God's love for man. Without this there is no marriage at all, neither Christian, nor any other. The marriage contract is simply part of the sacramental reality, not an act which can stand apart, or to which a sacrament can be added! There is no such thing as a "non-sacramental" marriage, although married people may refuse to acknowledge and live out the full significance of their union and the latter may be protected by law or custom. Marriage, therefore, is indissoluble because of what it is. If it is not indissoluble it is not true marriage. However, sacraments are also what are called "eschatalogical realities". They celebrate the covenant made by God in Jesus Christ, a covenant which introduces us into the full mystery of our being. Nevertheless, the full realization of this mystery, the full restoration of our humanity is still a future reality, and we live in hope of it because of the death and resurrection of Christ. Sacramental life involves us in a process of growth according to which we respond ever more intensely to God's offer of covenant love in Jesus Christ. When the marriage vows are publicly exchanged, the partners commit themselves to a growing sacramental reality, the task of living out an indissoluble relationship that shares ever more fully in the stability of the covenant between Christ and his Church. A marriage is realized, not simply in a contract, nor in the first sexual intercourse after the contract, but in all the dimensions in which husband and wife meet each other in love. The "consummation" of a marriage should be seen as the total involvement of husband and wife in signifying in their union the covenant of love in Jesus Christ; and this includes, obviously the sexual aspect.

19

Sacraments, as we have seen, are celebrations of the death and resurrection of Jesus Christ. This is true of marriage, and because of the particular way in which it expresses this mystery, it is more intensely experienced in marriage than in other sacraments. Because of man's sinfulness, marriage is constantly in danger of betraying its reality as a sign of the covenant. It is therefore part of the experience of marriage as a sacrament that it implies dying to oneself in one's self-gift to the other. Marriage as a sacrament must represent a dying of self and a rising with Christ. Evelyn Lebona, herself a Christian wife and mother, summed up her feelings about the indissolubility of marriage.[29] "To be able to live together 'till death do us part' needs faith and the grace of God. Christ, the author of indissoluble marriage, should be made the centre of this love-life. . . . Marriage is a permanent commitment, binding us to each other as spouses, to our children and to God, the infinite designer of matrimony and conjugal love."

2   Marriage as a Covenant between Persons

Reference is made several times in the course of this book to Walter Trobisch's well-known "garden concept" of marriage.[30] It is a symbolic way of referring to an emphasis on fertility in speaking and thinking about marriage. Although there is no human society whose concept of marriage is completely fertility-orientated, the temptation remains to give too great an emphasis to the aspect of fertility at different times and in different contexts. The garden metaphor is even used on occasion. According to this metaphor, the woman is a garden, in which her husband, the owner of the garden, plants seed. The children are the fruit of the garden and belong to the sower. A garden is valued for its soil fertility; so is the woman. Moreover, it is the sower who chooses the garden, not the garden which chooses the sower. If the sower plants seed in another man's garden, he deprives his own garden of nothing, but he is accountable for his adultery to the owner of the foreign garden.

The garden concept of marriage is a useful foil for drawing another emphasis, that of a person-orientated concept of marriage. This is the concept which emerges very clearly from the Yahwistic narratives in the first three chapters of Genesis. Axel-Ivar Berglund refers to the fertility-orientated concept in describing the hermeneutical setting of these chapters.[31] The Yahwistic passages were written in the time of Solomon, probably towards the close of his reign. It was a time of expansion and dramatic social change in the history of Israel. It was also evidently a time of moral laxity, as tribal and rural settings became dominated by a new urbanism, and the religion of Yahweh was threatened by materialism and the influx of foreign cults with their sexual deviations. In these circumstances, the call of the Yahwistic narratives for a revaluing of human relationships and for an understanding of marriage as a covenant between persons, rather than as a means of increasing family influence or ensuring one's posterity, must have sounded revolutionary.

The climax comes with the words of Genesis 2:24, "And they shall become one flesh". The Hebrew word *basar* implies the living, physical flesh and its functions, including the procreative act. The word is sometimes translated "body".[32] The two become one body, not in the sense merely of physical body, but the living body as a symbol of the whole person. We are being told in this passage that, like the man, the woman has a value in herself as a person. She is not valued simply for the children she bears. The oneness in flesh implies a very profound sharing between husband and wife. It is a communion of life in which the partners disclose themselves as persons to one another, and share with one another at every conceivable level. It would not be going too far to say that this mutual acceptance also implies a constant readiness to forgive one another. The personal relationship is a developing relationship which generates personality through the procreation and upbringing of children.

Earlier in the verse the condition for this oneness was laid down "a man shall leave his father and mother and shall cleave to his wife". In the strongly patrilineal society of the time, it goes without saying that there was no question of uxorilocality. It was the wife who went to live with the husband's family, not the husband who went to live with the family of the wife. The Yahwistic writer is challenging a view of marriage and family in which persons could be subordinated to familistic ideals. He is not preaching the superiority of the nuclear over the communitarian family, but he is stressing that persons matter and that marriage is, above all, a covenant between persons. Both husband and wife "leave" their parents, both form a new unit, both create a new home. The Hebrew word for "cleave" is also a very forceful one, conveying the idea of oneness in a striking manner.

From what has been said above by Louis Peters about the sacramental function of marriage in society and by Axel-Ivar Berglund about the compatibility of the personal covenant with the patrilineal family, it follows that Christian and Biblical ideas of marriage do not in any way conflict with the communitarian approach to marriage that is typical of African societies. On the contrary, the community would mean nothing if the personal aspect were lacking, for the community is the very field of personal relationships; and the person would mean nothing if he or she were not a person in community. The family is the basis of community. It is both an efficient cause of community, and also the community's primary care and concern. In seeking a solution to the declining church marriage rate and to the apparent incompatibility of Christian and African concepts of marriage we must look both to the sphere of personal relationships and to relationships within the community.

III   Models for Pastoral Action

1   *The Inadequacy of Purely Legal Solutions*
Everyone is disturbed by the very large number of Christians who are denied communion or who are under some form of discipline in their churches because of failure to marry in church or to obtain their church's recognition for their customary marriage. However, a solution is not going to be found either by ignoring Civil and Canon Law or by manipulating the law itself. Moreover the disciplining of such people is of no use whatever, if it is not accompanied by serious and practical measures to help them achieve church marriage. The situation will not be remedied either by simply admitting them to communion as if no problem existed. Obviously, people become hardened and even alienated from the Church when they are told that they are "living in sin", especially if they are not conscious of having done anything seriously wrong or find themselves in a dilemma that is not of their own making. There is a case for greater leniency in dealing with such people, perhaps even of restoring to full communion those who are on the road to a Christian marriage and who are responding favourably to the invitation to put their situation right. Nevertheless, as we have seen, it is not simply a question of converting a stable, customary marriage into a Christian one, it is one of helping to give

essentially unstable unions a greater stability—ultimately, indissolubility. As we have seen in the example from eastern Uganda, there was no problem about solemnizing customary marriages in church in the early days of the mission, since they were ordinarily stable, life-long unions. The problem now is how to confront unions that lack stability and, as the Mityana survey showed, run the risk of remaining in this "temporary" state forever. In the South African example from the Ciskei we saw that the problem was on the Church's side. In this case it is for the Church to legalize the situation, but even here elopement and trial marriage are undermining the stability of customary marriage. In general, no purpose will be served by recognizing "customary" marriages that lack the requisite stability. In any case, the nub of the problem is that people in such unions do not want a stable, church marriage. Those who do can have their situation put right with comparative ease. On the other hand, if a pastor brings pressure to bear on a couple to marry in church, he may find that a union that has lasted for decades breaks up in a matter of weeks or months. This is because a whole delicate balance of mutual expectations has been disturbed, and new expectations have been created which are not mutually accepted. There is a fundamental difference between Christian marriage and the union that consciously excludes indissolubility.

If the civil law of a given country or its administration is unhelpful or unjust, then representations must be made, and it may even be necessary to sidestep the law. Ordinarily, however, pastors have the duty of seeing that Christians derive the fullest possible benefit from the law of the country as it concerns marriage. As we have seen, the future can only lie with statutory law. In so far as church law is concerned, the various canonical solutions that have been proposed are unrealistic or untheological or both. To begin with, the various ways of legalizing or validating a marriage apply, as we have seen, to unions that were stable from the beginning, or to unions which have become stabilized (perhaps as a result of pastoral action). We shall deal with them towards the end of this section. One suggestion that has been made is that it should be admitted that Christians can contract natural marriages.[33] The argument is that if a convert can live happily in a natural marriage with a non-Christian partner, it should also be possible for Christians to contract a valid, natural marriage without envisaging an

23

indissoluble, sacramental marriage immediately. There would be a growth into sacramentality and indissolubility, seen as a marriage ideal, rather than as the condition for the marriage of Christians. Apart from the practical problem of persuading Christians to convert their marriages from natural ones into sacramental ones, there is the further question whether the distinction between "natural" and "sacramental" marriages is theological. If we accept Louis Peters' argument that a marriage that is not indissoluble is not a true marriage even in purely natural terms, then such a distinction cannot be made. That, however, is very far from saying that there is no growth in sacramentality. Obviously, there is a growing understanding and experience of what indissolubility means. The solemnization of marriage by the Church demands a commitment to the task of achieving indissolubility. If people are not ready for this, and do not even understand its necessity, then any union they may contract is obviously dissoluble, and though the churches should be sympathetic to such people, it is a question for debate whether they should deliberately encourage such unions as a matter of policy. Accepting them as a necessary evil, and adopting positive pastoral attitudes towards them is another matter. If it is not very theological to distinguish between "natural" and "sacramental" marriage, it is obviously possible to make a distinction between marriage as a "natural sacrament" and marriage as a "Christian sacrament". The Christian sacrament comes into existence solely because of explicit faith in Jesus Christ, and the churches have a right to testify, in a public act of witness, that such faith exists. If it is accepted that a baptized Christian who believes in Jesus Christ can also think that Jesus Christ has nothing to do with his marriage (and where religious education is deficient this is conceivable), it is not certain how the distinction between the natural marriage of Christians and Christian marriage will help him face up to the problem of indissolubility.

Another canonical suggestion is that marriage could be made conditional upon its fertility, just as marriage in the case of doubtful potency is conditional.[34] This solution assumes that fear of childlessness, rather than fear of indissolubility, is the reason for delaying church marriage. As we have seen, fear of childlessness plays a relatively small part in the whole problem. Patrick Whooley discovered in Ciskei that premarital pregnancies occurred not so much to test the girl's fertility, as to stake a claim on a particular bride.[35] And at Mityana the vast majority of married people were delaying church marriage in spite of having borne large numbers of children. We shall deal with the theological problem of childless marriages in a subsequent chapter, but we may anticipate the discussion by saying here that it does not seem possible that childlessness can invalidate a marriage. Finally, yet another canonical suggestion, which is open to the same objections, is that sterility be simply declared by the Church to be a diriment impediment to matrimony, rendering a marriage null and void when it is ascertained beyond reasonable doubt.[36] As we said at the beginning of this section, canonical sleight of hand is not going to solve the intractable problem of the declining Church marriage rate.

2 Marriage Catechumenate and Marriage by Stages

To begin with, the word "catechumenate" is often used in a very broad sense in the marriage context to refer to any planned programme of preparation for marriage or marriage catechesis. Edmund van Huet, for example, proposes, as a first stage of such a catechumenate, a series of "friendship days".[37] Friendship days are a series of full days of discussion, worship, and social activity in which young people are helped to come to terms with their life situation, and particularly with such experiences as dating, friendship and preparation for marriage. Such days should be held preferably on a Sunday. The second stage of the marriage catechumenate he envisages as a week-end seminar for engaged couples which would involve some six sessions altogether. After marriage, the marriage catechumenate would be followed up by parish seminars for married people on marriage and family life.

This is just one formula for marriage preparation, and it is clearly necessary to organize sessions of one kind or another if any contribution to a solution of the church marriage rate problem is to be made from a catechetical angle. We have already seen that the problem is partly a catechetical problem, and our theological reflection was intended to provide content for a marriage catechesis. To rely on the general religious education given to school children, and then two or three instructions on the eve of the wedding itself is totally inadequate. Even a purely catechetical effort is bound to fail, if it is not accompanied by structural innovations that will help to give stability to the unions. The phrase "marriage catechumenate", therefore, is more usually used in a strict sense to refer to what is also known as "marriage in stages".

In 1972 Melvin Doucette made a proposal for a marriage catechumenate in Zambia that would exploit the processual aspect of customary marriage, especially in so far as it has been exaggerated by rising bridewealth and the battle between the generations for control of the marriage institution.[38] He advocated a period of years between engagement and final, sacramental commitment when the partners would be getting to know one another socially, psychologically and even sexually. They would also be receiving instructions and would be improving their own material situation by laying the foundations of a new family home. Doucette is far from being alone in making such a proposal. The well-known Roman Catholic moral theologian, Bernard Häring, has let it be known that he also favours this solution.[39] Häring argues that we are in a period of transition between parental control of marriage and the freedom of choice of young people. In this situation the churches should not work through sanctions, but through patient education. The young people should have every intention of finalizing the marriage, unless obstacles supervene, and this would make their union essentially different from the uncontrolled use of sex which we usually call "fornication" or the deliberately temporary sexual community that we usually call "concubinage". To call this inchoate marriage "sin", or "fornification" or "concubinage" is not only unhelpful, it actually renders the union more unstable and makes it even more of a trial. Häring compares marriage in stages to the stages of initiation to the religious life, the novitiate with temporary vows. He also appeals to European examples from Bavaria and Sicily where the marriage of pregnant women is almost the rule. After the imposition of a penance or a fine the marriage is solemnized in church.

The Roman Catholic Bishops of Chad, West Africa, have adopted marriage in stages as a tentative solution, and a very interesting version of the proposal has been made in Ethiopia, in the Roman Catholic Vicariate Apostolic of Jimma.[40] The proposal is as follows: Marriage is arranged according to custom and the day of the marriage (a Sunday or Feastday) decided upon. On that day the couple manifest their mutual commitment to the whole Christian community gathered in church. This commitment includes the intention to live together and in due course, after consultation with the elders of the parish and the pastor, to have their marriage sacramentally confirmed. If, according to the local understanding, the marriage has a reasonable chance of surviving, the couple will consult the elders and the priest, and if they receive positive advice will be bound under pain of excommunication to marry according to the law of the church. During the period between the formal engagement and the celebration of marriage, the couple will live together as man and wife and will continue to receive the sacraments of the church. This proposal was enthusiastically received by the Christians of the area.

Christian moralists have always been lenient towards engaged couples who go too far in their manifestation of love towards one another, and, perhaps, the idea of "pre-marital" sex in this situation is less objectionable than other aspects of the proposed marriage in stages.[41] The chief consideration is whether this approach to marriage will encourage real, indissoluble, Christian unions. A marriage which begins on the basis of a trial becomes a different kind of relationship from one which begins on a basis of mutual commitment and responsibility. Both may achieve stability, but the first type rests on a nice equilibrium of input and output, on respect for each other's independence in certain spheres, provided certain minimal, mutual expectations are fulfilled. Each holds the other at a distance, imposing limits on the development of the relationship and accepting the limits imposed by the other. As we have already pointed out, however stable such a union may become, its delicate balance may be upset by its conversion into a church marriage. In fact, its very existence depends on a negative attitude to the totalitarian demands of Christian marriage. This was the lesson of Mityana.

Marriage in stages has the fundamental contradiction of formalizing the trial element while at the same time insisting on the declared intention to finalize the marriage in accordance with the Christian ideal. It might be worth experimenting with the proposal, but the experiment would have to be judged by its failure rate, and this brings us to another objection. Is the local community able to absorb the failures? Most African societies are able to care for illegitimate or unwanted children through the structures of the family community, but not so the "unwanted woman". In former days polygamy catered for the barren wife and reduced the chances of separation for this and other motives. Today, the rejected wife faces a life of loneliness, perhaps even of prostitution. In spite of the prevalence of sex before marriage in contemporary Africa, young men are still anxious to marry virgins, and parents are anxious to marry off their daughters at a young age "before they are spoiled". When husbands reject wives or parents break up trial marriages because bridewealth has not been paid, or because they hope for a bigger bridewealth elsewhere, it is usually the girl who suffers more than the boy. Marriage in stages can only be justified when the number of casualties of the system is small.

In the various sociological, theological and pastoral discussions sponsored by CROMIA, opinion tended to oppose the idea of marriage in stages. On the other hand, it tended to favour a tolerant attitude towards young couples caught in the dilemmas created by contemporary, social instability. Patient education, rather than sanctions, should be used, and great caution should be exercised in judging whether the couple is ready for the commitment to indissolubility. Above all, as we shall now see, patient education must be accompanied by social action and community building. Nobody is playing down the urgency of the problem, and it would seem that a massive campaign is needed, but the situation is complex, and there is no easy solution.

3 *Christian Marriage and the Community*
Marriage is a human institution, belonging to the human community, and the churches have no right to undermine such institutions. Their aim is to strengthen them and build them up. The churches, therefore, must work with the community, not in opposition to it. Everything must be done to minimize the distinction between the customary celebration of marriage and its Christian celebration. There are frequent anomalies in the Christian celebration of a marriage that has also been celebrated in customary form, and these must be removed. Nowhere is this more evident than when a church marriage is performed long after the couple began to live together, and long after the birth of children. Even the very texts of the Christian marriage service which speak about "entering into marriage" and which pray for the birth of children make nonsense of the rite. What is to be done?

Roman Catholic Canon Law (Canon 1098) admits the validity of a marriage between two church members even when there is no priest present, provided there are two witnesses and provided there is a grave reason, such as danger of death, or (apart from the danger of death) when the absence of the priest is foreseen as liable to last for a month or more. It might be that, under the provisions of this canon, a great many customary marriages between Roman Catholics in Africa are valid in the eyes of the law. Apart from the fact that African Roman Catholics are universally unaware of the existence of this canon, it does not seem that the canon is very helpful because the priest would have to ascertain later the validity of the marriage, and if the couple were serious in their desire for Christian marriage, a renewal of consent could always be made, and a marriage in canonical form duly celebrated. The Lutheran and Moravian Churches in East Africa invite Christians who have married according to custom to receive a blessing in church, and Roman Catholics sometimes have a similar practice when it is a question of regularizing a customary marriage. In the Roman Catholic diocese of Jinja, Uganda, a practice was started six years ago that has the Bishop's private approval. It is known as *Okukakasa obufumbo* in the language of the Basoga, and is described by the Bishop as "a regularization of customary marriage before the Church by renewal of consent in canonical form (before the parish priest and two witnesses) in a private ceremony".[42] The ceremony takes place usually in the couple's home and is followed by the blessing of the priest and the entry of the marriage in the church register. The main reason for the private character of the ceremony is the avoidance of an expensive wedding feast which might otherwise be demanded if the marriage was held in church.

Another Roman Catholic practice is *sanatio in radice* or "radical healing". This is a fiction in Canon Law, according to which an invalid marriage is validated retrospectively after the impediment to validity has been removed or dispensed from. It can even be carried out without informing the couple if they were unaware of the invalidity of their union. The power to grant *sanatio in radice* is delegated to local bishops and permission must be sought by pastors from them. Patrick Whooley in South Africa recommends an extension of this legal expedient to cover the marriages of Christians according to customary law.[43] It can be used to regularize marriages which are invalid because of lack of canonical form (the presence of the priest and two witnesses), when there is a grave reason. This method has the advantage of dispensing with all further ceremony, even simple renewal of consent. All that needs to be done is to record the fact that the marriage has been validated. As we said earlier in this section, none of these measures is meaningful, if the couple are not committed to the idea of an indissoluble, sacramental union.

Ultimately, if marriages are to be stabilized and indissoluble unions entered into from the beginning, the churches must effectively contribute to building a stable society. It is no use teaching young people in school that they should exercise freedom of choice in marriage, and then to side with the parental generation over bridewealth when it comes to marriage itself. The churches must educate the community, teach parents to be reasonable and help them do everything in their power to encourage stable marriages for their children. Young people must feel that they have the backing of their church community, as well as of their family, in embarking upon married life. This means that the churches must draw the threads of society together again at a time when traditional structures are breaking down and when the family itself is threatened by rapid and far-reaching social change. This is what is usually called "community building" and it is urgently required of the churches. The African Independent Churches appear to be considerably more successful than the older churches in giving their adherents the experience of community. The church community must take over many of the traditional functions of the old village society, and must help the family become an active and creative element in its midst. The church community will, in fact, be a community made up of family units.

In the modern situation, particularly in the urban situation, where there is an interplay of different cultural elements, the churches must help to bring about an integration, and Christians must be encouraged to resolve any duality or contradiction that exists in their thinking about marriage. It is not simply a question of bringing customary and Christian marriage rites together, or of the church community partici-pating in the marriage ceremony. The church community must create its own structures for marriage preparation and marriage counselling, and it must be actively involved in all the stages by which marriages are arranged and finalized. In the final chapter of this book we shall discuss community building at length and its importance for almost every aspect of marriage and family life. We shall also discuss the question of adapted marriage rites in detail. Let us simply repeat now that one of the major conclusions of the CROMIA project was that a solution for the falling marriage rate will be found primarily in the creation of active church communities through which Christian faith and practice—particularly in all that concerns marriage and the family—can be articulated and made relevant to a modern, pluralistic society.

References: Chapter One

1 Hastings, 1973.
2 Murray, 1969, p. 224.
3 cf. Shorter, 1973, CROMIA/22 and 1975a, 1975b.
4 Hulsen and Mertens, n.d., Chap. 8.
5 *Ibid.*
6 Shorter, 1975b, pp. 21–6.
7 Hastings, 1973, pp. 47–50.
8 Boerakker, 1975.
9 Shorter, 1973, CROMIA/22.
10 Hart, 1973, CROMIA/24, pp. 11–12.
11 Kasaka, 1976.
12 Whooley in Verryn (ed.), 1975b, pp. 245–378.
13 Conway, 1975.
14 Hastings, 1973, p. 49.
15 Hastings, *ibid.*, p. 102.
16 Conway, 1975, p. 35.
17 Aquina, 1975, I and II. Our contributors have used the name "Rhodesia", and this name has been retained throughout this book. We recognize, however, the increasing popularity of the name "Zimbabwe".
18 Thomas and Chisanga, 1976.
19 Hastings, 1973, p. 169.
20 Kauta, Welshman, Gastonguay *et al.*, 1975. The situation has, however, changed drastically in 1976. Recruitment for the mines has been stopped.
21 Spiegel, 1975, in Verryn (ed.), pp. 435–97.
22 Hastings, 1973, p. 42.
23 Hastings, 1973, p. 42, fn. 4.
24 Peskin, 1975, in Verryn (ed.), pp. 379–434.
25 Communication at Chilema meeting, 1975.
26 Peters, in Verryn (ed.) 1975, pp. 25–50.
27 cf. Brian Hearne, "Theology, Basic Course", AMECEA Pastoral Institute, Eldoret, 1976, p. 30.

28 Hearne, 1975.

29 Lebona in Verryn (ed.), 1975, pp. 133–4.

30 Reference was made to this concept in Axel-Ivar Berglund's paper presented to the La Verna meeting in 1974. In the published version of his paper in Verryn (ed.) 1975, he preferred to withdraw the reference. The authors are using it here on their own responsibility.

31 Berglund in Verryn (ed.), 1975, pp. 1–24.

32 Berglund in Verryn (ed.), 1975, p. 20.

33 Lufuluabo, 1969, p. 91; cf. also Ulbrich and van Driessche, 1972.

34 Lufuluabo, 1969, p. 86.

35 Whooley in Verryn (ed.), 1975b, p. 324.

36 Lufuluabo, 1969, p. 86.

37 van Huet, 1975.

38 Doucette, 1972.

39 Häring, lecture delivered at Gaba, August 19th, 1974.

40 Zwarthoed, 1973, p. 16.

41 However, the *Declaration on Certain Questions Concerning Sexual Ethics* published in January 1976 by the Roman Congregation for the Doctrine of the Faith, is concerned with the sexual aspect of relations before marriage, rather than with initiation into a stable, indissoluble union. Its condemnation of pre-marital sex for psychological reasons and because of external circumstances, even when there is a firm intention to marry, appears to be based entirely on western cultural presuppositions. There is no reference to African or other non-western marriage customs in the document. cf. *L'Osservatore Romano*, January 22nd, 1976, N 4 (408), pp. 5, 11–12.

42 Letter of the Bishop of Jinja, October 16th, 1974.

43 Whooley in Verryn (ed.), 1975b, p. 376.

Chapter 2

Divorce and Remarriage

I Case Material

1   *The General Picture in Contemporary Africa*

A major conclusion of the first chapter was that reluctance to marry in church is a result of social instability in general and the instability of marriage institutions in particular. As Hans Boerakker pointed out, the fear of young people in eastern Uganda that their marriages are liable to break down is far from being a groundless fear.[1] All the evidence points to an alarming increase in broken marriages. In western Uganda, Melvin Perlman drew a picture of marital instability among the Toro people in the 1960s that dovetails perfectly with Boerakker's.[2] In the past, the significant differences in attitude on the part of men and women to the marriage relationship were rendered less disruptive by the parents' careful choice of marriage partners. Today young people do not choose as carefully. They lack experience and they act hastily, cohabiting before negotiations are completed or even begun. People have become used to divorce and efforts at reconciliation are no longer made. Most divorces occur among young partners.

It is difficult to collect material about divorce, still more so to collect reliable statistics on divorce in Africa. Divorce was possible according to the customs of most African ethnic groups before the coming of the missionary and the colonial administrator. However, it was largely offset by the possibility of polygamy as an alternative, especially in the case of child-lessness. Today, although statutory and customary divorce procedures are foreseen by the legislation, comparatively few divorces actually come before the courts, and even when they do, the courts are often forced to accept a *fait accompli*. Brendan

33

Conway shows that the legislators in the various countries, while trying to make customary divorce proceedings available at the level of the local magistrate or district commissioner, have also tried to prevent divorces being obtained too easily.[3] In some cases, as in Kenya, divorce law follows the much criticized English model. This was rejected by the Spry Commission which, although it also opposed divorce by consent, recommended that each divorce case should be dealt with on its own merits. It also recommended that no divorce suits should be heard during the first three years of marriage and before an attempt at reconciliation. The Kalema Report in Uganda recommended the introduction of reconciliation committees, and the Tanzanian Law of Marriage Act has insisted on a two year limit before divorce suits can be introduced, as well as on reference to a reconciliation committee. These committees are set up by the government, or they are voluntary bodies which have been designated by the government as reconciliation committees.

Perlman found that most customary courts in western Uganda dealt with the return of bridewealth as evidence of divorce, although they usually considered other evidence such as lack of support. In this way *de facto* divorces were converted into *de jure* divorces.

Adrian Hastings noted that in many places divorce proceedings are begun by wives, and he considered this evidence of a greater independence of women a reason for the increase in marital breakdowns.[4] Sister Aquina found an increase of litigation begun by women in Nambya, Rhodesia, not only on grounds of cruelty and ill-treatment, but also on grounds of infidelity. One of the cases she records is as follows:

Mrs. Matthew discovered that her husband was having an affair with another woman who was currently seeking a divorce at the chief's court. She went to her own headman to sue her husband, but her headman cautioned her to desist, because if it were publicly known that her husband was sleeping with a woman who was still married, her husband would be heavily fined. However, she insisted that her case be taken to the chief's court and that she be given the opportunity of accusing her husband for sleeping with another man's wife. The court hearing took place and the husband was charged $140 for adultery. He agreed to pay, but reminded his wife at court that from that day onwards he was going to work for damages and that he would not be able to buy anything for her or her children until he had paid off his fine; she herself would have to look out for the family. He also declared publicly that he was going to marry the other woman as soon as she had obtained her divorce, for otherwise he would have lost $140 for nothing. The men at court blamed Mrs. Matthew for having caused great trouble to her husband and reminded her that men had the right to sleep with more than one woman. Soon after the court hearing Mrs. Matthew left her husband and went to her parents, thus dissolving her own marriage. Within a week the other woman had obtained her divorce and married her lover.[5]

Hans Boerakker makes the point that, because women nowadays take their husbands to court, one should not conclude that women initiate divorce proceedings more frequently than men.[6] All it proves is that women need the courts and men do not. Moreover, men can marry a second wife before they dismiss the first one, if, indeed, a dismissal is necessary. Successive polygamy which involves the effective desertion by the husband of the first wife is increasingly common. Nevertheless, Boerakker records 1,351 separation proceedings in the sub-county courts of Western Budama, Uganda, between 1957 and 1972. Of these, 1,258 or 93% had the wife as plaintiff!

Usually, the local courts have no jurisdiction over Christian, statutory marriage and this makes it less easy for Christian wives to sue their husbands in court. Magistrates and chiefs dismiss the case when they learn of an existing church marriage. If they have not been married in church, women can hold out separation in court as an ultimate weapon against their husbands, should the marriage be a failure. Here we have, incidentally, another reason for reluctance to marry in church, and it is noticeable that Christians without a church marriage figure very largely in the court cases. Boerakker studied all the separation cases of 1965 in three subcounties of eastern Uganda. There were 126, and all of them involved at least one Christian. Njelu Kasaka, studying marriages and divorces in a village settlement in central Tanzania (Tumbi), found that 59% of those without church marriages had experienced a divorce or separation, while only 15% of those with church marriage had been separated.[7] Partners were more likely to have had a non-Christian family background where church marriage had ended in failure, but this was not the case for those who separated after a customary union.

In Rhodesia, Sister Aquina came to the conclusion that

divorces were not numerous compared to other countries, and this is probably due to the fact that the patrilineal, customary system is still resilient and backed by civil legislation and high bridewealth.[8] Divorce was higher on the tea estates than in the Tribal Trust Lands, and considerably more men were divorced and remarried than women. Although women may be able to initiate divorce proceedings through the courts to end an intolerable marriage, they are the ones who suffer by the divorce. Men can remarry without difficulty, but divorced women find it hard to remarry. Many drift to the towns to enter into casual unions with migrant labourers or to become prostitutes. Another fact discovered by Sister Aquina was that divorce escalates. The percentage of divorces in second marriages is much higher than in first marriages. Examining divorce and remarriage from the point of view of religious allegiance, it was found that the independent church, the Vapostori, had a very high divorce rate. The Methodists were the next highest, then came the Church of Christ, the Zionists, and finally the Roman Catholics whose very small number of divorces is probably due to the strong prohibition of divorce in their church. Non-Christians had a divorce rate only slightly bigger than that of the Methodists. In Nambya the proportion of divorces in the whole community was comparable to that in eastern Rhodesia. Only 3% of the Nambyan men in the sample were divorced and only 2% of the women. Only one Catholic man and one Methodist woman in the sample had been divorced and remarried.

Sister Aquina accepts Max Gluckman's conclusion that where there is high bridewealth operating in a patrilineal family system with virilocal residence, divorce is likely to be comparatively rare. High bridewealth was traditionally an indication of a wider interest in a marriage. More relatives, and associates, benefited by the marriage and by its continuing stability. This accounts for the relatively low divorce figures in Rhodesia and for places like Kigezi in western Uganda, where the low divorce figures were contrasted by Adrian Hastings with high figures in Toro (also in western Uganda).[9] However, bridewealth becomes a problem in these communities when a money economy is introduced, and cash replaces cattle or other livestock in the marriage transactions. Bridewealth tends to be computed in cash according to the value of the number of cows which would have been traditionally transferred. High cash bridewealth encourages elopement, but so far, in Kigezi, even marriages which begin with elopement have turned out to be fairly stable. Yeld studied 140 marriages in Kigezi and found that 30% of them involved an elopement. Less bridewealth was paid when the marriage was negotiated after an elopement, but the elopement marriage was as likely to last as a negotiated marriage.[10]

Most African communities are unable to cope with elopement, and resulting marital instability is the common experience. In this situation another fact becomes apparent. Church marriage really does tend to confer stability, and Christians who feel unable to contract an indissoluble marriage are right to fear it. We noted above the evidence of Tumbi in central Tanzania. In Mityana, Uganda, 8% of the male Christians interviewed and 13% of the Christian women, stated that their present marriage could not be blessed by the Church because of a previous church marriage which had now been broken. This was, in fact, a small percentage beside the broken customary marriages. As much as 45% of the respondents had experienced some kind of union or liaison other than their present marriage, (excluding church marriage). Approximately, a third of the sample had church marriages, and of these slightly less than a quarter had broken down.[11]

In the urban communities of East Africa the pattern is not very different from the rural areas. Joseph Ssennyonga who studied Nagulu Housing Estate in Kampala City, Uganda, in 1972, concluded that church marriages—particularly marriages between Roman Catholics—showed more stability than other forms of marriage.[12] W. B. Lamousé-Smith, conducted research in 1970 among migrants in East African towns. Surprisingly, he found that although 52% of the migrants were unmarried, and of these the Christians were a majority, there was not a single broken church marriage in the survey, while 13% of the non-Christians were separated or divorced. The absence of divorces among Christians is probably partly due to the young age of the migrants.[13] At Kitwe, the Zambian Copperbelt town, Thomas and Chisanga found that the majority of Christian marriages were characterized by fidelity, and that it was the minority of inactive church members whose marriages were in danger of breaking down.[14] The inner community of the church acts as a means of social control.

Everywhere the reasons for marital breakdown are very similar. On the man's side it is personal incompatibility, wife's

37

infidelity, desertion, laziness, drunkenness or illness. On the side of the woman it is personal incompatibility, husband's drunkenness, violence, infidelity, desertion or refusal of support. The failure to have children is also mentioned, but appears to play a very small role among the motives for divorce. In the urban situation tensions are created by the greater independence of the woman, and we shall examine this in detail in a subsequent section on labour migration and the towns of Southern Africa. It is interesting to compare divorce statistics from the population censuses, although these figures are certain to be an understatement.[15] Thus in East Africa in 1969, Kenya's percentage of divorced and remarried people was 4·22% of the married population. In Uganda, in the same year, it was 10·72%. In Tanzania in 1967, the percentage of divorced and remarried in the country as a whole was 6·31%, while in the tiny, predominantly Muslim country of Zanzibar, it was 20·56%, a figure clearly due to Muslim permissiveness about divorce. The Tanzanian census offers a comparison between rural and urban divorces in the country as a whole: Rural: 6·20%, Urban: 9·01%, not a very significant difference. We may conclude this section by remarking that the stability of church marriages is maintained at a price in most of the areas discussed, the price of a low church marriage rate. In spite of this a small percentage of broken church marriages exists. Marriages that are not solemnized in church tend to be considerably less stable.

2   *Matriliny and Divorce in Africa*

In the first chapter we already noticed that matrilineal, family systems favour divorce, because there is a basic tension in the husband-wife relationship. This observation is amply borne out by the statistics. The study made by Kauta, Welshman and Gastonguay in Central Malawi was among Christians, mainly belonging to the Presbyterian Church.[16] In spite of the fact that many, if not most, of the interviews were conducted at the church door—therefore, among practising Christians—23% of the respondents were either separated or divorced. Slightly more than a third of those who were definitively divorced were divorced because of one or another aspect of the migrant labour system. The divorces of the other two thirds were all caused by local "behavioural" problems connected with the family system. In this study it was mainly Chewa people who were interviewed. Among the matrilineal, uxorilocal Yao of Malawi it

38

is reckoned that 41·3% of all marriages end in divorce.[17] The Ndembu of Zambia are matrilineal, but their residence is virilocal. This situation also favours instability and 52·7% of Ndembu marriages end in divorce.[18] The matrilineal Tonga of Zambia are neolocal in residence, and 29·8% of their marriages end in divorce.[19] Sister Aquina studied the Rhodesian Tonga who are the only matrilineal people in Rhodesia.[20] She discovered that their divorce rate was higher than that of other ethnic groups in Rhodesia. In her sample 19% of the men and 7% of the women had divorced and remarried. Most divorces in Tongaland are initiated by men, and not by women. Sister Aquina writes:

A husband who intends to divorce his wife first removes one of the three cooking stones from her kitchen and places it in her basket, instructing her to take it to her parents as a sign of her rejection. After that he will remove the door from her kitchen so that the kitchen becomes an open shelter for goats. This makes it clear to everyone that the household, centering round the woman's kitchen, has been dissolved.

On seeing her kitchen dismantled, the wife may appeal to her parents-in-law to persuade their son to forgive her and to take her back. If he does, the marriage continues, but if he refuses, she will return to her parents. Her parents will only take action and report the matter to the chief, if they want the husband to take back their daughter. If not, the matter rests there and the woman is free to remarry.[21]

Divorce is not a very recent phenomenon among matrilineal peoples. In the 1930s Audrey Richards presented divorce percentages on three samples of marriages from the Bemba people of Zambia. In a random sample of non-Christians in Chinsali she found that 20·5% of the married people had experienced divorce, that 18% had been divorced once, and the remaining 2·5% more than once. In a random sample of men from Kasama and Mpika, 35% of the married people had experienced divorce, of which 24% had been divorced once, 6% divorced twice, 4% divorced three times, and 1% divorced five times. Finally in a random sample of women from the same area, she found that 44% of the married people had experienced divorce, of which 38% had been divorced once, and 5% divorced twice.

Richards also demonstrated that divorces were on the increase and were more prevalent in the new villages. Whereas in an old village only 16% of the marriages ended in divorce and those involved had been divorced only once, in two new villages the percentages of divorces were 48% and 58% respectively. Of these 9% and 7% represented people who had been divorced more than once.[23]

A large cluster of matrilineal peoples is centred on the adjacent countries of Malawi, Zambia, southern Tanzania and Rhodesia (the Tonga only); but there are also matrilineal peoples in West Africa. Ghana is the West African country where matrilineal systems predominate, and yet divorce does not seem to create the same problems as in Central Africa. Mary Douglas has argued that matriliny has a far greater flexibility and a wider range of association and alliances than patriliny. The looseness of its ties permits this wider collaboration and encourages an open recruitment of manpower. When the economic field is restricted matrilineal fathers tend to favour their sons, and the demand for things is higher than the demand for men. In a situation of economic expansion the reverse is the case, and matrilineal kinship possesses great advantages.[24] In Central Africa there is not the type of economic expansion that favours matriliny. Men are drawn away as migrant labourers to other places, the Copperbelt, the mines in Rhodesia and South Africa, precisely because of a lack of economic opportunity in their own homelands. In Ghana modern market conditions and an expanding economy may have created more favourable conditions for matriliny than in Central Africa. The matrilineal system appears to generate fewer tensions and to be inherently more stable in conditions of steady economic growth. The incidence of polygamy in Ghana is also high, since polygamy favours an even wider range of alliances and collaboration. Polygamous tendencies are bound up with fear of indissoluble marriage in Ghana and help to account for the low marriage rate there.[25]

In the study carried out by Kauta and others in Central Malawi among married Christians, it was found that 63% had church marriages, a percentage slightly lower than the figure based on church records.[26] There was also a growth in the percentage of church marriages over the years in the sample. When those who had church marriages were asked to give their reason for it, a very large majority gave stereotyped answers, referring to the fact that they were Christians, that it was their Christian duty etc. About 6% stated that it was their own choice, and 9% that it was the choice of their parents. Twelve per cent of the respondents went further and spoke about the advantages of church marriage as something strong, long-lasting and holy. The remainder of the respondents mentioned motives such as ease of obtaining a church marriage and the usefulness of a marriage certificate for obtaining a passport. The percentage of divorces among these Malawian Christians was certainly higher than, say, among Christians in East Africa, but it was lower than the average quoted for most of the matrilineal peoples of Central Africa as a whole. The conclusion is that, not only is church marriage desired by Christians in this matrilineal area because it is thought to confer stability, but that church marriage does, in fact, confer a greater stability.

3 Labour Migration and Divorce in Africa

The migrant labour system is frequently blamed for the high rate of marital breakdowns in South Africa, particularly in the urban areas. There was plenty of evidence from the studies made in South Africa that the system does contribute to marital instability. Yet, the phenomenon is a complex one and deeply rooted in contemporary social processes. It is part of the whole movement of modernization in southern Africa—a fact of modern, social life. However, it is not the only cause of marital instability, and there are other aspects of modern living which are a source of tension.

Patrick Whooley, studying marriage in Ciskei, found that labour migration was essential to a man's full initiation. Coming out of the initiation school, the young man is known as *ikrwala*. He paints his face red and will be recognized as a full man when he takes a train and goes off to work in some big centre. Students return to their schools or places of education, but the vast majority go off to work. Very few wives manage to accompany their husbands to work for any length of time in this area. The man leaves after about a month of marriage, and returns every year for a month thereafter. Many return to settle down with their wives when they are past middle age. Wives visit their husbands in town for short periods also, usually to get a baby. Men who are away at work are not faithful to their wives and much of their wages may be spent on lovers in the city. The usual reason given by women who separated from their husbands is that they received little or no support. A smaller number leave because of love affairs with other men.[27]

41

Andrew Spiegel's study of marriage and migrant labour in Lesotho revealed a dramatic increase in migration over recent years.[28] As we saw in the previous chapter, there is a correlation between migration and marriages that begin with elopement. At the time of Spiegel's stay in Ha Mokgatla 55·2% of the marriages in the village were currently split by migrant labour and 14·9% had been previously split by it. 18·4% were widowed and 9·2% were broken by divorce. In only 2·3% of the cases was it possible for both spouses to live together as migrant labourers. The proportion of divorces was not noticeably high and the causes of divorce were varied. Spiegel gives three cases.

In the first case the husband went away to work in the mines, leaving his wife with her parents-in-law. However, she soon became pregnant by another man and decided to abandon her marriage to the migrant. She was not expelled by her parents-in-law.

In the second case a man who had never been recruited as a migrant labourer had his wife leave him. Probably, his refusal to go away and work influenced her decision to desert him, since great social stigma attaches to a man who does not become a wage-earner (which, in practice, means becoming a migrant labourer). Moreover, the wife needed money and migrant labour is the only way poverty can be alleviated in the short term.

In the third case the husband had been a migrant labourer for ten years. He then returned to settle down with his wife in the village. Shortly after his permanent return to the village, his wife left him. Spiegel notes that this case suggests that incompatibilities between spouses may not be realized during the period of migrant labour, when the only contact they have is a brief annual holiday during which the husband is not expected to work in and around the village.

Spiegel found that the wives of absent migrant labourers necessarily enjoy a great deal of authority and freedom which they would not do if their husbands were at home. This has a debilitating effect on marriage if the men cannot adapt to it on their return. It is often the basis for disputes between husbands and wives. There is even a further development created by migrant labour which certainly undermines the Christian ideal of marriage. In a normal situation, with the husbands present, the interpersonal links between married women in their husband's village are through his relatives. With the men absent, the focal points of these relationships are no longer there. Common lovers tend to replace the husband as a focal point for relationships. Married women find their relationships strengthened by sharing a concubine. They also commonly regard concubinage as necessary for health, and the practice is not necessarily a basis for tension with their husbands.

We have already seen (in the previous chapter) the part played by the church blessing of marriage in the migrant labour system. In this section we have seen how the system undermines the concept of Christian marriage in practice. Migrant labour has many far-reaching economic and social effects. It deprives the rural areas of the labour force necessary for its development and it tends to make the migrant labourer himself more conservative, placing his security in the traditional character and structure of his home village. In Lesotho, for example, people become more and more dependent on cash and consumer goods from South Africa while the potential of Lesotho actually declines. Short of making it possible for wives and families to accompany the migrant husbands, the only possible way of ending the system is to provide an alternative source of income at home. This would involve a very painful transition but marriage and family life would be normalized. In the next section mention will be made of some of the other causes for marital breakdowns in urban South Africa.

4 The Churches and Divorce

We shall deal more fully with the churches' pastoral practice concerning divorce and remarriage in the third part of this chapter—Models for Pastoral Action. We consider here the practical influence which the churches' pastoral activity may, or may not, have had on marital instability.

Hugo Huber, in his recent study of marriage among the Kwaya people of northern Tanzania, offers an interesting sidelight on the attempt by missionaries to restore marital stability to a matrilineal society.[29] The Kwaya are a relatively small ethnic group possessing a matrilineal family system and a partly uxorilocal rule of residence. Before the coming of Roman Catholic missionaries to the area, bridewealth was paid as a means of acquiring foreign wives from neighbouring patrilineal tribes. Such wives, it was reckoned, would be faithful and would not be tempted to return to their families after a few years of

43

marriage. The practice was certainly a method by which men could transfer property to their own children, as well as stabilize their marriage, but it was also in the nature of things disruptive of the whole matrilineal system. Missionaries have been "apostles of bridewealth" at many times and in many places in Africa. Realizing the importance of bridewealth for the stability of a marriage, they have sometimes insisted rigidly upon it, and in some areas they have even been instrumental in introducing the custom where it did not exist before! Bukwaya was a case in point. During the 1940s the missionaries hoped to extend the practice of paying bridewealth to marriages of Kwaya men with Kwaya women, but the campaign met with no success. On the one hand, maternal relatives proved too strong for the missionaries and managed to undermine the new system. On the other hand, economic conditions forced the amount of bridewealth to new heights, often sanctioned by the colonial government, thus placing its payment beyond the means of many Kwaya men. After the failure of the missionary campaign, new factors contributed to marital instability in the area. One factor was the—by now familiar—relaxation of parental control and family pressures on the marriage partners. Another is the rise of a money economy and the increased facilities for travel and mobility. Huber also finds a preponderance of females over males a factor in the trend towards greater marital instability. Husbands, deserted by their wives, have little difficulty in finding others, and polygamy flourishes. Oddly enough, polygamy in Bukwaya is not, as it frequently is elsewhere, associated with marital stability. On the contrary, Huber found that polygamists with two or three wives had often had as many as five or eight, but had been deserted by them.

Let us now turn to another aspect of the churches' pastoral activity—not the prevention of instability—but the work of reconciliation and pastoral care of marriages threatened by breakdown. Martin Peskin offers us two cases from Soweto, the African township of Johannesburg, and it is interesting to note that these do not concern marriages split by labour migration, but marriages of couples living together in town.[30]

The first case concerns Kenneth, a not very fervent Roman Catholic and Susan, a Methodist. Susan was received into the Roman Catholic Church before their marriage according to Roman Catholic rites in Johannesburg in 1959. They settled in

Soweto and Kenneth was employed as a driver-messenger by a large firm. At night and at week-ends he practised as a herbalist, while Susan earned a little extra for the house by working as a seamstress. For four years the marriage was happy until Susan became ill and Kenneth diagnosed her symptoms as a sign from the ancestors that she should become a spiritual diviner. Susan disagreed in spite of the confirmation of Kenneth's diagnosis by other herbalists and diviners. A white, medical doctor was consulted who prescribed tranquillizers and analgesics, but the symptoms persisted. Kenneth's aunt, a prominent member of a Zionist church, was of the opinion that the illness indicated a call to join the church and Susan was persuaded to do so by the local bishop.

Susan became involved in the affairs of the Zionist church. She underwent training as a spiritual healer in the church and began to travel to the city, healing people, attending church meetings every week-end, during the week and at night. She was sometimes away from home for days on end. In Kenneth's opinion she no longer acted like a wife. Arguments developed and the stalemate was only resolved by the intervention of Susan's parents who urged her to obey her husband. She did so and left the church. Subsequently their marriage became sound and Susan fulfilled her role as wife satisfactorily. Once again we see these urban married people operating at various levels to solve their problem, traditional medicine and beliefs, western hospital medicine, the Church. Since Susan's cure coincided with her emancipation from her traditional role, it can be assumed that her illness was related to frustration in her role as wife. However, the greater independence which church membership brought her conflicted with her husband's more traditional expectations. It is noteworthy that the church, having been the cause of this conflict, did not provide a solution or compromise. Reconciliation was effected in a traditional way, through the family.

The second case is that of Elizabeth and John, a couple born and educated in Soweto. John was a truck driver in Johannesburg and before marriage lived with his widowed mother who ran a vegetable stall at a Soweto taxi rank. Although both were financially independent, John gave her a large percentage of his earnings. Since there was ample room in the house, John continued living there with Elizabeth after their marriage and Elizabeth helped the old lady with her vegetable stall. Three years after the beginning of the marriage, Elizabeth could tolerate it no longer and accused her mother-in-law of interference in their marriage, denying her freedom and exploiting them financially. She applied for a house and got one. The widow appealed to her late husband's relatives to bring pressure on John to return to his mother's house. Meanwhile Elizabeth found work at a Medical Research Centre in Johannesburg. After a year of this independence John insisted that Elizabeth start working for his mother again, and for the sake of peace Elizabeth agreed. However, she and John soon ran into financial difficulties, while the mother-in-law's business flourished. There was no alternative but to go to work again. Elizabeth regained her job, but pressure from the in-laws increased. The mother-in-law became ill, and John felt it his duty to return, but Elizabeth refused to follow. John and his family demanded that she stay at the place of his choice and he removed all their possessions from Elizabeth's house. When Elizabeth tried to interfere, he assaulted her, and continued to threaten her with violence for some time afterwards. Eventually she filed a suit for divorce, and an order was passed preventing him from molesting or interfering with her. Although Elizabeth was a practising Anglican and John a Baptized Methodist, neither of them thought of taking their problem to a minister of religion. Peskin notes that this failure is typical. Ministers are not expected to offer any practical advice, but simply to restate doctrinal positions. No one expects a priest to be of any help. Like Elizabeth and John, people turn to their families, and when these fail, to the courts. The husband and his family usually expect a problem to be solved on traditional lines, and the churches also make the saving of the marriage their primary concern. A woman like Elizabeth, bent on emancipation, is not going to remain unhappy to please the Church! Evidence collected by Norman Thomas and Daniel Chisanga in Kitwe, Zambia, indicates a similar state of affairs. Although the churches contribute in Kitwe to an active and wide-ranging counselling service, their attitude tends to be more judgemental than positive in a situation in which divorce is frequent and easily obtained.[31]

At the end of this section we can draw several conclusions. Firstly, church marriage—as a rule—confers stability on the union, and is known by people to do so. Secondly, even outside matrilineal areas, a proportion of church marriages must be expected to break down. Thirdly, mechanisms for reconciliation provided by the churches are largely unsuccessful or irrelevant. The question to be considered in the theological and pastoral sections of this chapter is: If the churches can admit a more positive pastoral attitude to divorced and remarried Christians, will this necessarily undermine the stability of church marriage?

II   Theological Reflection

1   The New Testament and the Early Church
Our theological discussion of the subject of divorce and remarriage has been guided by the contributions of Brian Gaybba and Anthony O'Flynn.[32] Both are in substantial agreement. Our conviction is that Jesus totally rejected divorce and remarriage. In other words, Jesus rejected any system which can speak of "grounds for divorce". Whatever the famous Matthean exception may mean, and if Jesus himself pronounced it, it cannot mean an exception in the sense of a ground for divorce. Otherwise, Jesus would have been favouring the very Mosaic concession which—in the context—he is criticizing. If someone had approached Jesus and told him that his or her partner had committed adultery, would that person have received the answer: "That is sufficient ground for divorce"? The texts of New Testament do not allow us to think so. Instead, it is much more likely that Jesus would encourage the person to put into practice the love demanded by the situation, a love that manifests itself in forgiveness. Marriage demands a loyalty and a faithfulness that rises above injuries even as grievous as adultery. If a person who had been separated from his or her partner had approached Jesus and asked him whether he or she could remarry, would he have just said: "Go ahead and remarry"? Again, nothing in the New Testament texts suggests that this would have been his answer. On the face of it, it seems likely that he would have asked the person to remain loyal to his or her spouse. For Jesus there was no circumstance that could justify breaking the bond forged by marriage, nor was there any circumstance that could justify married people forging a new bond in the lifetime of their partners. We believe that the tradition of the Western Church is basically correct and faithful

47

to the mind of Jesus Christ in refusing to allow any intrinsic dissolubility of marriage.

However, we must also accept that, for Jesus, there could be no possible reason for ceasing to forgive others, and for refusing to be reconciled with them whatever wrong they might have done. Jesus looked to the heart—to a man's attitude. He would have had no time for "ways out" or for "grounds for divorce", but does that mean to say that he would not have looked with compassion on an abandoned spouse, especially on one who had remarried and who was now in a situation that could not be undone? We think he would have been disposed to grant reconciliation to such a person, and we think further that the Eastern Church has had a valid theological insight in making allowances for human weakness, and in accepting the principle of *oikonomia*, according to which the Church claims from Christ the power to find a pastoral solution in individual cases which the general law cannot solve.

Divorce is mentioned by four New Testament writers: Matthew (Mt. 5:32; and 19:3–9), Mark (Mk. 10:2–12), Luke (Lk. 16:18), and Paul (I Cor. 7:10–16). O'Flynn, following Karl Lehmann, points out that two writers (Mark and Luke) express the unequivocal opposition of Jesus to divorce, while the other two (Matthew and Paul) introduce restrictions upon this directive of Jesus. The Matthean "fornication" clauses may be an attempt—which is typical of Matthew's Gospel—to make allowances for human failings. The so-called "Pauline privilege" is much clearer. After the explicit statement of Christ's prohibition of divorce, Paul gives his own authoritative interpretation that there is a situation in which the Christian may not oppose divorce, namely if the pagan partner in a mixed marriage demands and effects the divorce. Paul's concession implies the absolute character of the original directive as a binding precept, rather than simply an "ideal" to aim at, but both the Apostle Paul and the Matthean church regarded themselves as authorized in certain circumstances to concede the possibility of divorce. It should be noted, however, that separation is not imposed in these passages, nor is remarriage recommended.

The duality of viewpoint found in the New Testament is found also in the Early Church. Origen in the 2nd century makes the following statement in his commentary on Matthew:

Already some of the leaders of the church, contrary to what is written, have allowed a wife to marry in her husband's lifetime. In this they are, it is true, acting contrary to the words of Scripture where it is said: "A wife is bound to her husband as long as he lives" (I Cor. 7:39) and "Accordingly, she will be called an adulteress if she lives with another man while her husband is alive" (Rm. 7:3). And yet their action was not entirely without foundation, for it may be supposed that they permitted it to avoid worse, though certainly in contradiction to the law established in the beginning and according to the words of Scripture.[33]

Gaybba notes that Origen also speaks about permitting widows to remarry, remarking that these marriages (like those of the divorced) do not have an incontestable sacramental quality in the Eastern tradition, even nowadays. Lehmann asserts that testimonies like those of Origen can easily be multiplied, and Gaybba wonders whether the recurring ban on the remarriage of divorced women in the post-apostolic tradition does not mean that divorced men were readmitted to communion after remarriage. Connected with this is the notable lack of statements ruling out all possibility of remarriage on the part of men. A few examples, moreover, make it clear that the Early Church did accommodate second marriages, especially in the case of an innocent husband.

Is this simply a meaningless juxtaposition of contradictory attitudes in the New Testament and the Early Church? According to Lehmann, the principle of indissolubility has an inherently higher normative force than the concession of milder practice in particular cases. The concessions of the Early Church, following the principle of choosing the lesser evil, drew attention to the obligatory character of Jesus' directive, and ensured that, as far as possible, it was maintained in practice. Such concessions must not be allowed to turn into an independent system opposed to Christ's explicit command, but they provide a basis for the pastoral practice of readmitting divorced and remarried people to communion.

2   Theological Basis for the Pastoral Options

The western Church came to express the doctrine of the indissolubility of marriage through the idea of the *vinculum* or bond. Basically, the concept is a juridical one, and stems from the overdeveloped identification of contract and sacrament. Adrian Hastings is right to criticize the concept of the bond

49

when it is seen primarily as an ontological fact, objectively preventing a further marriage in any circumstances.[34] It should, he argues, be seen as a required intention or moral obligation. It was precisely because of this notion of the bond, that the Roman Catholic Church was obliged to make use of the expedient of nullity in attempting to find a solution for the problem of broken marriages. Although the procedures have been conducted with extreme caution, and great care has been exercised in trying to establish the actual facts of each case, there is, nevertheless, something hypocritical in declaring a marriage null and void on the basis of factors that may have nothing to do with its actual breakdown, let alone the case of an annulment being used to justify the break-up of a genuine human relationship in favour of a second marriage.

Latterly, however, there has been a considerable widening of interpretation of the grounds for nullity in the Roman Catholic Church, so much so that in some respects nullity procedures seem to be coming nearer to the actual causes of breakdown and to be joining hands with some of the other solutions proposed. There remains, nevertheless, the basic unwillingness to call a spade a spade. Gerard Taylor indicates the ways in which nullity cases are developing.[35]

The canon (1083) which declares a marriage invalid in which there is an error regarding the person was presumed for centuries to refer to the person's physical identity. It is now being taken to refer to a person's social status and to the qualities which make a person what he is in relation to others, e.g. previous criminal record, previous civil or attempted marriage, previous practice of prostitution, pathological defects and perversions. Another canon (1086) declares invalid a marriage in which either party excludes an essential aspect of marriage by a positive act of will. For a long time this canon was interpreted in the light of another (1084) which declares that a simple error of the mind about the indissolubility of marriage does not vitiate matrimonial consent. In the absence of an explicit statement or sign, the presumption was that an indissoluble marriage was intended. It is now recognized that this presumption may be belied by the facts, that certain groups of people may not accept marital indissolubility, and that in certain circumstances a mental error easily turns into a positive intention.

Roman Catholic canon law has for long defined matrimonial

consent in the light of one specific, determining element, its character as a procreative union. The Second Vatican Council (*Gaudium et Spes* 48) describes marriage as a community of "life and love" and it has been proposed that this wider description of marriage should be incorporated into the reformed Code of Canon Law. It is now seen by canonists that a personality disorder which renders a person unfit for the common life that is marriage cannot validly marry. Finally, yet another broadening of canonical interpretation is the recognition that matrimonial consent may not only be absent, but that it may be half-hearted or inadequate.

Another course of action into which the Roman Catholic Church has been forced by its overdevelopment of the marriage bond concept is to extend the notion and practice of the Pauline Privilege. The so-called Petrine Privilege eventually made it possible to dissolve the marriages of non-Christians who had become separated and who, on the conversion of one of the partners, were unable to communicate with one another. The dissolution held good even if communication was later re-established or it became known that the other party was baptized. Finally in the 20th century popes began to grant a dissolution of disparate marriages between baptized and unbaptized persons, including marriages contracted in church with a dispensation and of marriages between two unbaptized persons. The reason for permitting the dissolution could be to allow the conversion of the petitioner, or to make it possible for one of the parties, or even a third party, to embrace the faith or receive the sacraments. From 1971 the Holy See began to restrict its practice and to grant dispensations in favour of the petitioner alone. In 1973 new norms were issued which refuse to grant a dissolution to a Roman Catholic partner in order to remarry a non-baptized person. Some theologians have suggested that the Petrine Privilege could even be extended to include the dissolution of ratified and consummated marriages of baptized people. On the other hand, there are canonists who hold that these are not really dissolutions at all but permissions to remarry, granted to people in very difficult situations. Gerard Taylor remarks that if this is the case, then Roman Catholics are, in fact, approaching the principle of *oikonomia* practised by the Oriental Churches.

Before leaving the realm of canon law we might mention a further canonical suggestion which is simply to reverse the favour of the law. Previously, in a case of divorce and remarriage in which grounds were being sought for the annulment of the first union, the previous marriage always enjoyed the favour of the law. The suggestion—and it is still only a suggestion—is that the law should now favour the existing marital situation, rather than a marriage which has irrevocably broken and which does not visibly exist.

Two theological opinions deserve consideration before we examine proposals for the restoration of divorced and remarried people to communion or their remarriage in church. One of these is that Christian marriage is an ideal, rather than an absolute, and that it should be recognized that some people fail to achieve the goal. We have already indicated that our findings are not in sympathy with such an idea. To say that the marriage bond is a moral obligation, rather than an ontological fact, is not to say that it is not a reality. In our opinion the indissolubility of marriage is a binding precept from Christ himself. Yet another opinion is the idea of certain theologians that a marriage can die, and that the death of the marriage itself dissolves the union, as much as the death of one of the partners. In fact, this theory is of limited value. Everyone accepts that a marriage can break down to the extent of being completely irretrievable and of there being *de facto* no community of life or love in existence. Even if this situation were to be recognized theologically by a doctrine of the "death of marriage", we would still be faced with the inherent contradiction of a person entering twice into a life-long union with the blessing of the church. Moreover, the phrase "life-long union" is a tautology if the "life" in question is merely the life of the union.

We must now study two practical proposals which seem to be more obviously in line with the theological thinking and pastoral practice of the Early Church, the restoration of divorced and remarried people to church communion and the remarriage of such people in church. In some provinces of the Anglican communion, for example the Church of Uganda, Rwanda and Boga-Zaïre, divorced people not only cannot be remarried in church, but there is disagreement as to whether they should be re-admitted to communion. In some cases they are admitted to the sacraments, but the dioceses follow different norms. In the case of the Roman Catholic Church discipline demands that divorced and remarried people should on no account be re-admitted to the sacraments. This ruling, not only has never been repealed, but it was reiterated in a strongly worded document issued by the Roman Congregation of the Faith in 1973.[36] However, a pastoral solution which does not yet have the force of law in the Roman Catholic Church, but which is widely and increasingly practised, is the so-called "Good Conscience Solution". This is based on the recognition that certain divorced and remarried people are living in good faith, believing that their present situation is the will of God for them. Under these circumstances they approach the sacraments, and are encouraged by pastors to approach them, in good faith. This is not a juridical decision by the pastor to disregard the church's law and admit such people to the practice of the sacraments. It is a decision made in the internal forum of conscience on the part of the persons concerned. The pastor recognizes a good conscience where it exists and encourages people to be in good conscience. In order to avoid scandal— especially liable to arise in the rural parishes of Africa—the pastor also ensures that the community as a whole is able to recognize the good conscience of those divorced and remarried people who approach the sacraments. Experience has proved that such cases can be accepted without scandal once they are understood. The "Good Conscience" solution receives ambiguous support from official church documents which exhort pastors to do all they can pastorally for people in these difficult situations, and it is analagous to the decision of a number of Roman Catholic Bishops' Conferences which recognize the good faith of many married people who use contraceptives for the common good of the family in defiance of the general ruling against the practice.[37]

O'Flynn, presenting the mind of the Roman Catholic theologian, Karl Lehmann, would go further than the recognition of a good conscience. He proposes a change in church discipline which, with adequate safeguards concerning the impossibility of remaking the first marriage and concerning the stability of the second union and the absence of scandal, would allow pastors to admit divorced and remarried people to the sacraments in particular instances.[38]

The practice of remarrying divorced people in church is followed by some provinces of the Anglican Communion, notably those of Central Africa and West Africa; by other churches in specific cases accepted as fulfilling the Matthean exceptive clause (thus, the Lutheran and Moravian Churches in Tanzania); and is practised by the Oriental Churches on the principle of *oikonomia* already mentioned. Although the Roman Catholic Church rejected the Protestant Reformers' appeal to the Matthean passages at the Council of Trent, the conciliar documents deliberately avoided condemning the Greek practice, and an earlier declaration in favour of the Greek tradition made in 1439 was repeated when the Tridentine texts were approved.[39] Adrian Hastings, following the Church of England's Commission on the Christian Doctrine of Marriage, also approves of the practice.[40]

In many ways remarriage in church is both a more logical, and a more theological, solution to the problem of the divorced and remarried. It acknowledges that, whatever the rights and wrongs of the marriage that failed and which cannot be restored, here now is a stable, loving relationship from which the love of God in Christ cannot be absent. Instead of tolerating a union that is recognized only in the consciences of the partners themselves, its sacramental quality is recognized and given expression in Christian celebration.

There are two problems connected with this procedure. The first is the acknowledgement that there exists a contradiction between the first and second marriage. In the Early Church second marriages were only permitted after the performance of a heavy canonical penance, and there is still a penitential note in the celebration of such marriages in the Oriental churches. We should not necessarily have the same presuppositions. As the Church of England's Commission points out, it is unsatisfactory to "cloud the life beginning with the shadow of the life that has passed".[41] However, an occasion must be presented, before the celebration of the second marriage, for divorced and remarried persons to express their sorrow for any responsibility they may have incurred in the breakdown of the first marriage and for the contradiction which their second marriage implies. This penitential rite should properly take place separately from the rite of marriage itself. However, the Church of England's Commission suggests that a declaration of intent be incorporated into the marriage rite to reassure the church community that the second marriage is not being lightly undertaken and that the church authorities are satisfied in this case that the partners accept all the conditions of Christian marriage.[42] It also goes without saying that if the churches recognize that a marriage celebrated in church has ceased to exist, they must make sure that it has also ended according to civil or customary law, and that all responsibilities arising out of the first marriage have been fulfilled.

The second problem is connected with the first. The "Good Conscience" solution assumes that we are dealing with divorced people who have already remarried according to civil or customary law. The Church of England's Commission is dealing with divorced people who desire to remarry, and argues that it is untheological to hold two marriage celebrations.[43] Marriage begins with the exchange of consent of the spouses, and it would be more logical to make the church ceremony coincide with the civil ceremony at the beginning of the second marriage. Against this point of view, a number of contributors to our theological discussion of the problem did not think that a pastor would be justified in recommending remarriage to Christians separated from their marriage partners. Although Adrian Hastings apparently adopts the view of the Church of England's Commission on the Christian Doctrine of Marriage,[44] pastors in Africa, as Archbishop Arden pointed out, are usually dealing with Christians who remarried according to customary law many years previously.[45] The question of a unified ceremony does not, therefore, arise. The church's recognition of the second marriage's validity could take the form of a renewal of consent according to canonical form, a church blessing, or even the unobtrusive process of radical healing if this were necessary.

Will the options examined here undermine the stability of church marriage? Given the fact that the churches are catering already for divorced and remarried people in various ways, it would seem not. Lehmann's principle has been accepted that these cases should not be allowed to become the norm. "Hard cases make bad laws" but "hard laws make bad Christians"! We have been more concerned in this section with a "theological re-ordering" of existing practices, rather than with the introduction of solutions that are entirely new.

III   Models for Pastoral Action

1   An Initial Case History

To illustrate the kind of situation which we have in mind, during this theological and pastoral discussion, we give here the case which is the starting point of Archbishop Arden's reflection on the subject.[46] The case is as follows: James is a Christian man living in a Muslim area of Central Malawi. In 1948 he took as his wife Dorothy, a girl from a Muslim family who was baptized before their marriage. James and Dorothy were married in church and lived together very happily for three years. They had two children. In 1951 James joined the army and was posted to a barracks in a country to the north. He was obliged to leave Dorothy and the children behind, and very soon she stopped writing to him. Eventually James learns that Dorothy has renounced her Christian faith and has married a Muslim man. In 1956 James was discharged from the army and returned to his village where he made every effort to get his wife back. She absolutely refused to return to him, and his marriage was regarded by everyone as being at an end. James lived alone for three years, and finally, in 1959, he married Margaret, a Christian girl from the same village, according to tribal custom. That was seventeen years ago! James and Margaret have remained together and have a large family of children. Their marriage bears every mark of a Christian marriage and both the parents and all the children are exceptionally keen church members. They have become virtually the leaders of the Christian community in the village. In 1976 the pastor now asks: Can they be allowed to communicate? Can they be allowed to marry in church? In the following paragraphs we shall see the various courses of action open to the churches.

2   *The Hard Line*

Two contributions to our discussions took what might be called the "hard line". In 1975 a seminar was held at St. Cyprian's Anglican Theological College at Lindi in Tanzania, involving three priests, eleven deacons and eleven Readers. The subject of the discussions was a series of questions that emerged from Adrian Hastings' Report on Marriage.[47] One of the questions was: Is it allowable in any circumstances to bless the wedding of a Christian who has already a lawful partner from whom he is separated? The answer was an unequivocal "No". A note appended to this answer reveals that there was a strong feeling that an undisclosed pregnancy by another man at the time of marriage should be considered a ground for nullity.

Stephen Kakokota also follows the traditional, hard line.[48] Sticking closely to the official discipline of the Roman Catholic

Church, he asks: What can be done pastorally for divorced and remarried people who are denied the sacraments? His answer is: "Pastors should do their best to try and settle such cases, if, however, there is no other way out, pastors should treat the people concerned kindly, and keep a fatherly eye on them, so that whenever there is a danger of death, they come to their rescue and save their souls."

Presumably, Kakokota's phrase "try and settle such cases" does not only mean "trying to restore the first marriage". He has also in mind the search for a regularization of the second union through nullity procedures. To these we now turn.

3   Nullity Procedures

Nullity is the speciality, as we have seen, of the Roman Catholic Church. We have also noted that the grounds for nullity are currently being extensively widened. In principle, therefore, a nullity case is a possible answer to many, if not most, of these problem cases. The question, however, is: are nullity proceedings practical? Does the machinery exist for dealing with such cases?

Until 1971, nullity cases in the Roman Catholic Church were tried in the first instance by a diocesan tribunal composed of three judges who were priests. If the sentence of the court was in favour of nullity, then the case had to be tried all over again in another diocesan tribunal which acted as an appeal court. If the sentence was upheld, the marriage could be declared null after a lapse of ten days, but if one of the parties appealed against the nullity during that time, the case would have to be tried yet again by another appeal court. Naturally, this cumbersome procedure ensured that very few nullity cases were ever heard in African countries. It was very difficult to find priests with the specialized training needed to become judges of such tribunals. Gerard Taylor tells us that, until recently, only two or three of the twenty-six Roman Catholic dioceses in Tanzania had a marriage tribunal for such cases.[49]

In 1971 new legislation came into effect. This allowed for the setting up of regional tribunals with an inter-diocesan membership, thus making better use of trained personnel. It also permitted a tribunal to be constituted with only one priest-judge, and it simplified the appeal procedure. The appeal court merely examines the sentence of the previous tribunal and does not try the case again, unless one of the parties lodges an appeal against the sentence. If the opinion of the second tribunal goes against the sentence of the first, the case must be forwarded to Rome.

These developments have greatly eased the situation. Rhodesia now has, since 1974, two regional marriage tribunals, and in Tanzania the Bishops' Conference has established a network of regional tribunals to cover the entire country. Moreover, from 1973–4 a series of training sessions were held up and down the country in order to find and train sufficient personnel to staff the tribunals and to handle the day-to-day problems concerning marriage in each diocese. If the law is meant to help people, and if the appeal to nullity is to mean anything in practice, then obviously Roman Catholic Bishops in other African countries must emulate Tanzania by setting up an organized system of regional marriage tribunals and taking steps to train the staff for them.

4 The "Good Conscience" Solution

We have already noted that some Provinces and Dioceses of the Anglican Communion admit divorced and remarried people to the sacraments under certain conditions. It is also becoming an increasingly frequent practice for Roman Catholic pastors to recognize the good conscience of such people in approaching the sacraments. Karl Lehmann lays down five conditions for admitting divorced and remarried people to the sacraments.[50]

(i) The obligatory, basic form of an indissoluble marriage must in no way be called into question. The parties concerned and the community as a whole must be made thoroughly aware that the situation is exceptional, and that help is only given in clearly circumscribed emergencies.

(ii) Any fault or responsibility for the breakdown of the first marriage must be acknowledged and repented, and any possible wrong or damage inflicted must be made good as far as possible. In certain circumstances this might even include a return to the first partner.

(iii) If a return to the first partner is impossible, it must be convincingly shown that, with the best will in the world, the first marriage cannot be restored. Particular attention must be paid to whether the first marriage has broken down for both partners.

(iv) A subsequently contracted marriage must have stood the test of a considerable space of time, as an indication of a determination to live together permanently, and must have proved itself as a moral reality. It must also be considered whether the maintenance of this second union has not become a new moral obligation in relation to the partner and to children that have been born. The partners must demonstrate that they are trying to live by the Christian Faith and are asking to share in the sacramental life of the Church for religious reasons and after serious examination of conscience.

(v) Both partners and the pastor responsible for them must see to it that no justified scandal is caused in the congregation and that the impression is not created that the Church no longer takes the indissolubility of marriage seriously.

In discussing the question of scandal, our contributors frequently said that they experienced no difficulty in practice. A Christian community very quickly grasped the situation when a difficult case was presented to it. It was found that Christians spontaneously opted for understanding and tolerance. The behaviour of the elder son in the parable of the Prodigal Son was often a useful example to take in discussing the right or wrong attitude of the community to such cases.

5   Remarriage in Church

Two examples from Tanzania offer us a stricter and more legalistic approach to the problem, before we examine Archbishop Arden's presentation of the canons of his province of the Anglican Communion. The Lutheran Church permits remarriage in church in specific cases, such as long separation, epilepsy or madness of one of the partners and some other cases which are held to fulfil the Matthean "fornication" clauses. People who divorce for any other reason are excluded from communion and there is a very long procedure before they can be readmitted.[51]

The Moravian Church allows separation more easily, but does not tolerate remarriage, even if the partner is mad or incurably sick. When partners separate, the guilty partner is excommunicated but the remarriage of the innocent partner is at least theoretically allowed. In practice, however, there are lengthy legal procedures before this can happen. It is for a series of councils and boards to hear the cases and the appeals before

59

the first marriage is dissolved and the innocent partner can be held to be free to marry again.[52]

The Church of the Province of Central Africa (Anglican), which includes dioceses in Malawi, Zambia, Rhodesia and Botswana, adopted a revised canon in 1969, permitting remarriage in certain cases.[53] In justification of this step, Archbishop Arden, the Metropolitan of the Province, firstly rejects the "brother-sister solution"—according to which the couple continue to live together and fulfil the obligations they have contracted for the sake of the children, but are not allowed to sleep together! He accepts the admission of the couple to communion, but notes that the denial of a second church marriage is a contradiction, since it casts a shadow of doubt over their whole relationship. Are they living in sin or not? The Archbishop then goes on to justify the revised canon on the following grounds:

(i) The Gospel is one of redemption and forgiveness, not of rejection.

(ii) The object of Church Law is to enable those who have a vocation to marry to fulfil this in a stable and deep union, and it is the pastoral experience of many priests that second marriages are often deeper and richer than the first marriages.

(iii) Previous Church Law did not accord with the consciences of many concerned lay people.

(iv) If a couple conscientiously feel that by remaining together and caring for their children, they are committing lesser evil than they would commit if they separated, then they are not guilty of sin.

(v) Reports suggest that the revised canons in West Africa and Canada are operating well and have not led to a flood of applications.

In Central Africa the new canon has been in operation now for six years, and there has not been a large number of applications. Applications are filtered through various levels to the bishop who gives the final approval. However, he does not always have to consider the details of the case in person. The new canon ensures that every possible attempt at reconciliation has been made, that an adequate time has elapsed for second thoughts and that the proposed remarriage is a real and deep relationship with every hope of being life-long. Everyone appears to be quite satisfied with the way the new legislation is working.

We may conclude this chapter by remarking that, in the experience of those who use them, the pastoral approaches represented by the so-called "Good Conscience" solution and by the practice of remarrying divorced persons in church under certain conditions, appear to work satisfactorily. There is no evidence that they are undermining the institution of indissoluble marriage; rather, they seem to be safeguarding the values of Christian marriage by acknowledging that these are exceptional measures taken to meet exceptional circumstances.

References: Chapter Two

1 Boerakker, 1975.
2 Perlman, 1963.
3 Conway, 1975.
4 Hastings, 1973, p. 39.
5 Aquina, 1975, II, pp. 70–1.
6 Boerakker, 1975, pp. 15–16.
7 Kasaka, 1976.
8 Aquina, 1975, I, pp. 133–7.
9 Hastings, 1973, pp. 175–8.
10 Yeld, 1966, Tables 1–12.
11 cf. Shorter, 1973, CROMIA/22.
12 Ssennyonga, 1972, CROMIA/17.
13 cf. Swantz, L., "The Migrant and the Church", *Sharing*, II, 6, August 1970, pp. 5–6.
14 Thomas and Chisanga, 1976.
15 Population censuses 1967 and 1969.
16 Kauta, Welshman, Gastonguay *et al.*, 1975.
17 Colson, 1958, p. 181.
18 Turner, 1957, p. 62.
19 Mitchell, 1956, p. 186.
20 Aquina, 1975, I, pp. 134–7.
21 Aquina, 1975, II, p. 72.
22 Richards, 1940, pp. 46 and 120–1.
23 Richards, *ibid*.
24 Douglas, 1969, pp. 121–36.
25 Hulsen and Mertens, n.d., Chap. 8.
26 Kauta, Welshman, Gastonguay *et al.*, 1975.
27 Whooley, in Verryn (ed.), 1975, pp. 320–3.

28 Spiegel in Verryn (ed.), 1975, pp. 475–6.
29 Huber, 1973.
30 Peskin, in Verryn (ed.), 1975, pp. 406–22.
31 Thomas and Chisanga, 1976.
32 Gaybba in Verryn (ed.), 1975, pp. 82–92; O'Flynn, 1975.
33 Quoted by Huizing, P., 1973, in "Canon Law and Broken Marriages", *Concilium*, VII, 9, September, pp. 13–21.
34 Hastings, 1973, p. 86.
35 Taylor, 1974.
36 Communication of April 11th, 1973.
37 cf. Pastoral Directive on Family Planning from South African Bishops' Conference, *AFER*, XVI, 3, 1974, pp. 345–8.
38 O'Flynn, 1975.
39 Häring, lecture delivered at Gaba, August 19th, 1974.
40 Hastings, 1973, pp. 87–8.
41 Commission on the Christian Doctrine of Marriage, 1971, p. 73.
42 *Ibid.*, pp. 75–6.
43 *Ibid.*, p. 69.
44 Hastings, 1973, pp. 87–8.
45 Arden, 1975.
46 Arden, *ibid*.
47 Lamburn, 1975.
48 Kakokota, 1975.
49 Taylor, 1974.
50 O'Flynn, 1975.
51 Communication from Bishop Mshana at Nairobi, 1974.
52 Communication from Pastor Nkaisule at Nairobi, 1974.
53 Arden, 1975.

Chapter 3

Polygamy and the Care of Widows

I   Case Material

1   *Polygamy in Africa Today*

It is unfortunate that the Second Vatican Council equated polygamy with "the plague of divorce" and "so-called free love", and called it a "disfigurement" of marriage.[1] The institution of polygamy in traditional Africa was certainly not merely a means of satisfying male lust. It had a number of well-defined social functions and advantages, and it certainly helped to stabilize the institution of marriage and to integrate the family with society. It had nothing to do with "free love", and it was often a remedy for divorce. Strictly speaking, the word "polygamy" is a generic term, referring to either kind of plural union: the single husband with several wives, the type of union called polygyny; and the single wife with several husbands, the type of union called polyandry. Polyandry is sufficiently rare in Africa—and indeed, in the world—for the terms "polygyny" and "polygamy" to be equated in common usage. For the purposes of our discussion, the word "polygamy" will be taken always to refer to the union of a single husband with several wives.

It should be noted in passing that polyandry is not entirely absent from traditional Africa. African apologists often strenuously assert that polyandry is a thoroughly un-African idea, and yet polyandrous institutions have been reported. An example of a polyandrous sexual union is provided by the custom of *busweswempe* among the Lele, Wongo and Djembe peoples of Zaïre.[2] In order to cater for the sexual needs of men whose wives were pregnant or breast-feeding and who were forbidden to have sexual intercourse with their husbands, as

63

well as for the needs of men for whom wives were not available, a young girl was designated by the elders of the village to be *nsweswempe* of a group of men from the same age-group. Each husband gave some bridewealth to the family of the girl, and the latter was installed in a special house to which the husbands came by turns. One husband could eventually become the girl's exclusive spouse, if he compensated the other men for the bridewealth they had paid.

Polygamy (polygyny) also traditionally had the function of catering for the sexual needs of men and of minimizing the chances of promiscuity and prostitution. More importantly, polygamy helped to satisfy the need and the desire of having a large family, while at the same time keeping the fertility rate of the women at a low level. Polygamy also catered for the childless union and offered a kinder solution than that of divorce when a wife was barren. Polygamy was a form of security and a guarantee of prosperity when a large family community was necessary to exploit the environment and provide for basic needs. Finally, polygamy helped to stabilize the institutions of marriage and the family through multiple marriage alliances with several families. It helped to tighten the bonds of society and broaden the circle of relatives and associates.

Allied to the institution of polygamy, but not to be confused with it, was the leviratic union, according to which a man (whether already married or not) could cater for the procreative needs of his brother's widow, or the widows of other close kinsmen. Eugene Hillman, in his comprehensive study of African polygamy, makes the common mistake of confusing levirate with polygamy.[3] As we shall see in a later section, the levirate is not marriage. Polygamy, today, is also taking new forms which are really functions of the general, contemporary social instability, and which certainly do not contribute to the strengthening of marriage and the family. We shall also consider them in their place.

How polygamous is contemporary Africa? David Barrett has estimated that in 34% of all sub-Saharan tribes polygamy occurs with an incidence of over 20%.[4] In 44% of the tribes polygamy is common but restricted to certain types, either sororal (co-wives are sisters) or non-sororal. For the remaining 22% polygamy is very limited, restricted, infrequent or non-existent. These estimates should be used with care. They are based on an elaboration of representative samples of tribes, and on ethnographic and church records of differing dates and reliability. Furthermore, they were made for the purposes of a study of African independent churches, and they, therefore, do not include the northern, Islamic African countries where polygamy is, of course, also well established.

Hillman calculates the polygamy rate, following Dorjahn, for the whole of sub-Saharan Africa, excluding the East Horn and Eastern Sudanic areas, and concludes that there is an average of 150 wives to 100 husbands, or a ratio of 1·5 wives to each married man.[5] Census figures do not necessarily distinguish between monogamously and polygamously married men, and the ratio given by Hillman is what is known as the crude polygamy rate, the ratio of married women to married men. As it stands, the crude polygamy rate is the most generous estimate of polygamy in a given area. A high proportion of the excess of married women over married men is accounted for by differential reporting, i.e. by different standards of judging whether a woman is married or not. Also the crude polygamy rate can make it appear that a high proportion of married men are polygamous—in this case 50%. In fact, this is not the case, since many polygamous men have more than two wives. An example can illustrate this point. Central African Republic is a country which in 1960 had a relatively high crude polygamy rate of 1·4; however only 12·5% of the married men were polygamous.[6] Hillman also quotes Dorjahn's estimate that 35% of all married people in sub-Saharan Africa are polygamous.[7] This would mean that, if no polygamous husband had more than two wives, the average number of polygamous marriages would only be 27%. In actual fact, of course, it would be much less. This is shown by the findings of a rural study like that of Hans Boerakker in eastern Uganda, who found that 12·4% of his sample of 428 married men were polygamous in 1974, considerably below the estimated average for all countries of sub-Saharan Africa.

Polygamy rates appear to be lower in East, Central and Southern Africa than in West Africa. One can compare, for example, Gabon 1·41; Ghana 1·35; Ivory Coast 1·40 with Kenya 1·21; Tanzania 1·25 and Uganda 1·18, these figures all being taken from the 1960s.[8] In Tanzania the crude polygamy rate increased from 1·20 in 1957 to 1·25 in 1967, and the rates of certain regions show how local factors may influence the practice. Iringa Region had a rate of 1·50; Kigoma, 1·48; Mara,

1·37 and Mbeya, 1·37, all well above the national average. The same is true of Uganda where the national rate was 1·18 and the local rates in the Eastern and Northern regions both 1·25.[9] Generally speaking, there is no polygamy rate for urban areas, since married men usually outnumber married women in towns. This does not, of course, mean that there are no polygamists in towns. What it means is that married women often remain in the rural areas while their husbands are at work in the urban areas.

Oddly enough, in spite of an apparently low percentage of polygamous unions in a given society, it is possible for a large proportion of married men to experience polygamy. The percentage of polygamous unions increases with the older age groups, a fact overlooked by Hillman. Thus, to take the example of the Central African Republic, although 21·5% of the married men were polygamous in 1960, in the group of married men aged between forty-five and fifty-four the percentage of polygamists was well over 30%; and in the age group of fifty-five to sixty-four, the percentage was still 26·5%. In the age group of the seventies the percentage had fallen, although, at 21·7%, it was still slightly above the average for all age groups. Obviously, an increasing number of married men had three, four or more wives, as the age scale rose.[10] Thus the chances of becoming a polygamist improve with age.

A popular, but misleading idea in Africa, is that polygamy is made possible, if it is not actually demanded by an imbalance in the sex ratio. This is not likely to be the case. Normal populations everywhere in the world show a slight preponderance of females over males, and while more males are born than females, the male mortality rate is higher than the female mortality rate at all ages. A number of African countries have populations with a preponderance of males over females, for example: Angola, Egypt, Equatorial Guinea, Gambia, Ghana, Kenya, Libya, Mauritania, Namibia, Nigeria, Spanish Sahara, Sudan, Tunisia, Uganda, Upper Volta and Zanzibar.[11] Even countries with a high polygamy rate, such as Ghana, have a preponderance of males; and the difference in the polygamy rate between Kenya, which has a male preponderance, and Tanzania, which has a female preponderance, is extremely slight. The unusual male preponderance may be caused by the fact that women were not available in some places to be enumerated. Special factors such as external migration and immigration, which more usually concern men than women, may affect the sex-ratio. Generally speaking, we can say that the sex-ratio has little or nothing to do with the incidence of polygamy.

A much more important fact, as Hillman recognizes, is the age of marriage. It is enough for the male age at marriage to be postponed seven years from puberty to allow nearly a quarter of the male population to be polygamous. To allow the older men to acquire junior wives, the young men must postpone their marriage to a first wife. Only a very small percentage of men marry before the age of twenty, while already some 10% of the women are married before twenty. The percentage of married women under thirty is nearly twice that of married men under thirty. In the three countries of Kenya, Tanzania and Uganda, the latest census figures reveal that nearly 60% of the married women are under thirty, while only 25% of the married men are under that age.[12] In South Africa the discrepancy between the ages at marriage is less striking. For the Black population, 50% of the married men were under thirty in 1965 and well over 80% of the women were under that age. This was a sharp contrast with the white population in which the percentage of sexes, married under thirty was almost equal, at around 80%.

We may sum up this section by saying that polygamy is still a significant phenomenon in African countries. It is difficult to say whether it is increasing or decreasing. As we shall see, there are factors which favour polygamy in contemporary society, but there are also other factors which discourage it. Very few countries have legislated against polygamy, and the law has little effect in those countries which, like Ivory Coast, have done so. Other countries, like Uganda and Tanzania, have been more realistic in passing legislation to put polygamous marriages on an equal footing with monogamous ones. In any population the actual number of polygamous men is small, at the most a quarter. The older, wealthier men have polygamous marriages while at least three-quarters of the married men have monogamous marriages, the majority of which are, of course, potentially polygamous.

2   Socio-Economic Causes and Effects of Polygamy

Polygamy obviously demands a modicum of wealth, both for the outlay required by multiple bridewealth and for the upkeep of several wives and their children. However, in the rural situation, once the initial outlay has been made, polygamy becomes more of an asset than a liability. It increases the labour force, and assists food production. A large family community renders all the operations of rural life more efficient, clearing land, building, making artefacts and utensils, guarding the fields against marauding birds and animals, and so forth. It also makes co-operation in communal work less demanding, since there are more representatives of the family available to participate.

Polygamy is also an advantage for pastoralists as well as for cultivators. In Somalia where Islamic polygamy is practised (a maximum of four wives at any one time), it is most unusual for a man of from forty to sixty years old not to have married at least twice. In a sample of seventy-seven men between the ages of thirty and sixty, 36% had two wives; 13% had three wives and 5% had four wives. In this society the incidence of polygamy is unusually high, and the number of wives increases with age and status. Larger herds and flocks are required to meet the bridewealth payments involved by more wives, but also, according to a vicious circle, larger herds and flocks require more wives to tend them.[13]

As we have seen, polygamy has usually been the privilege of a few, rather than a rule for the majority. In many rural areas of Africa the practice is receding. Patrick Whooley in Ciskei, South Africa, found very few cases indeed over the last thirty years. Polygamous marriage either involved older people, or was the result of special cases, mostly cases of childlessness.[14] In Rhodesia Sister Aquina found that very few marriages indeed were polygamous, an exception, however, being Tongaland where 25% of the men were polygamists. There is, nevertheless, an indication that modern settlement schemes and co-operatives may encourage polygamy. Sister Aquina found that there was an incidence of polygamy, higher than the average for other parts of the country, on tea estates in Rhodesia. She put this down to the fact that there was a high percentage of traditionalists and illiterates among the workers, and little contact with agents of change, such as teachers and missionaries. Njelu Kasaka, however, in Tanzania, found that, while there was little or no polygamy in the older, competitive agricultural schemes, like that of Tumbi in Tabora, the newer, co-operative schemes (known as *ujamaa*) can favour polygamy.[15] The heavy work of tobacco farming in Matwiga *ujamaa* village was an encouragement to marry more than one wife. Since every working member of the family is paid a wage, the income of the polygamous family is also attractive. Moreover, a larger food plot is allocated to a big family, and this is often an important consideration where soil has a low fertility. Kasaka's findings coincide with the results of enquiries made by Francis Lubowa during a visit to ujamaa villages in the Iringa region of Tanzania, a region which already enjoys a high polygamy rate.[16] The impact of change agents from school and mission is also often at a low level in these new villages.

Both Patrick Whooley and Sister Aquina thought that polygamy was largely absent from towns in southern Africa for socio-economic reasons. Sister Aquina, in particular, believes that the companionship aspect of married life is now coming to the fore, as against the procreative aspect. Moreover, low wages and lack of adequate housing discourage large families.[17] Such a trend is not so characteristic of the largely non-industrial towns in other parts of Africa. In the great, mining complex of Kitwe in Zambia, Thomas and Chisanga found many of the traditional factors operating in favour of polygamy. Kitwe has more of the character of a huge, mining camp, than of an administrative, commercial and manufacturing centre. In the mine compounds, restrictions have recently been lifted on the keeping of more than one wife in rented accommodation. The traditionally polygamous Bemba are the largest ethnic group in Kitwe, and recent increases in wages and salaries make it possible for Bemba men to support more than two wives in town, although the polygamy rate in general remains low.[18] This is a different state of affairs from Abidjan, the capital of Ivory Coast, where Raymond Deniel found in 1970 that although a small number of polygamists were still defying anti-polygamy legislation, the cost of living in the town made the practice prohibitive.[19]

In Nairobi, Dar-es-Salaam and Kampala, as well as in the other towns of East Africa, polygamy may be a social and economic asset to a family. In these towns there is a high level of under-employment, and the urban wage-earner often has one or more food-plots in peri-urban or rural areas. Co-wives who are left in charge of such food-plots are important contributors to the total family income. In Ssennyonga's sample of thirty marriages in Nagulu housing estate, Kampala (Uganda), there were five cases in which he suspected a second wife stationed in a rural homsestead. In one case the husband openly revealed her existence to the researcher.[20] James Holway, in his study of marriage in Nairobi (Kenya), stresses the social advantage of a second wife.[21] Polygamists in Nairobi are usually well-to-do, middle aged men who have come to the city and made good. In their youth they married a wife who was ill-educated and rustic, unable now to mix with sophisticated urban society. This wife, therefore, stays behind in the village, and the man takes a second wife, a young, educated girl, who runs a city home for him in a sophisticated manner. "These are the so-called 'parlour-wives', who help the men to entertain their guests, and who go with them to parties and receptions, where European and Asian men go with their wives."

In Central African Republic where there was a high percentage of polygamy in 1960, the difference between urban and rural areas was not very great. In fact, the figures show that one out of four householders in the urban areas was a poly-gamist, as against one out of five householders in the rural areas.[22] It was also noted that the incidence of polygamy was higher among the middle-income groups (cadres moyens), than among the poorer or the very highly salaried classes. In general, we can conclude that the traditional forms of polygamy are becoming more difficult to maintain in the urban areas, and that low wages, high cost of living and inadequate housing are the major causes for this. However, there are still many places in which rural and urban life are closely interlocked, and here the middle-income groups and better paid classes can afford to be polygamous. However, as we shall see, there are many new forms of polygamy which go more easily hand in hand with town life.

Sister Aquina shows how running a polygamous family requires great skills.[23] Whether the co-wives are living with their husband in a single compound, or whether they are dispersed in several homesteads or settlements, tensions are bound to arise. To reduce these tensions, the first wife is usually given a privileged status and authority over the junior wives. The husband, in his turn, is expected to be absolutely fair in visiting the wives in rotation, eating the food they prepare for him and sleeping with them. To run a polygamous family smoothly, such rules must be strictly adhered to. The fact that the younger wives give their husbands more pleasure than the first wife, helps to counterbalance her influential position. On the other hand, the polygamous husband must be continually on his guard against giving in to pressure from one of his wives to obtain special favours from him. Many men are frankly afraid of becoming

70

polygamists because of the demands this type of marriage makes on the husband, and Eugene Hillman is right to speak of the "reluctant polygamist", who accepts the burdens of a polygamous marriage with hesitation, in order to fulfil social obligations, or out of economic necessity.[24]

3 Polygamy, Sexual Needs and Marital Stability

Contrary to popular ideas about the wicked women of the streets, prostitution is largely caused by male demand, as well as by male dominance. Mugo Gachuhi has argued that prostitution is a necessary counterpart to the institutional control of sex in marriage, and that it is caused partly by the desire of some women to escape this control by living promiscuously and partly by the desire of men for a sexual outlet outside marriage. In this way a small number of professional women are able to cater for the extra-marital sexual needs of a very large number of men, and to support themselves economically by so doing.[25]

It is undeniable that traditional forms of polygamy obviated the need for prostitution. Not only was the problem of the ageing, unattractive or sick wife solved by polygamy, but also the problems created by traditional taboos surrounding the period of lactation. In most African societies there is a traditional belief that the mother's milk will fail, if sexual intercourse takes place during lactation. Since baby foods did not normally exist, the period of breast-feeding was long and it was usually two years at least before a baby was weaned. This custom and belief imposed a very long period of sexual abstinence on the husband, and if he was not capable of it, he could only gratify his needs outside of his marriage, if he was monogamous. If, on the other hand, he was polygamous, he stood a greater chance of always having a legitimate sex partner at hand.

We have already noticed that one of the characteristics of polygamy is to create multiple alliances with different families. In many African societies a special, social bond is created between parents-in-law by the marriage of their children to one another, and there are specific ways of referring to this relationship. Polygamy creates larger and more complex affinal networks which have a stabilizing effect on the institution of marriage. It is frequently remarked by anthropologists that marriage is noticeably more stable where polygamy flourishes.

Melvin Perlman, for example, found that in Toro (western Uganda) polygamous marriages were not only more stable than monogamous ones in the 1950s, but that they did not give rise to concubinage. Very often, however, a stable concubinage led to polygamous marriage. Polygamists in Toro constituted about 8% to 9% of the married men.[26] It is well known, also, that polygamy existed as a kinder alternative than divorce, particularly when the first wife was barren. The sororate catered for this situation by providing a sister of the first wife as a junior wife, when the first wife had no children. Sororal polygamy also helped to reduce tensions between co-wives, although it limited the range of marriage alliances. Quite often, a man would take another wife, especially a sister of his first wife, at the first wife's request. Polygamy was acceptable to women who did not aspire to independent roles in society, and was appreciated among women for its socio-economic benefits just as much as among men. Traditionally, therefore, it was not a cause of desertion or divorce. Nowadays, on the contrary, the education and emancipation of women, and their desire for deeper companionship in marriage, makes them necessarily hostile to polygamy. As a woman in Abidjan told Raymond Deniel: "A boy with two wives is a big liar. Today he sleeps with one woman and tells her that she is the one he loves. Tomorrow, he sleeps with the other and tells her the same thing."[27]

4   *Polygamy and Childlessness*

Polygamy caters for the desire of having a large family, and the ideal in nearly all traditional African societies was to have as many children as was physically possible. Angela Molnos concluded from her East African Survey that there was "a pervasive sentiment that it was good to have a numerous progeny". She further noted that "the general and diffuse motives accompanying this sentiment were that children meant wealth, prestige and the blessings of God and the ancestors".[28] We have already spoken about the socio-economic advantages of the large family in the labour-intensive subsistence economy. Children were also a social and economic investment. By their marriage new family allowances were formed and bridewealth was obtained. In traditional African society it was desirable and necessary to have a large household of children.

Children belonged, not only to the nuclear household, but also to the extended family community as a whole. There was considerable co-operation in the upbringing of children by different categories of relatives, and it was relatively easy for children to be fostered or loaned to various households within the family community. Patrick Whooley cites cases of adoption among the Xhosa of Ciskei (South Africa), and also cases in which a woman whose husband was sterile found another man to be the *genitor* of her children.[29] There were also numerous examples in both East and West Africa of the legal fiction known as "woman marriage", according to which an heiress "married a wife" and was treated as the *pater* or legal father of the "wife's" children by another man. All of these were devices to obtain the all-important children for the prosperity and continuity of the family.

However, whatever fictions or devices were employed in order to procure children for one's household, the African was not usually satisfied with someone else's children. It was necessary to transmit life oneself to another human being, and this was regarded as an essential aspect of being alive. It was a share in the divine prerogative of giving life, and it was an insurance that one's memory would be cherished after death. The death of a childless man or woman was final, but the death of a person with a numerous progeny was less feared. The children would continue to invoke their ancestors within living memory and make offerings to them. Very common in East Africa was the concept of nominal reincarnation, the custom of naming children after their grandparents, and even referring to them by regularly alternating kinship terms. This verbal practice was backed by the belief that a special relationship existed between grandparent and grandchild, and that the grandparent acted as a guardian spirit or protector of the grandchild. The extreme importance of siring and bearing children can therefore be appreciated. It can be readily understood that child-lessness placed a very heavy—if not an intolerable—strain upon a marriage. Without the alternative of polygamy, divorce would be practically inevitable, and it was divorce that the practice of the sororate was designed to forestall.

Although the fear of childlessness is hardly in the minds of those who delay church marriage, and even pre-marital pregnancies are not necessarily the result of a deliberate trial of fertility, the desire for children is intense in Africa and lack of them places a marriage in jeopardy. Many Christians find in the teaching of their church a support for a procreative emphasis in marriage which harmonizes completely with their traditional outlook on childbearing. 88% of the male respondents and 83% of the female respondents in the Mityana survey in Uganda thought that Christian parents should have as many children as possible.[30] For the vast majority the attitude was one of passivity and fatalism in the face of God's creative activity. "One must simply accept whatever God gives." Some respondents, however, saw it in terms of a divine law. "It is God's law to have as many children as possible"; "God said: Increase and multiply" and so forth. A small number saw childbearing as a national or ecclesial duty—to swell the number of citizens or Christians, and one or two, faithful to traditional African thinking, linked childbearing with the doctrine of the resurrection. Childlessness, therefore, is certainly a motive for polygamy, although, as we shall now see, polygamy is no longer bound to traditional forms.

5 *Polygamy as a Function of an Unstable Social Situation*

In the struggle between the generations over the control of marriage institutions, and in the general instability created by the relaxation of family, and other social pressures, polygamy turns out to be one of the solutions to the dilemma in which young people find themselves today. It is fairly frequent to find young men courting two girls at the same time, in the hope that, if one refuses, the other will accept; and occasionally it happens, as Sister Aquina observed among the Tonga in Rhodesia, that the young man marries both girls shortly after each other.[31] A more frequent occurrence is when a young man is forced into a polygamous marriage as a result of labour migration or re-settlement. Njelu Kasaka provides a good example in a case history from Tumbi re-settlement area in Central Tanzania.[32]

Andrew is the son of a local chief of the populous Nyakyusa people in southern Tanzania. When Andrew was a young man in the early 1950s, his father tried to exercise his traditional prerogative by arranging a marriage for Andrew to a Nyakyusa girl at his home village. Andrew refused the arranged marriage and shortly afterwards left his father's village and migrated to the tobacco scheme at Tumbi in central Tanzania. Tumbi lies in the heart of Nyamwezi country and Andrew soon fell in love with a Nyamwezi girl with whom he started living as man and wife in 1959. Although Andrew is a member of the Moravian Church, he did not seek a church blessing for his marriage, and he was consequently excommunicated by his church. The main reason for Andrew's hesitation over a church marriage was because the whereabouts of the girl's father were unknown, and he wanted to finalize his marriage according to customary law. When Andrew's father got to hear of his son's proposed marriage, he rejected the Nyamwezi "wife" out of hand. In 1962, Andrew returned home on a visit and enormous pressure was brought to bear on him by his father and family to marry a Nyakyusa girl. This he did according to Nyakyusa custom, but without any intention of dismissing his Nyamwezi "wife". The Nyamwezi girl had proved faithful and reliable, and she had already borne him two children. Subsequent events confirmed Andrew's attachment to her. The Nyakyusa wife turned out to be unfaithful, disrespectful and quarrelsome, and Andrew decided to dismiss her and marry the Nyamwezi girl in church. In the meantime, however, Andrew's father was deserted by his wife in his old age and the family of Andrew's Nyakyusa wife undertook to care for the old man on the understanding that Andrew was their son-in-law. Andrew hoped to extricate himself from this awkward situation by inviting his father to come and live with him at Tumbi. The father would not hear of it, and no amount of pleading could get him to leave his homeland. Andrew could not afford to leave his tobacco growing, nor could he risk the displeasure of the family which was caring for his ageing father. He therefore decided to remain a reluctant polygamist. In 1971 the father of the Nyamwezi girl was finally traced. Bridewealth was paid, and Andrew is now the legitimate husband of two wives according to customary law.

Not every case of this kind finishes with a simultaneous, plural union like that of Andrew. More commonly, desertion and concealment make an appearance as factors in the story. Eugene Hillman, whose otherwise excellent account of polygamy in contemporary Africa appears to ignore these developments altogether, compares Western "serial monogamy" with African polygamy.[33] His contention is that the frequency of divorce in Europe and North America is tantamount to a system of polygamy. The practice of "serial" or "successive" unions in Africa is much closer to polygamy, since civil, or even customary, divorce hardly intervenes between them. It is becoming increasingly frequent for a married man to desert his first wife effectively when relations have become strained between them, when she no longer attracts him, or when she is beyond the age of child-bearing. The husband, in these cases, gives her little or no financial support and she either lives as a more or less independent woman, or else receives support from adult sons. If the woman does not wish to marry again and if the return of bridewealth is no longer possible, she may come to accept this situation. Successive polygamy of this type is economically feasible and many urban dwelling men are living in such marriages, taking a second, younger wife, having effectively deserted the first one.

Gladys Enderley of Cameroun, at an All Africa Conference of Churches consultation in Yaoundé in 1972, coined a term for another type of polygamous union. She called it "mono-polygamy".[34] This is really an early stage in successive polygamy, when the husband blackmails his first wife into accepting his liaison with another woman. The man keeps the other woman as a concubine and maintains this second household, threatening to dismiss or desert his married wife, if she objects to the arrangement. At this stage there is no legal second marriage, although the concubine may eventually demand this security. Another type of polygamy, related to this one, is "clandestine polygamy", according to which a rich man, already married, buys a farm in a different place from his home, marries another wife and settles her on the farm as manager without telling her about his first wife. James Holway was told by his informants in Nairobi, Kenya, that some rich men did this several times over, without any of the wives learning of one another's existence.[35] Besides having the luxury of several wives, such a man is able to build up a large holding of land as a means of investment. Much the same thing is happening in modern Kampala, Uganda. High ranking army officers have been able to acquire property in the city, particularly the residences of the Asians who were expelled from the country in 1972, and install a series of wives or concubines in the houses to manage them. This can also be a profitable concern since a good income can be obtained by letting out rooms and apartments to lodgers and tenants.

Polygamy of all types does sometimes involve divorce, since tensions and jealousies in the polygamous family may eventually result in a divorce action. Generally speaking, divorce is rare, as we have seen, in the traditional, simultaneous polygamous family, whereas it is often encouraged in situations of successive or clandestine polygamy. Even so, as Perlman noted in western Uganda, divorce tends to take place among the younger married people,[36] and it may even serve polygamy to the extent of providing secondary wives for polygamists. A divorced woman has difficulty in finding a husband and she may have to be content with becoming the second wife of an already married man.

To a considerable extent marital instability in modern Africa is aggravated by what might be called an outmoded polygamous mentality. An African, Roman Catholic Archbishop, a Cardinal, confided to one of the authors that, in his opinion, African men were twenty years behind the thinking of their womenfolk. They wanted to continue treating their educated and emancipated wives in the same way that their fathers had treated their mothers. On all sides there are complaints about the double moral standard, according to which married African men demand sexual freedom, while denying it to their wives. Male dominance demands that the sexual activity of women be strictly controlled and regulated by men, which is one reason for the horror with which African society often regards the promiscuity of prostitutes. The paradox, of course, is that male freedom in sexual matters undermines their control of female sexual activity in a non-polygamous society. The polygamous mentality demands that a wife be absolutely faithful to her husband, but it allows the husband to court an unlimited number of other women with a view to marriage. The husband's extra-marital sexual interests can always be justified in this way. The fact, however, is that the polygamous mentality is out of place when simultaneous polygamy is not feasible and when women are demanding a greater degree of married companionship. An outmoded polygamous mentality is one of the causes of successive and clandestine polygamy.

There seems to be some evidence that married Christians, especially married Roman Catholics, prefer polygamy to divorce. This was the tentative conclusion reached by Sister Aquina in Rhodesia, and it was the conclusion of Hans Boerakker in eastern Uganda.[37] Of the 136 church marriages in his sample, 10% had ended in divorce, but 19% had turned polygamous. In the Tonga region of Rhodesia where 34% of the men are polygamous, Sister Aquina found that 23% of the Christian men had become polygamists.[38] In northern Tanzania, Ron Hart found that a large majority of Roman Catholic catechists favoured a lenient approach to polygamists, particularly towards the Christian wives of polygamists. 78% thought they should be admitted to the sacraments, at least under condition.[39] In the Mityana survey in Uganda, a larger proportion of the married Christian men who answered the questions favoured polygamy, rather than divorce. 34·9% thought that Christians should be allowed more than one wife, but only 22·6% thought divorce should be allowed in certain circumstances. The women were less in favour of both divorce and polygamy, but they clearly favoured divorce. 15·6% thought divorce could sometimes be allowed, but only 6·6%, a tiny minority, thought polygamy should be allowed.[40] These figures accurately reflect differing attitudes towards polygamy on the part of the sexes, and they also show that many Christian men remain open to the option of polygamy.

6   The Leviratic Custom and the Care of Widows

As Paul Kalanda demonstrates very clearly, the popular term "widow inheritance" much used today, is highly misleading.[41] Widows are not heirlooms and they are not, nor ever were, inherited. More correctly, one should speak about the "care of widows", because the purpose of African customs concerning widows is to cater for them, their domestic, sexual and procreative needs within the family community into which they married. African marriage has a strong communitarian character. In patrilineal societies, a woman who is married enters the family community of her husband as a worker and bearer of children for the whole group. Her marriage is not only to a particular man of that group, her husband, but in a very real sense to the group itself. She is the "wife" of the whole family—"our wife". This does not, of course, mean that any other male, besides her husband, has the right of sexual access to the woman, but it stresses her communitarian role in the family. Bridewealth has been contributed by many members of the family, and she and her children belong to the family. When her husband dies, her marriage in the family is still regarded as being in existence and a surrogate or proxy-husband must be found for her from among the male relatives of her husband to take the latter's place. Michael Kirwen emphasizes very strongly that in no case can such an arrangement be called a new marriage.[42] No more bridewealth is paid for her and no marriage celebration takes place, for the original marriage is regarded as continuing in existence. If the surrogate happens to have a wife of his own, the provision he makes for the widow is not regarded as a second marriage. If he has no wife, then his relationship with the widow does not stand in the way of subsequent marriage, and she is not regarded as a wife, let alone a "first wife". In western and Christian thinking there is no category in which this relationship can be placed. It is an injustice to call it "marriage", just as it is unjust to call it "adultery" or "concubinage". Granted that it raises a complex moral problem for Christians, nevertheless it is not strictly polygamous marriage, nor is it a question of sexual relations outside marriage. Kirwen defines it as: "a marital adjustment in a continuing marriage in which a brother-in-law substitutes temporarily for a deceased legal husband".[43]

In some cases any children born to the widow and her husband's surrogate are regarded as the legal heirs of the deceased man. This is the true levirate. In other cases, the children may be counted as the surrogate's own. Yet even in these cases the union has a leviratic character, for not only do the children belong to the family community as a whole, but there is a link with the deceased man. One of Paul Kalanda's informants, who came from Ankole in western Uganda, was himself the child of such a leviratic union. His experience was that a "curious importance" was attached to him as a child, being one who had been born after the death of his mother's husband.[44]

In traditional society there was a need to house, feed and protect widows, whatever their age or condition. If the widow was still of childbearing age, it was essential that her procreative needs be catered for, and that "the children within her" be given an opportunity to be born. But even if she was past childbearing, it was still recognized that she had sexual needs, and the care of widows normally included sexual relations. This is still the case in many African ethnic groups, although greater freedom is now accorded to the widow either within the leviratic custom, or in avoiding the custom altogether.

Paul Kalanda presented three cases from Uganda.[45] Among the Langi of northern Uganda a widow must still be cared for by one of her brothers-in-law, but nowadays she is courted by them and is allowed to make her own choice. In Ankole, already mentioned, Christians have generally abandoned the practice, while among non-Christians it continues to flourish. Christians incur considerable odium because of their attitude, and they

79

themselves, are at a loss to understand the reason for the Church's condemnation of the practice. Among the Teso of eastern Uganda the family of the deceased man decides who is to take care of the widow, but she is allowed nowadays to continue living as an independent woman in her deceased husband's house. Michael Kirwen summarizes his findings in four ethnic groups in northern Tanzania as follows:

> *Luo:* Widows cannot divorce (from the deceased husband's family) and remarry, but must enter into a leviratic union, where sexual and domestic rights are always demanded.

> *Kuria:* Widows can divorce and remarry or enter into a levirate union. In a levirate union sexual rights are not always demanded.

> *Kwaya* (Matrilineal Descent): Widows return to their father's home with their children and can remarry; there are no leviratic unions.

> (Patrilineal Descent): Widows can divorce and remarry, enter into a leviratic union, or (apparently) live as single persons in their deceased husbands' homestead.

> *Sukuma:* Widows can divorce and remarry, enter into a leviratic union or live as single persons in their deceased husbands' homesteads.[46]

There is little doubt that, although it has been modified, the leviratic custom continues in many, if not most, African ethnic groups of patrilineal descent.

Finally, we should note the fact that, although the leviratic custom is not to be identified with polygamous marriage, polygamy contributes to the custom, by creating "a widow problem". When a polygamist dies he makes a number of women widows at the same time, and statistics show that the proportion of widows is high in polygamous societies. For example, in Central African Republic in 1960, the number of women in their fifties in polygamous marriages and the number of widows were both around 40% to 50% of the age group as a whole.[47] Polygamy, therefore, helps to create the problem which the levirate is intended to solve.

II   Theological Reflection

1   *Polygamy*

The traditional approach of western theologians to the question was that polygamy is a sin, comparable to adultery, "indirectly opposed to natural law" and forbidden in the New Testament by positive Divine Law. To quote the missionary conference at Edinburgh in 1910, "It is simply one of the gross evils of heathen society which, like habitual murder or slavery, must at all costs be ended."[48] However, as the positive aspects of African and Asian polygamous marriage came to be recognized by missionaries, this extreme, negative attitude was modified. It came to be understood that prejudice played a large part in the total condemnation of polygamy. The traditional verdict had been directed against the "adulterous polygamy" of princes in monogamous western societies, and even the canons of the Council of Trent were directed against the notion of some of the Reformers that polygamy could be tolerated as an exception in an otherwise monogamous society.[49] They did not envisage a situation where Christianity was being proclaimed in a society in which polygamy was an approved and preferred social practice. It was not until Christian missionaries from Europe came into contact with the polygamous cultures of the non-European world, that the Church was effectively confronted by polygamy. The distinction came to be accepted, which has been neatly formulated by Bernard Häring, between disordered, lustful polygamy on the one hand, and socially controlled and approved polygamy on the other.[50] Such a distinction, Häring argues, can even be recognized in the Old Testament where the polygamous Lamech represents the wild, threatening and disordered man, and the polygamous Abraham, the just man of peace who desires to ensure his posterity. Whatever the truth of this assertion, there are still, as Adrian Hastings observes, four basic positions a Christian can take towards polygamy.[51]

In the first position, polygamy is simply a sin, comparable with adultery. This is the traditional position from which, as we have seen, theologians and missiologists are just emerging. A second position would be that polygamy is an inferior form of marriage, not sinful where it is the custom but always unacceptable for Christians. This is probably the position of most pastors and church authorities today. It is the explicit position of two

81

contributors to our discussions, Robin Lamburn and William Blum.[52]

The third position is that taken up by Hastings himself. According to him, polygamy is a form of marriage less satisfactory than monogamy and one which cannot do justice to the full spirit of Christian marriage, but in certain circumstances individual Christians can still put up with it, as they put up with slavery, dictatorial government, and much else. Just as the early Christians tolerated the practice of slavery but undermined it by their teachings, so, Hastings advocates, Christians today should tolerate polygamy but undermine it by promoting the superior ideal of monogamy.[53]

The fourth position is that polygamy is one form of marriage, monogamy another. Each has its advantages and disadvantages; they are appropriate to different types of society, and it is not the task of the Church to make any absolute judgement between them. This is basically the position of Eugene Hillman. However, although he argues for both monogamy and polygamy to be placed on an equal theological footing, he finally pleads only for the "toleration" of polygamous persons and institutions.[54]

Following Sigqibo Dwane, the position we have favoured is really mid-way between that of Hastings and Hillman and it leads up to a practical conclusion that resembles theirs.[55] The position is that both monogamy and polygamy are manifestations of the reality of marriage as ordained by God, but that in monogamy this reality appears within a more intense relationship. In so far as the husband–wife relationship develops into real companionship, so polygamy becomes correspondingly less tolerable, and the Christian understanding of marriage is a call to this ever-deepening, unending process of sharing that leads those who experience it eventually into the abyss of God's own infinite love.

We would agree with Hillman's attack on the Church's narrow-minded intolerance of polygamy, and we would also agree with him that polygamy is nowhere explicitly condemned in the Old or New Testaments. Marriage theology has developed largely as a result of experience, and theologians have appealed to the Bible out of this experience. Hillman is right to condemn the literalistic interpretation of texts, such as the Genesis story of Adam and Eve, and the reading into them of doctrines which are already proposed independently of them.

Nor is it at all clear that the marriage symbolism of the covenant demands a monogamous understanding of marriage. All that is said about the covenant and marriage in the Old Testament is said in a context which is known to have been polygamous. Hastings makes the point that polygamy as an institution receded into the background in post-exilic Judaism and hardly existed at all in New Testament times, whereas Hillman makes the most of vestigial polygamy in the time of Christ. He is certainly correct in interpreting New Testament silence about polygamy as evidence that it did not pose a pastoral problem to the Early Church. But that was because it hardly existed. A very few rich people could afford polygamous marriages and Hillman seems to be thinking mainly in terms of the leviratic union, which as we have seen was not really marriage (in ancient Israel, as in Africa) and which was not proposed as an image of the covenant. [56]

On the other hand, Hastings is on shaky ground in suggesting that monogamous marriage must be accepted because it is the term of a whole trend within the communal experience of the Jewish people, and that the teaching of Christ and Paul, set against the background of this social trend, "surely presupposes a monogamous norm".[57] The existence of this trend appears to have a quite accidental relationship to the use of marriage as a symbol of the covenant, or to any other teaching concerning marriage and family life. One cannot say that there is a progression of thought from a communitarian to a personalist understanding of the marriage relationship, from polygamy to monogamy as the marriage ideal. Such an idea comes close to social evolutionism and theories of cultural progress which Hillman rightly condemns.

Polygamy, as Dwane points out, is like monogamy in being a relationship of love. Even though it serves socio-economic needs and the desire for children, and may not be associated with the concept of romantic love, nobody would deny that it is founded on the mutual attraction between man and woman, and that it is essentially a loving relationship. It is also a permanent, life-long relationship, as indissoluble as mono-gamous marriage. As an indissoluble, life-long relationship of love, polygamy is certainly sacramental, an effective sign of God's covenant love. Dwane goes even further than this, expanding on the paradoxical statement of Karl Barth that polygamous marriages can be, contrary to all appearances, monogamous in the sense of divine purpose.[58] They contain within themselves the divine invitation to deepen and intensify the marriage relationship. This invitation was made explicit in a Jewish society that was undeniably polygamous, but it must not simply be judged according to the social standards which it intentionally challenged. The Yahwistic writer in Genesis did not condemn the communitarian family in stressing the personal character of the marriage covenant, nor did he explicitly forbid polygamous marriage. He did, however, issue a challenge to the polygamous, fertility-orientated, familistic marriages of Solomonic times, a challenge to intensify the personal aspect of the relationship.[59] Hillman tries to water down the force of the phrase "one flesh", by making it refer exclusively to the carnal and social realities. "One flesh" in the carnal sense and "one kindred" in the social sense do not do justice to the full meaning of the phrase as "one living body".[60] Hillman is obliged to admit that in polygamy married love is extensive, not intensive, and that the relationship between the co-wives is more important than that between husband and wives.[61] For Christians it is the equality of love, the intensity of the relationship between husband and wife that matters. The New Testament takes up this emphasis on personal values, on qualitative, rather than on quantitative relationships, and insists even more strongly on it. There is no doubt that these ideas are in harmony with the aspirations of African women as they benefit progressively from modern education and economic emancipation.

2   *The Care of Widows*
The leviratic custom raises three problems for the Christian theologian. The first is whether or not the death of one of the partners to a marriage means the end of the marriage. This problem is closely related to the second one, if it is not, in fact, contained in it. This is the question of the widow's freedom to decide on her own future. As we have seen, the custom is being relaxed in some ethnic groups to allow the widow freedom of choice, and if the churches decide to tolerate the levirate, this freedom of consent must be guaranteed. In Kenya and Tanzania this freedom is demanded by Civil Law.

The third problem concerns the liceity of the leviratic union, if the deceased husband's surrogate is already married. Michael Kirwen argues very persuasively that the levirate is not an extra-marital relationship, and that it exists precisely to uphold and prolong marriage, as it is understood in traditional African societies. This is perfectly true, if one is speaking about the marriage of the widow herself, a marriage threatened by the death of her husband. The question is whether or not the leviratic relationship undermines the previous marriage of the surrogate, or, if he is unmarried, renders him incapable of contracting a subsequent marriage. For a married man, Paul Kalanda argues, the leviratic relationship is illicit.[62] Certainly, if the Christian vocation in marriage is towards an ever-deepening, personal communion, then the levirate, like poly-gamous marriage, is ultimately an obstacle to the fulfilment of this ideal. Kirwen argues that the mentality which would exclude the levirate on these grounds has an individualistic notion of personhood, and that, if one has a more communal understanding of person, the practice is not opposed to marriage.[63] We think, however, that one has to be beware here of a confusion of terms. Being a person means having an awareness of oneself in relation to others, having the capacity to enter into personal relationships. As soon as we speak of "person", we imply a relationship with other persons. Rela-tionships can be broadly divided into two classes: "networks" and "groups". In the one, the individual is aware of his relation-ship to other persons as single individuals; in the other he is aware of his relationship to other individuals because he and they share something in common. There is no doubt that the consciousness of group allegiance is strong in the African family community. This does not mean that conflicts between relationships do not occur within the family, nor does it mean that the individual is somehow absorbed into a "corporate personality". A wife may be "wife" of the family as a whole, but she still remains primarily the wife of an individual member of the family, and other men in the family are denied sexual and domestic rights over her. Thus, African custom also recognizes a hierarchy of personal values and relationships within the family community. The levirate is, of its nature, a temporary marital adjustment, which is more easily accepted by the polygamous mentality.

Eugene Hillman makes much of the fact that the practice of the levirate did not become a subject of discussion in the writings of the New Testament.[64] This is true enough, but Hillman totally overlooks the mention of other pastoral solutions to the problem of widowhood found in the pages of the New Testament, particularly in the Pastoral Epistles. Paul Kalanda points out that the creation of the seven deacons was occasioned by the presence of helpless widows in the early Christian community. At Joppa, they were the special object of Tabitha's industrious charity. Paul recommends widows not to remarry, but allows young lonely widows to do so, especially if they have no one to support them. An order of widows seems to have come into existence, composed of the older women whose task it was to care for the younger widows and young married women in their domestic duties.[65] So it does look as if the Church found new ways of caring for widows, other than the levirate, which respected their dignity and personal freedom.

3 Childless Marriages

In Chapter One we examined several canonical proposals designed to cater for childless marriages: the idea of natural marriage, marriage under condition and the impediment of sterility, and we rejected them as unrealistic and untheological. William Blum, however, carries the discussion further by proposing to broaden the concept of impotence, thus making it easier to annul childless marriages.[66] Normally a distinction is made between impotence and sterility. The first, which implies the inability to consummate the marriage renders it null and void. The second, which implies the inability to have children in spite of consummation, does not. However, for consummation to take place it must be possible for the man to inject true semen into the vagina. It has only relatively recently been established that a man can ejaculate seminal fluid which lacks spermatozoa, and it is being asked if this is "true semen". If the answer is in the negative, a male who is incapable of producing sperm may be classified as impotent, rather than sterile, but one would immediately have to ask whether females incapable of producing ova should not also be classified as impotent.

This would take care of a number of cases of childlessness, but it is still possible that cases might arise where spermatozoa and ova are present, but conception never occurs. If such cases could not be solved medically, what can be done about them? Blum realizes that a redefinition of impotence is not going to cater for all cases of childlessness. He also realizes that the social repercussions of such annulments in Africa will be harder on the women than on the men. Most important of all, he wonders whether such a line of solution does not proceed from a perspective that overlooks the real human meaning of marriage and the real meaning of sexuality in marriage.

It is an incomplete and defective understanding that sees procreation as the end of marriage, and sexuality as primarily, if not only, for procreation. This is also the argument of Hennie Pretorius.[67] Procreation was strongly emphasized in Old Testament Israel, and birth had a value for salvation history. Childbirth had a messianic perspective, since the promised saviour was to be born of Israel's posterity. With the advent of Christ, the all-important birth has taken place. It is not birth that matters now, but re-birth in Christ. We do not overcome death by bearing children, but by sharing in Christ's risen life. Womanhood is no longer defined in terms of the capacity to have children, but rather in terms of her relationship with a husband. Blum adds that man does not procreate so that God will love him, but because God loves man and invites some of us to join with him in the propagation of the human race. The procreation of new human life is not totally dependent upon man. However, the principal way in which the kingdom of Christ is being established is not through the propagation of new members or by the number of people who become Christians, but by the quality of life of those who are Christians. Our worship of God is not to be a material or physical worship, but a worship "in Spirit and in Truth".[68]

Patrick Whooley rightly objects that the New Testament does not make too sharp a break with the past, and that procreation held the place of importance in the Church's teaching on marriage, for centuries.[69] This fact is reason enough for showing toleration towards those who cannot accept childlessness. Nevertheless, there can be no ultimate denial that Christian love—the selfless living for others—is the essence of Christian marriage. A spouse that remains faithful to his or her mate despite the latter's sterility shows that his love is founded upon the dignity of the partner as a human person, and is not calculated according to the partner's capacity to procreate children. A childless marriage is not a defective marriage. The truly defective marriage is one in which true love is lacking, a marriage in which the spouses live for themselves and not for each other. Blum even adds: "Childless couples whose love is not deep enough to sustain the union despite the lack of children lack something important, if not essential, to the upbringing of children."[70]

A childless union, therefore, can be a sign of authentic married love. It can also be a sign of the value of suffering according to the Christian economy. Spouses who accept the suffering of childlessness, without losing their faith in God, must themselves grow in the love of Christ, and also help others to grow in it. All of these considerations suggest that we should not seek a solution to childlessness by encouraging a new marriage, but should help Chrstitian spouses discover a meaning and significance in the childless marriage itself. Childlessness represents a challenge to reflect more deeply on the authentic meaning of the Christian life and the vocation of Christian marriage.

III   Models for Pastoral Action

1   *Polygamy—Traditional Approaches*

Traditional missionary practice in Africa demanded that the polygamist send away all his wives but one, before he could receive baptism. Roman Catholics, in principle, maintained that the first wife in chronological order was the true wife, and she alone should remain. However, by an extension of the Pauline Privilege (the so-called Petrine Privilege), the polygamist husband was allowed to keep the wife he preferred, if he could not remember which one he had married first, or any one of his wives, provided that she also desired baptism. Wives of polygamists could not be baptized unless they separated from their husband, or unless it was the case of a first wife, who was regarded as the legitimate wife. This policy, in making the divorce of the secondary wives a condition for baptism, was certainly a cause of great hardship and injustice. It also clearly favoured the male partner at the expense of the female partners. Virtually all the Christian Churches followed a similar policy concerning the male polygamist, but some were more understanding regarding the wives. For example, the (Anglican) Lambeth Conference of 1888 allowed the local bishops to decide under what circumstances the wives of a polygamist could be admitted to baptism.[71]

Robin Lamburn is of the opinion that nowadays the break-up of a polygamous family is not so likely to involve hardship and injustice, since women have a greater independence in modern Africa, and solutions can be found for the support of divorced co-wives.[72] This is an arguable point, for it is not simply a question of material support. What is envisaged is the break-up of a loving, life-long relationship, not to mention the relationship of parent and children. However, Lamburn is prepared to consider the baptism of a polygamist and his household, if the break-up of the family cannot be carried out without injustice. On the whole, he does not favour even this. The problem for him is whether the polygamist is in good faith. He could be using the possibility of injustice as an excuse for retaining all his wives. Lamburn, therefore, prefers to admit the polygamist to the "Guild of Abraham", a kind of perpetual catechumenate in which certain promises are made, including that of not increasing the number of his wives. The wives, in Lamburn's view, could all be baptized.

William Blum sees the choice as being between refusing to baptize the polygamous household, and baptizing the whole household without condition.[73] His concern, very rightly, is to uphold and promote monogamy, and he considers that the chances are slim for the children of polygamous marriages to accept monogamy as the norm when their turn comes to marry, if polygamous households are baptized. If polygamists are to be baptized, he argues, then the children must be allowed to contract polygamous unions in their turn. Blum, in common with most Christian pastors nowadays, is opposed to the break-up of the polygamous family. He, therefore, opts for a solution, identical with that of Lamburn—the perpetual catechumenate.

Blum's argument about the children choosing polygamy, in their turn, is a hypothetical one, and he has no evidence to support it. Probably, one could find as many examples of children of monogamous families becoming polygamous, and of children of polygamous families becoming monogamous, as of children following a polygamous family tradition. There is also a generation and education gap, and many children are in revolt against parental ideals, particularly against unhappy childhood experiences of family tensions. The toleration by the Christian community of a polygamous household may speak more for Christian love and understanding than its rejection, and may inculcate in children a spirit which leads them to appreciate the value of monogamy.

Blum quite rightly questions the assumption that baptism is

necessary in these cases. Baptism is not conferred simply for the personal consolation of individuals. It is a sign of entry into a community that shares a single faith, which accepts specific ideals and lives by definite norms. It is right that the community should not have polygamists imposed upon it against the will of its members. Solutions must be found which are acceptable to the Christian community and its leaders. However, Blum goes further than this in suggesting that baptism is not strictly necessary for the salvation of the polygamist himself, and that faith is not indissolubly bound to the sacrament of baptism and the other sacraments.[74] Yet, although he is aware of the problem of the relationship of faith to sacrament, he does not, in fact, pursue the subject. Bernard Häring for his part, is strongly opposed to the separation of faith and sacrament.[75] Faith, he argues, demands sacramental expression, and, besides, how can the ordinary, African Christian be expected to accept such a subtle distinction, when baptism is demanded of others who fulfil the necessary conditions?

2   The Liberal Approach to Polygamy

Englebert Kofon, a pupil of Bernard Häring from Cameroun, offers a pastoral solution to the problem of polygamy which is much more liberal than those we have just considered.[76] Having studied polygamy anthropologically and theologically, and having traced the attitude of the Church to polygamy in history and in recent missiological practice, he proposes to admit polygamists and their wives to baptism and the sacraments on condition. The condition rests on a curious distinction, akin to the so-called "brother and sister" solution which is sometimes offered for divorced and remarried people. The distinction is between what Kofon calls "poly-marriage" and "poly-sex". Kofon sees no difficulty in baptizing persons involved in "poly-marriage", so long as they do not practise "poly-sex". In other words, a polygamist and his wives may all be baptized, on condition that sexual relations continue to take place only with the first wife, or a wife chosen according to the principles of the Petrine Privilege. The polygamist would be living as husband and wife with one of the women. With the rest, he would be living as brother and sister. It seems to us that this is neither a very theological, nor a very realistic solution, although Kofon's survey of parish councils in Cameroun suggests its feasibility. One may well ask; What sort of a marriage is it that is denied sexual expression? And is it fair for the man to impose absolute sexual continence on the remainder of his wives? As a female contributor to our discussions remarked, this is once again a solution devised by men, in favour of men!

On the other hand, Kofon shows some scepticism himself about his proposal, and he foresees that it will be difficult for the polygamous household to honour the undertakings they have made as a condition for baptism. He, therefore, counsels leniency. If "poly-marriage" does lapse sometimes into "poly-sex", then absolution must be easily given and the parties restored to communion. It is difficult not to conclude that these suggestions smack of hypocrisy and double-think. Would it not be better "to call a spade a spade" and allow polygamists to be baptized unconditionally?

Such a proposal would be the logical outcome of the argument of Eugene Hillman.[77] If polygamy is to be placed on an equal footing with monogamy, then, obviously there can be no objection to the baptism of polygamists and their wives. Nor can there be any objection to Christians contracting polygamous marriages after their baptism. If one accepts Hillman's position that it is at least an open question whether monogamy is superior to polygamy, would it be necessary to preach and uphold the idea of monogamous marriage in a community which prefers polygamy? Hillman betrays no anxiety on this score. Monogamy has its spokesmen already, and his concern is more for the toleration of polygamy than for the survival and safeguarding of monogamy.

3   The Limited Toleration of Polygamy and Levirate

The proposal that follows is based on the assumption that monogamy must be upheld and promoted as the ideal and the normative form of marriage for Christians. It assumes that baptized Christians should not be allowed by the Church to contract polygamous marriages. That being said, the proposal can be outlined as follows:

(a) Persons involved in polygamous marriages and in leviratic unions can be admitted to baptism and the other sacraments.
(b) It is understood that these are "socially approved" cases of simultaneous, plural unions.
(c) It is understood that the parties involved remain in these unions freely of their own accord.
(d) It is understood that these are compassionate exceptions in a

91

context where the traditional teaching on monogamy is strictly recognized and applied.

(e) It is understood that these exceptions are made with the explicit consent of the local Christian community as a whole, and with the approval in principle of the local church (diocese, country) and its leadership.

(f) On the same conditions, cases of Christians who have lapsed into polygamy, or who have entered into leviratic unions, under social or economic pressure or the burden of childlessness, should be treated with equal consideration and sympathy, and even readmitted to Communion if these plural unions cannot be dissolved without grave hardship to those concerned.

These are very general principles, and it would be the duty of local churches to apply them with discernment in their own, local situations. The indiscriminate baptism or readmission to Communion of all polygamists is definitely not recommended. The reasoning behind the proposal is that polygamous marriage does have positive value, even in Christian terms, that compassion must be shown, and that the lesser evil must be preferred to the greater. The proposal follows fairly closely those of Bernard Häring, Adrian Hastings, the regulations of the Liberian Lutheran Church and the recent recommendations of the Anglican Consultative Council.[78]

4 Helping Childless Couples

In the final section of this chapter we offer some suggestions made by Hennie Pretorius for helping childless couples discover a Christian significance in their situation.[79] Firstly, following the spirit of New Testament teaching, they should be brought to understand that the childless union is a sign of authentic married love and that it is creative in innumerable ways. Secondly, it is important that they should be clear about the role of sexuality in marriage. From a psychological point of view, the expression of oneness in love is the principal end of sexual intercourse in marriage. The biological passion to procreate may overshadow, and become a threat to, this love. Thirdly, childless couples must be warned against, on the one hand, turning their disappointment into an obsession or mutual reproach, and on the other hand, satisfying parental instincts in their relationship towards one another. Fourthly, the childless couple should be encouraged—where this is feasible—to have a thorough medical examination and eventual treatment for any physical or psychical causes of childlessness. In the fifth place, the couple should be encouraged to be socially and spiritually creative through active witness in their community. Finally, they must be encouraged to have a deep prayer life, in which, through setting their mind on God's kingdom, the problem of childlessness loses its overwhelming importance for them.

References: Chapter Three

1 *Gaudium et Spes*, 47.
2 Communications from Zaïrean participants at the Jos Congress, Nigeria, September 1975.
3 Hillman, 1975, *passim*.
4 Barrett, 1968, p. 116.
5 Hillman, 1975, p. 94.
6 *Demographic Study of Central African Republic—1959–60*. This country is now renamed Central African Empire.
7 Hillman, 1975, p. 94.
8 cf. 1969 *Censuses of Uganda and Kenya*; the 1967 *Census of Tanzania*; the 1960 *Census of Ghana*; *Ivory Coast Ministry of Finance Statistical Bulletin I*, 1966; and the *Gabon Census*, 1960–1.
9 cf. *Tanzania Census*, 1967; *Uganda Census*, 1969.
10 *Demographic Study of the Central African Republic*, *1959–60*.
11 *United Nations Demographic Yearbook*, 1971.
12 *Censuses of Uganda and Kenya*, 1969; *Census of Tanzania*, 1967.
13 Lewis, 1962, p. 8.
14 Whooley in Verryn (ed.), 1975, pp. 332–3.
15 Aquina, 1975, I, pp. 137–42, and II, pp. 73–4; Kasaka, 1976, and 1972, CROMIA/14.
16 Lubowa, 1974, CROMIA/28.
17 Aquina, 1975, I, p. 138.
18 Thomas and Chisanga, 1975.
19 Deniel, 1975, pp. 117–20.
20 Ssennyonga, 1972, CROMIA/17.
21 Holway, 1974, p. 11.
22 *Demographic Study of the Central African Republic*, *1959–60*.
23 Aquina, 1975, I, p. 140.
24 Hillman, 1975, p. 120.
25 Gachuhi, n.d.
26 Perlman, 1963.
27 Deniel, 1975, p. 122.
28 Molnos, 1973, III, p. 7.
29 Whooley, 1974.
30 Shorter, 1973, CROMIA/22.

31 Aquina, 1975, II, p. 74.
32 Kasaka, 1976.
33 cf. Hillman, 1975, p. 10.
34 Enderley, 1972, p. 28.
35 Holway, 1974, pp. 11–12.
36 Perlman, 1963, chap. 9.
37 Boerakker, 1975, p. 20.
38 Aquina, 1975, II, p. 74.
39 Hart, 1973, CROMIA/24.
40 Shorter, 1973, CROMIA/22.
41 Kalanda, 1974.
42 Kirwen, 1974, p. 258.
43 *Ibid.*, pp. 259–60.
44 Kalanda, 1974.
45 *Ibid.*
46 Kirwen, 1974, p. 175.
47 *Demographic Study of the Central African Republic, 1959–60.*
48 Quoted in Hastings, 1973, p. 15.
49 cf. the very full discussion of this subject in Hillman, 1975, Appendix, pp. 217–40.
50 Häring, lecture delivered at Gaba, August 19th, 1974.
51 Hastings, 1973, p. 73.
52 Lamburn, 1974a; Blum, 1972.
53 Hastings, 1973, p. 79.
54 Hillman, 1975, p. 206.
55 Dwane in Verryn (ed.) 1975, pp. 221–37.
56 Hillman, 1975, pp. 163–7.
57 Hastings, 1973, p. 75.
58 Quoted by Dwane in Verryn (ed.), 1975, p. 226.
59 Berglund in Verryn (ed.), 1975, pp. 15–16.
60 Hillman, 1975, pp. 152 and 167.
61 *Ibid.*, pp. 122 and 123.
62 Kalanda, 1974.
63 Kirwen, personal communication, October 5th, 1975.
64 Hillman, 1975, pp. 163–5.
65 Acts 6:1–16; Acts 9:39; I Cor. 7:8–9, 39–40; I Tim. 5:3–16; Tit. 2:3–5.
66 Blum, 1974.
67 Pretorius in Verryn (ed.), 1975, pp. 108–29.
68 Blum, 1974.
69 Whooley, 1974.
70 Blum, 1974.
71 cf. Hastings, 1973, p. 14.
72 Lamburn, 1974a. At the Lindi Discussions (Lamburn, 1975), about half of the participants disagreed with Lamburn's point of view and thought the polygamist in good faith should be baptized.

Lamburn himself interprets the Anglican Consultative Council's Resolution 25 in favour of his "guild of Abraham" solution, since it speaks of "receiving into the Church" and not about "baptism", cf. Lamburn, 1974.

73 Blum, 1972, pp. 56–7.
74 *Ibid.*, pp. 63–4.
75 Häring, lecture delivered at Gaba, August 19th, 1974.
76 Kofon, 1974.
77 cf. Hillman, 1975.
78 cf. Häring lecture delivered at Gaba, August 19th, 1974; Hastings, 1973, pp. 78–9; Resolution 25 of The Anglican Consultative Council, July 1973.
79 Pretorius in Verryn (ed.), 1975, pp. 123–9.

Chapter 4

Husband–Wife Relationships, Fatherhood, Sexuality

I Case Material

1 Husband–Wife Relationships

Variations and shifts of emphasis in different societies apart, Axel-Ivar Berglund describes as fairly widespread the concept of husband–wife relationships which is fertility-orientated.[1] This has also been popularized as "the Garden Theory" by Walter Trobisch and was referred to in Chapter One.[2] It must be said right away, however, that this understanding of husband–wife relationships is not biblical although passages may be found in the Bible which allude to it as a tendency in biblical cultures. It is also certainly not the African ideal of relationships in marriage as the research reports show. But this is not to say that it is entirely lacking from, or is completely foreign to, the African view of marital relationships. A restatement of the theory will help to show in what respects it agrees with, or differs from, the understanding of relationships between husband and wife in Africa.

In the last analysis, fertility is the determining factor of all man–woman, husband–wife relationships in the fertility-orientated image of marriage. The birth of children is the foundation-stone of the marital union in this understanding. The purpose and primary duty of the woman is to receive the male seed, nurture it within herself and bring forth offspring. The woman, therefore, does not exist in her own right or for her own sake. She exists first of all as mother of her husband's children. Apart from this necessary requirement, she is of little importance. If no offspring is forthcoming, all material relationships flounder.

On the other hand, and almost diametrically opposed to the woman in this theory, is the man, the husband. Whereas the woman is weak and inferior, the man is strong by common presumption and dominant. He is the bearer of the seed of life, the destiny and activator of human life. The initiative in any undertaking, including sexual relationships in marriage, is his. The woman is, as it were, a passive receptacle. It is up to the man to choose his wife, never the other way round. And, as can be expected, his choice is governed by the woman's potential to bear children. The man pays the *lobola* (or whatever name is used for bridewealth) to ensure that the woman is in his hands and that, therefore, he has the right, recognized by society, to have his children through her. Hence, rightly understood, *lobola* is not bride-price but actually child-price.

In view of fertility-orientated marital relationships, therefore, the wife is really the property of her husband. She is bound to him, to only one husband; but the man is not bound to one wife. While there can be ordinarily no thought of a woman taking several husbands simultaneously (polyandry), there are, as we saw in the last chapter, a number of motives which can lead a man to take another, or several other wives at any one time (polygyny). Infertility, for instance, or the poor condition of children, which are invariably blamed on the wife, can act as motives for a man to enter into other marital unions. Another motive may be the lack of birth of male children. Sons are a major concern in marriage. It is they who continue and propagate the life of their father, the family and the clan. Daughters are only important primarily because they are future mothers of children of other men in other clans.

The fertility idea governs even sexual morality in this view. An adulterer does nothing wrong to his wife because he does not deprive her of anything. He does wrong only to the husband of the wife or the father of the daughter with whom he commits adultery. This is because he plants his seed in another person's "garden" where he has no right to do so. Any adulteress, on the contrary, wrongs her husband or her father and his clan because she receives foreign seed.

Determining all husband–wife relationships in this view of marriage, then, is fecundity. Such values as love and sharing, loyalty and confidence, female personality and female human dignity for its own sake are liable to be bypassed or sometimes even completely disregarded. In sum, Berglund points out the following four characteristics as indicative of the fertility-orientated husband–wife relationships:

(i) The concept is patriarchal in approach to the family, the clan and society.
(ii) The concept is potentially polygamous (in the form of polygyny).
(iii) The concept is discriminatory against women, giving them an inferior role to play in the family, clan and society.
(iv) The concept is fertility-procreatively centred.[3]

With the main characteristics of the fertility-governed image of marital relationships now before us, we can ask whether or not these characteristics appeared in traditional African marriages. Evelyn Lebona enumerates a number of factors in marriages in South Africa which seem to suggest that some aspects of the fertility-directed concept of marriage were present in, and applicable to, Africa. For example, the question of love between spouses was disregarded when the parents were the only ones solely responsible for the choice of the spouses for their sons and daughters. Another factor was the commercialization of the "bridewealth" by the bride's parents. They made it very high as a way of enriching themselves. Both of these factors affected relationships in marriage. Forced, as it were, to live with a partner one did not choose, either of the two could very easily, and perhaps justifiably, put all the blame for difficulties encountered in that particular marriage on the parents: "Look, it's my parents who married you, not I." Or again, faced with a fantastic sum of *lobola* to pay in money or cattle, young people, as we noted in the first chapter, not infrequently opted for elopement—where the girl was abducted "against her will". In this case, the young man or his guardian paid much less cattle or money in "damages" to the parents of the girl than he would otherwise have done in the actual form of the *labola*. At other times, and especially today, young people evade arranged marriages or too high forms of *lobola* by simply deciding to live together with all the privileges of married life but without its bonds. In such circumstances the marital relationships will be loose, with either of the partners relatively free to walk away for another union the moment he/she feels like it.[4]

Yet, although some, or all, of these aspects of husband–wife relationships may be found in the concept of marriage in Africa, they are by no means typical of African marriage. As Patrick

Whooley points out, to understand husband–wife relationships in traditional Africa, marriage must be situated within the context of family relationships as a whole. One must avoid the temptation of making simple comparisons between Western and African attitudes to marriage. It is not possible, Whooley notes, to treat husband–wife relationships usefully where Africa is concerned without considering a whole list of other relationships: a husband's relationships with his mother and sisters; a wife's relationships with her father, brothers and mother, and everybody's relationship with their clan. And then all these must be placed within the setting of the values, attitudes and structures of the culture within which the marriage takes place.[5]

As a concrete case, Whooley studies carefully the marital relationships and attitudes of the Xhosa-speaking people of South Africa. A wife's first duty, according to the Xhosa, is to respect her husband and his people. A newly-wed wife had to observe many restrictions in her husband's home in order to show this respect. There were, for instance, strict standards of dress, prescribed in detail by tradition which she had to observe. The observation of these standards was insisted upon by her mother-in-law and other senior women of her husband's kraal. She obeyed her husband's demands for sex whenever possible, but custom discouraged her from showing open or direct interest in sex or to take the initiative in soliciting sexual intimacy from her husband.

A man's access to the world of women was primarily through his sisters and through his mother. No other relationships in Xhosa life rival these. They are characterized by intimacy, warmth and reverent respect. To refer disrespectfully to a person's mother would be the greatest of insults. And the greatest confidante of any Xhosa man is his sister. "At a boy's initiation rite", Whooley reports, "I have seen girls slip in and out of the kraal for long whispered chats with the initiate. 'It's his sister', an informant will tell you as sufficient explanation. One notices the outgoing self-assurance of a woman who comes forward to offer a friendly greeting. 'This is my brother's place. Here I am at home' is a typical explanation. 'Home' for a Xhosa woman is always the place where she was born, the kraal where her brother is now married. Her husband's place is her 'homestead'—never her 'home'."[6] The Xhosa men's attitude towards husband–wife, brother–sister, son–mother relationships may be summarized in sayings often heard among the Xhosa people such as this one: "You have only one mother (or sister); you can always get another wife."

The value of respect among the Xhosa must be emphasized as it governs relationships not only in marriage but in almost every aspect of life. That is why it is accentuated and thus driven home to the boys during their initiation rites as well as to young wives by their mother-in-law or other women of their husbands' clans. Respect simply means knowing and keeping to one's place in interpersonal relationships. A person who drives dangerously under the influence of alcohol has no respect because he endangers other people's lives. The adult man who associates with young boys has no respect as well because his place is with his fellow adults.

Other forms of respect by the Xhosa woman to her husband and his people are that she does not use his name or that of his father and she shows reluctance to speak in her husband's homestead unless she is spoken to. As she bears children, however, her status in society changes. She gains complete freedom to mix with the women who sit side by side with the men at feasts and beer parties when her child is ten or more years old.

For the men, it is disrespectful of his wife and quite undignified to be too much in her presence or in the presence of the other women of his homestead. He simply does not belong there. It is a sign of dignity and respect if a man identifies with other men of his age-group. Most of the time a man should leave the women, including his wife, to lead their own life. It follows, therefore, that the man who helps his wife out with the house chores "has no dignity" and everyone, men and women, often have grave reservations about such a one. They ridicule him and pity his "unfortunate" wife. It is dignified to disclaim publicly before fellow males any affection for one's wife. But this does not necessarily mean that one is cold or that, in private, one lacks affection for one's wife.

It can now be seen from this example how marital relationships in Africa were based on roles which the man or woman was expected by custom to play. Questions such as that of equality between husband and wife, in the cut and dried sense of the word as understood in western European and American marital relationships, did not arise. Maqalaka Mahara reporting on a group of Sotho people in the Orange Free State,[7]

Patrick Whooley researching among the Xhosa-speaking Nguni people of South Africa[8] and J. A. Nkaisule speaking with southern Tanzania in mind,[9] all agree that there can be no question about equality in traditional African marriages because there are established sex-roles and the sex-line must not be crossed. At no time and at no age may a male undertake a female role or participate in jobs set aside for women. Neither may a woman, for that matter, assume a male role. Among the Xhosa this sex-division was maintained in social life where men and women (and boys and girls) sat on different sides in the house; in marital life where husband and wife each had a separate sleeping mat and only the man could cross and join his wife on her mat.

There was also an obvious division of labour. Women took care of the children, collected firewood, fetched water, cooked and in some places did all but the heaviest work in the garden. The men saw to cattle, did the heavier work in the garden such as clearing and fencing and built the houses.

In the patrilineal societies of Africa, marriage meant the incorporation of the bride into the family or clan of the bridegroom with the consequent rights and duties belonging to the different members of the family or clan towards one another. These rights and duties were determined by the traditional customs and laws governing the clan. Traditionally, the position of the African women in the family was not as bad as it would seem on the surface. Her position, as Mahara points out, can really be seen from two points of view. Out of doors under public scrutiny the wife may be like an adult child. Indoors, however, she is mistress over her household. To her husband she is an indispensable partner and supporter. She has a say at every stage of many of the affairs of the family. She can moderate or even overrule the husband's decision!

A survey conducted by the Catholic Church in Ghana on marriage and the family[10] shows that there are new realities impinging upon the relationships of man and woman in marriage. This is borne out by Norman Thomas and Daniel Chisanga in their survey of marriage in Kitwe, Zambia,[11] and by Martin Peskin in his research about Christianity and marriage in Soweto, South Africa.[12] Besides the well-known factors influencing relationships in marriage in Africa: namely, infertility of the wife, incompatability, adultery of the wife, and illness, the liberation of woman today threatens to change the traditionally accepted role of explicit male dominance in the home. Even in those societies which were matrilineal, men posed as sources of greater wisdom and controlled the economy of the family. Today, however, the wife may be more educated than her husband and her position as breadwinner is accepted more and more. But the strains this development brings to relationships in marriage are considerable. Because now the husband is not the only source of wisdom in the family, and he is not the only source of income, he is often suspicious and jealous. No longer dependent on her husband as she was before, the wife may even clothe and educate the children without counting on the husband's earnings. The man may then resort to chasing after other women and neglecting his wife as a way of punishing her. This behaviour will in turn arouse the suspicions and jealousy of his wife. Thus suspicions, jealousies and other tensions grow which in the end may wreck the marriage.

Migrant labour is another source of tension in marriage in Africa today. Men leave their wives and go to work far away from home and for a long time. Some men exploit this situation to enter into casual unions with other women. Sometimes they completely neglect to provide for their families back home. To feed herself and the children, the woman may consequently turn to prostitution. This, as can be imagined, is the beginning of the end of that particular marriage.

Especially in the urban parts of Africa, the extended family relationships are being eroded. This means that husband and wife are thrown more together. But aspects of the old system do not disappear completely. In spite of its urban character, the prevailing social life in Kitwe (Zambia), for example, is one of separate networks for husbands and wives. When the men go out in the evening to drink, they leave their wives at home with the children. Thomas and Chisanga note in their report that an average of 10% of the family income will be spent on alcohol by the father of a family in Kitwe. This may result in the non-support of the wife and children and the marital relationships may, therefore, become strained to breaking point.

But in Kitwe as among the Nambyans and the Tonga of Rhodesia[13] beer drinking is by no means an exclusively male activity. At beer parties, females are available as drinking companions. Husband and wife may be attending separate beer parties and rivalling one another in infidelity. Unfaithfulness multiplies until the marriage breaks down.

Industrialization, western civilization and Christianity have all contributed their share to the confusion in relationships between husband and wife in Africa today.

2 Fatherhood

Life and the sharing of life are universal values. They are also frequently proposed as being pre-eminently African. For in traditional Africa, to live meant also to transmit life. As we saw in the previous chapter, one was not fully alive if one did not, or could not, bear children. Implicit or explicit requests for children formed the content of many prayers. But for a few exceptional ritual or other roles, there was no role in traditional African society for bachelors or spinsters. The childless person was an object of reproach or pity. There being no descendant to carry on his name after him, such a person was consigned to oblivion after death. To transmit life was to share in the divine creative powers. It was an act of triumphing over death. "Many children mean rising from the dead."[14]

In the act of transmitting life, the position of the father was paramount. Among the Shona people of Rhodesia it is believed that the father of a child has greater life-force (*simba*) than the child. The father is looked upon and treated with respect and even with fear by his children. His authority cannot be challenged by them and his orders are unquestioned. "As long as a father lives, a son does not become fully independent, but has to refer all important decisions to him. The father in turn feels great responsibility for his son and intercedes for him with the ancestral spirits. When a father grows old and infirm, a son works hard to support him. The easiest way he can do this is when he lives with his father in the same village."[15] The father has to pay *lobola* (bridewealth) for his sons so that they, too, may become parents—as much like him as possible—and perpetuate his and his father's name.

A father's sons in most patrilineal societies of Africa are his heirs. It is in their hands that he entrusts the guardianship of his dependants when he dies. One of the interests in his daughters is that when they marry, the *lobola* he receives helps towards getting wives for his sons.

Full fatherhood means a large number of children, as many as one can beget. That is why, if a marriage remains childless for a long time, marital bonds become loose. A man who cannot get children in his marriage is therefore very likely to do one of two things: either he will divorce his present wife and remarry or he will accept polygamy. Women also know how hard it is not to have children. If a Shona wife knows she is barren, she will urge her husband to take another wife. If childlessness is due to the sterility of the husband, his wife will have no qualms about sleeping with other men. Whatever children are born will be the children of her husband. Sometimes the man, knowing that he is sterile, will ask his brother to sleep with his wife and bear children for him.

Whereas in the patrilineal societies the children belong to the husband and he keeps them when he sends his wife away, in the matrilineal, uxorilocal societies such as the Mang'anja of the Lower Shire Valley of Malawi, the husband has no legal claim over his own children. By custom, they belong to his wife and her people. The role of the father is only to be genitor of the children. *Mkamwini*, which is translated "son-in-law" in English, means in fact "he who belongs elsewhere". This is significant. The husband cannot gain any status among matrilineal peoples in the lineage group of his wife. He can only be a person of importance in his own village of origin. There he may have the same status of authority and prestige as the brother of his wife in her village.[16] Amid his wife's people, a man is careful not to incur upon himself their displeasure. He must be cautious even in disciplining the children. As these belong to the wife, only she and her people may discipline them in any way they see fit. If the wife and her people no longer like the husband, they divorce him.[17]

The maternal uncle or mother's brother controls his sister's children in African matrilineal societies. Yet the child does not cease to regard his father as important. The belief is that the child is so mystically linked to his father that not even his uncle, with all the legal authority he has over the child, may sever this relationship. Also, the child calls upon himself fatal consequences for any disrespectful behaviour or insult towards his father. In spite of the fact that they are not legally bound to him, the children live with their father and serve him faithfully until he dies. The father can, and often does, reward the thoughtfulness of his children by placing them before his sister's children, for example, for inheritance of his property although the latter have the legal right to inherit from him.[18]

However, matrilineal systems in the strict sense are now on the wane in many places in Africa.[19] From the matrilineal peoples of Ghana to the Ehansu of Lake Eyasi in Tanzania, the transition from matrilineal to patrilineal inheritance and succession, to mention only two aspects, is being felt (although, it is argued by some that matriliny is more stable in Ghana). As wealth increases and the man keeps control over his property the matrilineal principle seems to be doomed. Strains in matriliny, not the least of which is the repression of the emotional interest of the father in his children, are proving unbearable. What Elizabeth Colson says of the Plateau Tonga is true also of many matrilineal groups elsewhere in Africa:

The importance of the matrilineal group wanes before the increasing demands of the household and the family for the loyalty of its members. New economic possibilities emphasize the importance of the household working team, and give rise to clashes between the interests derived from membership within a matrilineal group. The development of cash-crop farming, with the possibility of accumulating wealth either in the form of savings or in capital goods, is creating tensions in a system based on a male-centred household combined with matrilineal inheritance. More and more the Tonga are demanding, where a clash occurs between the interests of the two groups, that the matrilineal group should give way.[20]

Where the father has control over his family, the children develop a strong attachment to his dwelling place. This is their home. Here members of the family feel most secure because they see this place as their "base". Here their forefathers lie buried. Here, too, they have rights to land. It is here that those single men who go to work far away are received when they come back after their retirement. And for the married man who must work away from home, his wife represents his interests—especially as regards land.

3 Sexuality

The attitude of traditional Africa towards sex and sexuality can be summarized in the following observation: "Infertility and sterility block the channel through which the stream of life flows; they plunge the person concerned into misery, they sever him from personal immortality, and threaten the perpetuation of the lineage."[21] And because the generation of life was a matter of concern to the whole community, there were strong sanctions against people who indulged in sex for selfish reasons. Sexuality and its powers were understood as permeating every level of human existence: interpersonal relationships and matters of ritual. Sexuality was looked upon as mysterious and sacred. If it were misused, evil surely resulted.

Initiation rites prepared the adolescent for the right use of his/her sexuality, to get married and raise a family. But today things are falling apart. Initiation rites are fast dying out. Although traditionally appropriate sexual and marital behaviour was worked out and structured so that men and women knew what was expected of them at different well-defined stages of their lives, these structures are now crumbling as well and giving way to western influences. The so-called sexual liberation is spreading out rapidly from Europe and America and bringing in its wake both values and dangers.[22]

There is a lot to be said for this present development. Fundamentally, it tries to promote a sincere understanding of human sex and sexual activity. It encourages men and women to accept their sexuality seriously and honestly without false inhibitions, guilt complexes or shame. In its own way, it strives to make clear that although sex is a force for reproduction, it has an equally important part to play in strengthening interpersonal relationships, communication among people and bringing happiness. Also, it aims at dispelling fears brought about by ignorance and confusions which are not conducive to mature human sexuality. Thanks to this development factual information about sex and sexuality which is free from cheap moralization is beginning to be disseminated.

These may have been areas lacking in an earlier way of looking at sex and sexuality. But, as we say, this tendency, which has been called by some people "permissive" could easily deteriorate into a misuse of sex and sexuality. Then sex becomes nothing but "fun". No duties, no responsibilities, no obligations: just fun. This can lead, and in fact has led, to psychosexual puerility in relationships, to sex being turned into a commercial commodity. Then, early, casual, and discriminate sexual relationships, damaging to the human personality, will result.

In order to survive, there is need for society to regulate its sexual activity. If old structures are now falling apart, perhaps for the good of society, new and more relevant ones must replace them for the same social good.

II Theological Reflection

1 *Husband–Wife Relationships*

Neither of the two creation narratives in the Bible, Gen. 1–2:4a and Gen. 2:5–25, seek to give an historical account of the beginnings of man and the universe. The message they want to bring across is theological: it is that of the greatness of God and the dignity of man created in the image of God himself. "So God created man in the image of himself, in the image of God he created him, male and female he created them."[23] Man and woman are assigned an equal status by God at creation and sex is given a clearly defined role in their relationship: "God blessed them, saying to them, 'Be fruitful, multiply, fill the earth . . .'."[24] But the marriage itself is the priority which God blesses and from it comes fruitfulness. The emphasis therefore is not on fertility but on the man-woman relationship in marriage not conditioned by anything else: "This is why a man leaves his father and mother and joins himself to his wife, and they become one body."[25]

The biblical view of marriage is that in marriage a new union of man and woman is formed not only, or even not primarily, for the sake of offspring thereby, but for the sake of those entering into the union themselves. Their union is exclusive, they "cleave" to one another. This certainly seems to suggest that the biblical ideal of the marital union opposes the polygamous liberties which the fertility-orientated systems of man–woman relationships permit. Cleaving implies total commitment and belonging to one another. Such commitment and belonging does not allow interference from any other quarter. Man and woman must live and act in marriage actually like "one body".

The woman is first and foremost a partner in marriage. The biblical ideal of the relationships of husband and wife is not so much equality, however, as mutuality, sharing at every level of life. The quality of input may differ, and does indeed differ, but what is essential is that each is given the opportunity to be himself or herself. This is what is foremost in Paul's mind as he gives his theological insights on marriage and speaks to husbands and wives:

Give way to one another in obedience to Christ. Wives should regard their husbands as they regard the Lord, since as Christ is head of the

Church and saves the whole body, so is a husband the head of his wife; and as the Church submits to Christ, so should wives to their husbands, in everything. Husbands should love their wives just as Christ loved the Church and sacrificed himself for her to make her holy. He made her clean by washing her in water with a form of words, so that when he took her she would be glorious, with no speck or wrinkle or anything like that, but holy and faultless. In the same way, husbands must love their wives as they love their own bodies; for a man to love his wife is for him to love himself. A man never hates his own body, but he feeds it and looks after it: and that is the way Christ treats the Church, because it is his body—and we are its living parts. For this reason, a man must leave his father and mother and be joined to his wife, and the two will become one body. This mystery has many implications; but I am saying it applies to Christ and the Church. To sum up: you too, each one of you, must love his wife as he loves himself; and let every wife respect her husband.[26]

Each of the partners in marriage has value as a human person. Like the man, the woman has value and importance in her own right and not necessarily in her children. Neither the man nor the woman is an instrument for an end, be it genitor or childbearer. The value of man and woman in marriage cannot be subordinated to any other purpose. "Sex belongs to the man–woman relationships of marriage to the extent and depth that the two, in reality and essence, become one flesh. Herein lies the mystery of human togetherness in marriage, a mystery applicable also to the unity between Christ and his Church (according to Ephesians). There is, in the fulfilment of the divine concept of marriage, a physical completeness which transcends the spiritual, includes it and is interwoven into it."[27]

Loving and tender sexual fascination is proper to husband and wife. It is obviously not condemned in the Bible. On the contrary. When he is given woman, for instance, man exclaims with unmistakable joy, pleasure and satisfaction: "This at last is bone from my bones, and flesh from my flesh!"[28] Fascination and desire, which are not merely egoistic, belong to proper relationships in marriage. This enhances candour, joy in sharing, simplicity and trust. It is an essential element towards being one in marriage. Perhaps this is what is meant by standing before each other naked and without shame.[29]

The biblical *ideal* of man–woman relationships in marriage appears, in short, to be the following:

(i) God's view of man–woman relationships in marriage is of such importance that the relationship is analogous to the relationship between him, incarnated in Christ, and his Church. The loving care that God has for his people should be reflected in the care that husband and wife have for each other.

(ii) In the total biblical view of creation, man and woman in togetherness are of singular importance. They are "one body". In the sum of both of them, God chooses to continue his creation.

(iii) Both man and woman have a worth and dignity equal to each other given them by God at creation. Neither is superior or inferior to the other. Neither's worth is increased or decreased by fertility or infertility. Children are a blessing granted by God to a couple. They come from the unity of man and woman in the oneness of the body but the marriage does not rotate or hang upon them. In other words, children do not constitute marriage.

(iv) In marriage husband and wife form a new centre of gravity, as it were, and forces pulling them to other directions must be reduced to a minimum.

(v) One husband cleaves to one wife in total commitment and belonging. There is no room for divorce or polygamy.[30]

The biblical ideal is a constant challenge to men and to the Church. It is original, holy, sinless. It is the ideal of man–woman relationships in marriage that must be realized slowly as man journeys towards the Kingdom. However, the present realities of imperfect man are different from the ideal, and the Scriptures make allowance for the weakness of man, for his "hardness of heart". Room must be given for the striving of man to grow from imperfection to perfection, to the ideal of marriage which is always before us.

But even given this allowance, three things can be said of marriage in the present human condition: first, that marriage involves a personalization of sexuality; second, that marriage involves some kind of commitment which is permanent in nature; and third, that ordinarily marriage should be open to procreation.

For the sake of the married people themselves and for the sake of the children who may be born of the union, marriage cannot be a temporary, transient affair. It is a permanent commitment which always grows. Perfection in marriage is always a goal to be achieved. As Michel Quoist says to the married: "No matter how long you have been married, marriage is both a present reality and a goal to be attained. In marriage you must give yourselves to one another at all three levels of your human make-up—the

109

physical, the emotional and the spiritual—it is difficult not to take anything for self. Genuine love is not an easy attainment, but you have the whole of your lives to help one another to attain it. Remember, however, that your life of love will always be marked by a sign of contradiction—the Cross. This cross is a personal invitation from Christ to union.''[31]

Open to it, the gift of children brings great joy to the marriage, and tightens the bonds of the relationship. Yet, the lack of children must not be allowed to cause joylessness in the marriage union or loosen relationships. Conjugal love without procreation is quite possible and it can bring as much joy and happiness.

Order in inter-personal relationships, the order for which God created mankind, finds its supreme expression in marriage. Community is a composite of relationships of which the man–woman relationship in marriage is basic. In marriage, as in community, man and woman relate to each other in tension and complementarity in every stage of marriage at both the psychological and the physical levels. It is also, as Felicity Edwards emphasizes, at the level of psycho-physical unity that man relates to his environment and to God.[32] The alienation from God, from other persons and from one's own self brought about by sin manifests itself in such ruptures of relationships in community as androcentricity. This alienation, disruption of relationships and fragmentation calls for reconciliation. Reconciliation and full humanization come through Christ. It is in Christ that we become the men and women God wants us to become. In him we restore the relationships with God, with one another and with ourselves that were severed by sin. Persons, then, have worth in their own right, and may never be used as objects. Man's goal is growth and maturity in relationship with all his fellow men and in marriage, with his/her partner and children. Man and woman commit themselves to a shared life and interdependence in marriage. One is incomplete without the other. But, together, they need the community into which they and their children are integrated. The Second Vatican Council calls marriage "a community of love, a perfecting of life", and synthesizes the theology of marriage according to the Roman Catholic tradition, thus:

Authentic married love is caught up into divine love and is governed and enriched by Christ's redeeming power and the saving activity of the Church. Thus love can lead the spouses to God with powerful effect and can aid and strengthen them in the sublime office of being a father or mother. For this reason Christian spouses have a special sacrament by which they are fortified and receive a kind of consecration in the duties and dignity of their state. By virtue of this sacrament, as spouses fulfil their conjugal and family obligations, they are penetrated with the spirit of Christ. This spirit suffuses their whole lives with faith, hope and charity. Thus they increasingly advance their own perfection as well as their mutual sanctification, and hence contribute jointly to the glory of God.[33]

2 Fatherhood

Perhaps the best way to begin a theological reflection, in the African context, on the very important question of fatherhood is to quote the words of Pope Paul VI in praise of the place of the father in the African family:

Then in the family one should note the respect for the part played by the father of the family and the authority he has. Recognition of this is not found everywhere and in the same degree but it is so extraordinarily widespread and deeply rooted that it is rightly to be considered as a mark of African tradition in general.

Patria potestas is profoundly respected even in the African societies which are governed by matriarchy. There, although ownership of goods and the social status of children follow from the mother's family, the father's moral authority in the household remains undiminished.

By reason of the same concept the father of the family in some African cultures has a typically priestly function assigned to him whereby he acts as mediator not only between the ancestors and his family, but also between God and his family, performing acts of worship established by custom.[34]

The Pope's insight into the nature of African fatherhood has important theological implications. Comparisons have been made of both the patrilineal and the matrilineal father with the fatherhood of God. God, the Master of all creation, can be likened to the patrilineal father. Both are interested in their children and have unlimited power and authority over them. They protect their children and keep them from evil and harm. But they demand obedience, service and loyalty. Although they do not hesitate to punish when punishment is due, they are extremely tolerant. What they always hold before the children, however, and what they want the children to strive for, are the rewards they are so eager to bestow.

On the other hand, like the matrilineal father, God loves his children (the human race) for their own sake without expecting anything in return. Although they have no strict claim to the rewards he bestows, he nevertheless rewards them abundantly and beyond their wildest hopes.[35]

According to the Bible, the father has the duty to use his understanding of the faith to build up the same Christian faith in his wife and children. Albeit in another connection, this is what Paul instructs Christians in all Churches to do: "If you are a husband, for all you know, it may be your part to save your wife."[36] For the rest, let every father do everything for the glory of God.

The Hebrew emphasis on male domination shows itself clearly in the Pauline corpus of teaching on marriage in the New Testament. He insists on the wife's subjection and obedience to her husband.[37] Taken at its face value this is attractive to African husbands as it agrees with their patriarchical interpretation of marriage and family life. On the other hand, Paul's teaching is disregarded in the West as outdated because emphasis there is now on the equality of the sexes. What both attitudes miss in the Pauline teaching, however, is the biblical demand of self-giving, self-sacrificing love that Paul underlines as necessary for fathers in order to give direction and to provide a clear charter of life for the family. The father, according to Paul, has to look at all his duties through the cross of Christ. He must make the transition, that is, from his old sinful nature of selfishness and pride to the cross's ideal of self-denial and thus discover his new self. Only such discovery can infuse love into the family and make fatherhood a saving asset.[38]

True Christian fatherhood means a constant endeavour to inspire trust, not fear. Fatherhood is leadership in service to the family the father leads. The father is head of the family (the body) even as Christ is head of his body which is called the Church. As every true member of the Church is a cause of joy in heaven, so every member of the family is an important gift and should be a cause of thanksgiving to God. All members of the family are equally heirs to the life of grace[39] under one Father who is God.[40] With Christ as his example and guide, the father of a family needs to excel in the quality of fatherly, loving, self-giving—*agape*. He is entrusted with the duty of forming the

Christian attitudes of his family and to form their character by word and especially by example. However good it may be to have children, to keep them in the ways of the Lord is a great responsibility. Ecclesiasticus warns:

Do not long for a brood of worthless children, and take no pleasure in godless sons. However many you have, take no pleasure in them, unless the fear of the Lord lives among them. Do not count on their having long life, do not put too much faith in their future; for better have one than a thousand, better die childless than have godless ones.[41]

Husband and wife form a covenant to fulfil and express their personality. The covenant grows as their union becomes closer. In their union new human beings are born whose development as human persons depends very much upon it, and through it they are introduced into the wider human community.[42]

Fatherhood cannot be a reality without motherhood. It is the woman who enables the man to become a father and it is the man who enables the woman to become mother. Together they are the nucleus of the family. Together they are the image of God and source of life. Together they are co-creators with God. Like the man, the woman, who represents Christ's Church, has a redemptive mission towards her husband and her family. In the same breath as Paul says, "if you are a husband, for all you know, it may be your part to save your wife", he also says, and in fact he begins by saying: "if you are a wife, it may be your part to save your husband, for all you know".[43] The proper vocation of husband and wife is to be witnesses to one another and to their children about their faith in, and love for, Christ. The Kingdom to come is proclaimed loudly by the Christian family. And also through the family the hope for the perfect Kingdom is kept alive. The joy and completeness of husband and wife is found in one another.[44]

He who finds a wife finds happiness, receiving a mark of favour from Yahweh.[45]

A good wife is her husband's crown, a shameless wife, a cancer in his bones.[46]

3 *Sexuality*
Find joy with the wife you married in your youth, fair as a hind, graceful as a fawn.

113

Let hers be the company you keep, hers the breasts that ever fill you with delight, hers the love that ever holds you captive.[47]

Those are a few lines in the Bible in praise of sexuality. Furthermore, the whole book of the Song of Songs is, as Ashby notes quoting Andersen, "a witness to the soundness of passionate love".[48]

For a long time neglected, it is now being felt more than ever before that sex and sexuality must have their proper place in any theological treatment of marriage and marital life. The feeling now also is that these, as any other aspects of marriage, must be treated clearly, frankly and openly.

It is true that traditional theology was at times suspicious, even hostile towards sex and sexuality. Such uneasiness still persists today in the thinking of many people. Among not a few churchmen, Alex Chima argues, discussion on sex and love stir supposedly "righteous" emotions of indignation. When it is necessary to speak about sex and sexual love, these spokesmen of the Church, the definitive sign of whose members is precisely "Love", do so with reluctance and apologies! This attitude is no help towards a theological understanding of sex and sexuality. At present it is being challenged from all sides and in all manner of ways as being hypocritical and therefore unhealthy. Man is a sexual being who should be thankful for his sexuality to God. Helped and guided by the Church, the Christian has the duty of understanding himself, and this includes understanding his sexuality, in his relationship to God, to his fellow man and to the environment. Sex is a gift of God and it is being ungrateful to the Creator to call it dirty or obscene. Often it is a sign of a sick man to have unhealthy inhibitions about his sexuality and that of others. Ecclesiastical and cultural prejudices against sex have to be carefully uprooted.

Alex Chima traces the beginnings of the disregard for sex and sexuality from the time when the religions began divorcing the spirit of man from his body. The body was evil, and sex, which is carnal, became something to be ashamed of. Platonism, Manicheeism, Augustianism, Jansenism, Puritanism and Victorianism are all different manifestations of this view.

Particularly influential in biasing the Church against sex was the teaching of St. Augustine, although the puritanical strain of teaching goes back to Tertullian and Origen. According to Augustine, sexual relations even in marriage involve too much concupiscence, and so there is always a measure of sin in sexual intercourse. Procreation is a justification for intercourse, but even then continence is by far the most Christian course of action and it is a value superior to procreation. Sexual intercourse, apart from the necessity of procreation, can only be justified as a remedy for concupiscence.

Pope Gregory the Great was even more disparaging of sex and sexuality than Augustine. He taught that pleasure, taken in sex, is sin, notwithstanding the possibility of procreation. Intercourse is befouled if it gives pleasure, because sexual pleasure—and this is also the view of St. Thomas Aquinas—takes away, albeit for a brief moment, the use of the highest of faculties: reason.[49]

All of these theological positions were conditioned by the circumstances of their time. The general view of the traditional African religions on sex and sexuality appears not to have been too much off-centre. It is possible to say that in the African worldview sex was not biological only; it was also sacred. It was to be "used" with care; it was mysterious and like all mysterious things it belonged to the gods. The pleasure of sex was, of course, legitimate, but its outcome, whenever possible, was to be children. Childbearing was a religious and social duty. It follows, therefore, that in almost all parts and cultures of Africa, rape, homosexuality, bestiality—all sexual acts which did not fulfil both of these conditions—were condemned and severely punished. They could bring nothing but disaster not only to the people concerned but to the whole community.[50]

The right view of sex goes beyond mere coition. Pleasure and procreation are both very important aspects of sex the absence of any of which would undoubtedly spell disaster to the human race. But beyond that, sex is a reality by and through which the Christian married couple can worship God in love of one another. In intercourse the couple sum up the whole meaning of human relationships: in love sex can be positive and creative and thus bring people closer to God and to a deeper understanding of their fellow men; in selfishness it can be negative and destructive of interpersonal relationships and relationships between God and man. Thus, rightly used, sexual intercourse is a religious act. "It contains all the elements of worship: invocation, confession of faith, prayer, offering, communion, etc. It is the natural worship of man. It can be a worship offered to the Creator or an idolatrous worship. . . .

Sexuality is essentially a movement towards the depths, the height and the breadth of the love of God. With it man is totally turned towards God; the eternal penetrates and calls what is passing; the incorruptible, the corruptible; the infinite, the finite. It is thus that the celestial vocation of man is well and truly inscribed in the book of sexuality."[51]

In no other human togetherness do two people share so much so simultaneously as in sexual intercourse. The sexual experience, which is also true communication, cannot be fully described in words because it involves man's whole being. Part of the mystery of sexuality lies in this, that it is essentially existential. It defies analysis. Like the experience of God, there is much more to the experience of sexual union than can be put into words. Thus sexual intimacy points far beyond itself. It transcends the self of individuals and fuses two persons together. Is this the experience evocative of the unity of God and mankind? It might well be, for in the Scriptures the union of man and woman is the figure of the union of God and his people, Israel. As always, love is the driving force. The Song of Songs will remain as a witness to the soundness of passionate love as seen by the Bible. The song is about love "as we experience it, leading us to love as we experience it in God, couched in the language of our human experience".[52]

The Bible has no hang-ups about sex. It is clear in its affirmation of sexuality; that it is good, satisfying and blessed.

III   Models for Pastoral Action

Husband—Wife Relationships, Fatherhood, Sexuality
The disintegration and breakdown of marital relationships is caused, as we have seen, by the following factors: (1) Hostile pressures in the environment of the married couple such as extreme poverty; inadequate housing; unsatisfactory work conditions (e.g. migrant labour); and too much interference in the marriage by the other members of the extended family—especially the in-laws of both patrilineal and matrilineal societies. (2) Failure of the married couple to adjust to each other and this shows itself in frustration in sexual relationships and the frequency of extra-marital sexual relations. (3) Childlessness. (4) Individual inadequacies in the

husband or wife such as physical or emotional ill-health or gross selfishness on the part of either of the partners.[53]

Faced with all these disruptive elements in present-day Africa, the question is, what is to be done? In other words, what models for pastoral action could the Church adopt? In the work of stabilizing marriage relationships, the priest, the pastor in Africa has a great task to perform. His task is to use all means in his power to guide married people to gain a mature understanding of themselves, of each other in marriage and thus strengthen their marital bonds. For the trouble today is that everywhere in the world, and much more so in Africa, society is in a state of constant flux. This situation has many setbacks for Africa. In the old days when there was rigid adherence to the extended family, everyone's status and role in society were set, easily determined and accepted. Relationships entailed certain obligations and prescribed ways of behaviour so that everyone knew exactly what was expected of him and when. The complexity of society today makes things very difficult indeed. There are different ideas and convictions, various religious institutions, different norms of acting, divergent values, a variety of social classes and widely differing standards of education. Add to this the social evils of too much drinking and promiscuity and you have a fair idea of how roles and relationships are hard to determine. Often people do not know how they are expected to act because there are no guiding norms and principles, and if there are, they are confusing. In marriage, the result is disintegration and collapse of marital relationships.

The duty of pastors therefore is to disentangle the confusion and to build up healthy, Christian relationships in the family and in society as a whole. But whatever pastoral models are proposed for marriage, they will have to remain within the will of God as we find it in the Holy Scriptures, that is within the ambience: "This is why a man must leave father and mother and cling to his wife, and the two shall become one body."[54] Also, in Africa, they will have to be within the lineal system of the extended family. The pastoral task of the Church is the complicated one of strengthening husband–wife relationships within the context of the extended family group.

Everywhere in Africa, changes of mentality and practice have taken place in all members of the lineal communities. That is why Gerard Hochstenbach suggests that the stress of the Church's pastoral action should be on:

(1) Greater autonomy of the married adults of an extended family in their own domestic affairs. The African sense of family and respect for authority and the role of the head of the extended family should be maintained, but as circumstances and times demand, it should be redefined and reformulated. The authority of the head of the extended family over the private lives of the adult members of the family is now limited. It is up to the Church to encourage this. The Church should strive to build "that kind of social unit which allows greater independence for the adults in their private affairs but at the same time holds them together. Thus, it is a community of relatives, living and sharing common life together, accepting the head of the lineage as co-ordinator in everything concerning the whole group, helping each other, solicitous of the good name and reputation of the whole group and responsible to it for their moral conduct. Then within the extended family, the Christian spouses would be autonomous in their domestic affairs, the wives would be responsible primarily to their husbands, more accepted as partner than as mother and worker; the upbringing and education of the children would be primarily in the care of the parents. . . ."[55]

(2) Justice for both women and men in marriage. Rights and duties must go hand in hand in both patrilineal and matrilineal societies. To repeat, the wife must be accepted as a partner and not as a servant or a bearer of children. This must be worked for especially in patriliny. In the matrilineal societies the husband must not be looked at as a mere progenitor without any rights either over his wife or his children. Husband and wife must be encouraged to co-operate more and more closely in their marriage. Without neglecting the extended family altogether, they must be made to understand that their first responsibility is to their own family: that is, to take care of their children and to educate them. About the question of inheritance, it should be made clear that in case of the death of either partner in marriage, the living partner has a right to at least part of the family's savings for the sake of him/herself and for the sake of the children. The following points are therefore basic to the creation of a strong Christian family:

—the gradual diminishing and ultimate exclusion of polygamy.[56]
—the recognition of the spouses as partners and their co-operation in the education of their children.

—the freedom of the widow or widower to lead the life he/she wants after the death of one of the spouses.[57]

These values must be inculcated in patience and understanding. Customs and traditions which have taken centuries to solidify cannot be done away with overnight. The priest needs practical structures in his work to help him assist Christian couples in the realization of the potentials of the marital relationship. The following suggestions may be of help to the priest:

Pre-marital education. It is evident in many parts of the continent that husbands and wives are not sufficiently prepared for the responsibilities of married life either before or after marriage. Serious preparation on both the spiritual, physical and psychological aspects of marriage and family life should be given before, and if possible from time to time after, marriage. The duration and the frequency of the instructions must be left to the discretion of the pastor, but a more complete and more fitting instruction than that given hitherto is a matter of great necessity. Whenever possible the instruction should be done by competent people: a doctor or a dresser or a nurse and a priest.

Instruction could begin in the young people's last year or so of school. For the young men and women who do not attend school a way could be found through youth organizations, courses, holiday camps, etc., to gather them together for some time and give them this orientation for marriage. If government departments of social welfare are willing, this training could best be carried out in co-operation with them. We shall see the possible content of the instruction in the next chapter.

In addition to this remote preparation for marriage, there should also be an immediate spiritual preparation when the spouses are reminded finally before marriage what rights and obligations the sacrament entails. Ideally, this should be done during the time of the banns.

Remedial counselling. After marriage, every effort should be made to stabilize the relationships and to help the married people absorb the shocks that come out of living together. The idea is to make the family a viable unit. A form of Christian reconciliation council could be set up in every church and out-station. Many marital problems could be solved there. If this were difficult, these councils could be helpful sources of information to anyone dealing with those difficulties at the parish or diocesan level. A plea should be made here in favour of counselling methods based on "transactional analysis". This has been proved to be extremely successful by John Tau in his marriage counselling work for the Christian Academy in Southern Africa.[58]

A meaningful marriage celebration. The atmosphere of celebration at wedding ceremonies in the villages contrasts very much with marriages in Church. Ways must be found to make marriage ceremonies in Church impressive and meaningful to the people. It is the opinion of Hochstenbach that it may help for marriage ceremonies to take place on Sunday so that the whole community can be there and witness to a new marital bond. Church and village celebrations should as much as possible be on the same day, and not separated by weeks, for then the paradox of a double marriage ceremony would be removed. If village celebrations are not normally done on Sunday, then it should be possible to celebrate the Christian marriage on the same day as the village celebration in the homestead of the marrying couple.[59] A new rite (new rites?) more attuned to the cultures of the people is, of course, necessary, and we shall discuss this subject in the final chapter of this book.

References: Chapter Four

1 Berglund in Verryn (ed.), 1975, pp. 1–2; see also note 29 to chap. 1 of this book.
2 Trobisch, 1968.
3 Berglund in Verryn (ed.), 1975, p. 9.
4 Lebona in Verryn (ed.), 1975, pp. 137–40.
5 Whooley in Verryn (ed.), 1975a, pp. 164 ff.
6 Whooley in Verryn (ed.), 1975a, p. 176.
7 Mahara in Verryn (ed.), 1975, *passim.*
8 Whooley in Verryn (ed.), 1975b, pp. 245 ff.
9 Nkaisule, 1974a, pp. 4–6.
10 cf. Hulsen and Mertens, n.d., chap. 8, *passim.*
11 Thomas and Chisanga, 1976, pp. 8–20.
12 Peskin in Verryn (ed.), 1975, pp. 379 ff.
13 Aquina, 1975, II, *passim.*
14 Shorter, 1974a, pp. 3–4.
15 Aquina, 1975, I, p. 26.
16 Hochstenbach, 1968, p. 9.
17 Ncozana, 1975, p. 7.
18 Sarpong, 1967, pp. 166–7.
19 Douglas, 1969, pp. 123–4.

20 cf. Douglas, 1969, pp. 123–4.
21 Pretorius in Verryn (ed.), 1975, p. 119.
22 Nkaisule, 1974a, pp. 2–5.
23 Gen. 1:27.
24 Gen. 1:28.
25 Gen. 2:24.
26 Eph. 5:21–33.
27 Berglund in Verryn (ed.), 1975, pp. 20–1.
28 Gen. 2:23.
29 Gen. 2:25.
30 Berglund in Verryn (ed.), 1975, p. 23.
31 cf. Lebona in Verryn (ed.), 1975, p. 134.
32 Edwards in Verryn (ed.), 1975, pp. 51–75.
33 *Gaudium et Spes*, no. 48.
34 *Africae Terrarum*, no. 11. By "Matriarchy" the Pope seems to mean "matriliny".
35 Sarpong, 1967, pp. 165–7.
36 1 Cor. 7:16.
37 cf. Tit. 2:1–8.
38 AACC Yaoundé, 1972, pp. 18–22.
39 1 Pet. 3:7.
40 Eph. 4:4–6.
41 Ecclesiasticus (Sirach) 16:1–3.
42 Shorter, 1972c, pp. 18–22.
43 1 Cor. 7:16.
44 *Lumen Gentium*, no. 35.
45 Prov. 18:22.
46 Prov. 12:4.
47 Prov. 5:19.
48 Ashby in Verryn (ed.), 1975, p. 96; Andersen, B. W., *A Critical Introduction to the Old Testament*, London 1959.
49 cf. Chima, 1975, pp. 1 ff.
50 Nkaisule, 1975, p. 2.
51 Nomenyo, 1972, CROMIA/20, p. 7.
52 Ashby in Verryn (ed.), 1975, p. 97.
53 Tau in Verryn (ed.), pp. 211–14.
54 Mt. 19:5.
55 Hochstenbach, 1968, p. 25.
56 See chap. 3.
57 Hochstenbach, 1968, p. 26.
58 Tau in Verryn (ed.), 1975, pp. 200–20.
59 Hochstenbach, 1968, p. 31.

Chapter 5

Parent–Children Relations
and Sex-Education

I Case Material

1 *Parents and Children in Africa Today*

There can be no doubt that the influence of the family, let alone the wider family community and the clan, on the children is not as strong as it used to be in the past. This is because of a number of factors. Firstly, many children today do not live with their parents or in their own communities. The shift of African young men and women into towns and cities is increasing by leaps and bounds year by year. Also, it is well known that some uneducated or less educated parents are reluctant to exercise control over their own highly educated children who, in turn, may be contemptuous of what they would call the "low standard" of their parents and their homes. Other parents, on the other hand, are too severe. Their severity alienates their children and either makes them run away from home to the freer atmosphere which towns and cities offer or makes them grow to resent authority. Too much paternalism almost always paralyses the young so that they do not perceive the need for authority in the family or clan. At times the parents themselves do not make any effort to show the children the need of authority and to make them appreciate it. Their own attitude to civic or church authority may by no means be the best example to the children. When all is said, however, it is the parental dictatorial attitude which young people accept least of all. Whenever parents adopt such an attitude towards teen-agers, for example, and thus deprive them of freedom and initiative, tension in parent-children relations is bound to arise and develop.

The social sciences have demonstrated that young people have a tremendous creative potential and can be extremely difficult to work with. They are gradually becoming aware of the physical and emotional changes taking place within them. They experience powerful urges of self-expression and exploration and these frequently find unhealthy outlets. Their desire for freedom and independence leads, or may lead, to an attitude of being completely anti-authority and very often this results in a lack of communication with the very people—their elders—who are in a position to help them at this critical stage of their growth. As adolescents, they are also easily vulnerable because of their great need for love, stability and recognition. In many cases, their high ideals and ambitions put them at the mercy of unscrupulous employers and other adults.

In traditional Africa, the education of children was the collective responsibility of the whole community. With the diminishing allegiance of the nuclear family to the extended family and clan, the early education of the children falls, naturally, more and more on the shoulders of the father and the mother alone—it becomes the responsibility of the parents. These have to try to help the child to face the complexities of life today, not only, as formerly, to help the child to fit into the extended family and clan. And so, the parent today has a greater responsibility. But things are such that there is a time when he almost completely surrenders this responsibility to the school. Many schools do not concern themselves with the religious and moral formation of the children. Worse, there is little or no collaboration at all between the parents and the school in the task of the child's moral formation. This situation exposes the unprepared child to influences with which he cannot as yet cope—especially in urban areas.

The birth of the nuclear family in Africa has its own advantages. The nuclear family assures the children of their parents' direct care and protection until they grow up and can manage their own affairs. The parents have thus a direct control over their own children and the children have more loyalty and love for both parents. There is also a greater mutual respect between brothers and sisters than in the extended family. The big disadvantage of the nuclear family for the children comes in the event of the death of the parents when they (the children) are still minors and cannot take care of themselves. Then all at once they lose the security and protection that children in the extended family enjoy even in the absence of their parents. These have a sense of belonging and of community spirit—a sense of the clan's values, customs and traditions—which their counterparts in the nuclear family so often lack.

Even in matrilineal communities where the uncle was the authority in the family, things are changing as a result of urbanization, education and Christianity. Today their power is limited, and, as in the patrilineal societies, the parents shoulder the responsibility. The father is no longer "only the progenitor". Blame for faulty upbringing falls largely on the parents.[1]

Yet, as we have said, parental authority over many aspects of the children's life is slackening. For example, whereas in the old days the choice of marriage partners was made by the parents or the families, today this system is almost utterly rejected by the young people. They insist on making their own choice and in many instances the parents cannot but give in. There is very little they can do about it. Any show of resistance on the part of the parents can easily drive the young lovers to an elopement or a decision just to live together. The survey of the Church in Ghana has shown that according to reports by lay groups there, parental resignation and acquiescence in young people's wishes in marriage matters is widespread throughout the country. Although in the remote villages of Ghana the parents still have the final say, this is obviously rapidly changing. However, custom is still important in the eyes of the young people. They value it and will follow it in their marriage arrangements if they can. According to the Survey, not more than 3% or 4% of the youth marry without adhering to what custom demands, seeking the advice and possibly the consent of their elders. But the general pattern is that the role of the parents/extended family in the choice of marriage partners for their children is no longer dominant. It is declining. Today the situation is rather that "there is a balance between the initiative of the young people and the guiding, advising role of the parents or members of the extended family".[2]

But there are extreme cases when families are completely uprooted. This is the situation when father, mother and children are all separated by intent or necessity. The father may be working far away from home, for example, the children studying in a foreign country, and the mother might also take on a job in a different place from her husband's. In such circumstances it is little wonder that the children have an unhappy upbringing in an atmosphere where the parents are either ignorant of their responsibility towards their children's growth, or they are so preoccuped with other things that they do not want to take on this responsibility. The children respond by rejecting even the little guardianship of the parents there might have been, and all too soon decide to stand on their own without direction from any other quarter. Now the only way in which they can effectively do this is to stay as far away as possible from their parents. So young school leavers drift into urban areas lured by the gleaming lights of the cinema halls and the wild sounds of the jazz bands, but without any clear plans about what they will do there. The result of this is often disastrous to the children.

2 Sex-Education in Africa Today

The emancipation of youth from clan and parental authority, the breakdown of community consciousness, the introduction of the western type of education and employment possibilities in cities, urbanization and the Christian religion's assumption that the nuclear family is the only ideal family to be imitated and adopted by all good Christians—all these factors and many more have shattered practically all chances for many African communities to give the traditional type of education to their offspring. In Rhodesia, for instance, the Nambyans seem to be the only Shona-speaking people who still give some sex-education to their growing children. But then this is minimal and it is done only in the remote villages. When a girl has her first menstruation, she informs her mother about it, and her mother sends her to her maternal grandmother. Her grandmother prepares herbal medicines for her to regulate her bleeding. Then the grandmother and another old woman demonstrate to her the techniques for sexual intercourse which the girl is instructed to imitate so that when she marries she will please her husband.[3] After this, some more medicine is given to the young girl by her grandmother to make her sexually attractive. She is instructed to abstain from sexual contact during her menstruations and she is sent back home. There she begins tying beads around her waist for attraction.[4]

Sex-education for Nambyan boys begins with their first wet dream. When a boy notices this, he takes a cock and goes to the house of his maternal grandfather. His grandfather kills the cock which is then cooked stuffed with some roots, and it is eaten only by the two of them—grandfather and grandson. The boy is then told not to have sexual intercourse for four months afterwards so that the medicine may have time to work and to make him more virile. Even after the prescribed time of four months, he is allowed to have intercourse only occasionally when he is not yet married but he is warned never to approach a woman during her menstruation. If his grandfather is a medicine-man, he uses this time to show his grandson some medicines—especially those for sexual prowess should he need them later in life.[5]

Although sex-education among the Nambyans is minimal, it is better, compared to the situation among the Tonga. Tonga youths do not receive any sex instruction at all. Fathers merely tell their sons about the responsibilities of a husband and father around a fire at night and that is all! No direct sex-instructions are given. Washing in cold water once on an early morning without shivering is the only test a young man is given by his father or guardian to ascertain whether or not he is now grown up and fit to court girls and eventually marry. No sex-instruction is given to the girl either. At her first menstruation she is considered of marriageable age.[6]

Making things worse is the taboo in many parts of Africa against parents and children discussing sexual matters. Few parents are ready or able to give information about sex to their children. Sister Aquina reports a comment indicating desperation from a young Shona woman: "What makes the whole situation worse is the fact that African tradition does not encourage open and free discussion of such things, especially not between parents and children. I say this from personal experience. For years I tried to talk to my parents about sex and other related subjects but they never wanted to be engaged in such discussion. When I persisted they eventually forbade me to bring up such topics. So what could I do? I turned to friends and books. From these sources I got all kinds of information and advice."[7]

Two analyses of letters sent to advice columns of two newspapers separated in time and distance serve to prove the girls' complaint. The picture that emerges from the analyses shows a pathetic lack of sex-education not only at home but also, and especially, in schools. Young men and women have therefore no choice but to resort to popular, sometimes unscientific, cheap and un-Christian newspaper or magazine columnists for advice. It also shows that there are no adequate structures at the local level where people can seek Christian advice in difficulties pertaining to their sexual life.

Letters asking for advice sent to the *African Mail* of former Northern Rhodesia (now Zambia) in 1961 show that by far the greatest number of correspondents are concerned mainly with "how to contact girls", "how to overcome shyness", "how to persuade boyfriends or girlfriends to grant pre-marital sexual intercourse", "how to keep the affection of a girl or how to get rid of a girl one is no longer interested in". Eighty-three per cent of the correspondents have received formal education of up to Standard VI or more and are over twenty-one years of age. About half of the correspondents are still in school and about 74% are single. Over 350 letters, about a year's intake, were analysed.[8]

In 1974 Hubert Bucher analysed 180 letters written to an African columnist, "Sophie", in the *Weekend World* newspaper of Soweto, South Africa, between January and November 1973. Surprisingly the results are not much different from the above analysis more than a decade before! Most correspondents to the *Weekend World* are males, 66% as opposed to 34% females. The average age of the correspondents here, as in the *African Mail*, is twenty-one to twenty-two years and 70% of the letters ask advice concerning courtship and love. Let us put the categories of the correspondence to both the *African Mail* and the *Weekend World* side by side.

Categories of Correspondence[9]

	African Mail (1961)	Weekend World (1973)
1.	Approach to girls and romantic love; threatened or broken relationships; family interference in marriage—71%	Courtship and love: difficulties between lovers; prostitution; venereal disease; family planning; family interference—70%
2.	Multiple entanglements —9%	Marriage problems: unfaithfulness; concubinage; physiological inadequacies in sexual intercourse; barrenness—20%
3.	Miscellaneous—20%	Miscellaneous—10%

It can be seen from the above that although marriage comes late in life, boys and birls lead an active sex life before marriage. In 1974 alone, the number of girls who had to leave school in Kenya because of pregnancy was as high as 7,000.[10]

Premarital sexual intercourse is almost universal. It is described as "extremely common", "the common thing", "very common", "rampant", "it has become the custom", "common practice", "the usual thing", "they are the rule, not the exception".[11] Nowhere in Africa today have premarital sexual relations been described as non-existent or infrequent. In a survey in Ghana the percentage of sex relations before marriage ranged as high as 75–100%. Three reasons for this percentage are given by the survey:

1. The general climate of opinion, lack of control.
2. It is not seen as fornication by the young people, but as a necessary way to get to know each other. It is the natural way to prepare for marriage. "How can you marry without first trying it out?" they ask.
3. The young people make their own choice, and to have a boyfriend or girlfriend means sleeping together. The purpose is also to see whether the girl can become pregnant, in which case it is more difficult for the parents to refuse marriage.[12]

The young men and women interviewed in Ghana generally refuse to admit that sex before marriage is bad, evil or sinful, although those among them who are Christians are uncertain whether or not they should do it. In general, however, they regard it as a preliminary preparation for marriage and are strengthened in their opinion by its common occurrence: "Everybody does it", they say, "it is the usual way!"

But a distinction must be made. Premarital sexual relations are more common among the literates and semi-literates than among the completely illiterate. This applies to both Christians as well as non-Christians. It would seem that this is because the literate young people are more removed from the family and clan milieu and the influence of tradition and custom touches them in only a minor way, if at all.

II Theological Reflection

1 Parents and Children

In this time of change in Africa, a time when we are witnessing rapid transition from old ways of life to new ones, the Christian family is deeply affected and needs guidance. Pope Paul VI saw this need, and in his letter to Africa[13] he gives guidance to young people in their relationship with their elders. "There is the . . . sacred duty", the Pope says, "mentioned by the Fourth Commandment to honour father and mother. So while it is just that the young should have freedom of choice inherent in their marriage, this should not become a reason for them to loosen their family ties. They should consider it a precious heritage to be able to share in the common fortunes of their families; with love and generosity they should be ready to give aid to their parents, and if necessity requires, even to other relations, according to their means."[14]

The Pope, quoting the Second Vatican Council, goes on to say:

Married couples and Christian parents should follow their own proper path to holiness by faithful love, sustaining one another in grace throughout the entire length of their lives. They should imbue their offspring, lovingly welcomed from God, with Christian truths and evangelical virtues. For thus they can offer all men an example of unwearying and generous love, build up the brotherhood of charity, and stand as witnesses to, and cooperators in, the fruitfulness of Holy Mother Church. By such lives, they signify and share in that very love with which Christ loved His Bride and because of which he delivered Himself up on her behalf.[15]

In the Christian family the father and mother are the first evangelizers of their children. Theirs is an irreplaceable mission. Childhood is the best physical, psychological and emotional atmosphere for religious growth. Parents, mindful of their Christian duty to their children, should use this opportunity to the fullest advantage. This is the time when parents have the exclusive responsibility of giving the religious message to the children, that message of love which must be apparent in the parents' own daily lives. Without this love between the parents, or when the parents do not live together at all, the children are deprived of a precious Christian aspect in their development. "The Christian is integrated in the universal priesthood by Baptism and Confirmation which confer on him the responsibility of proclaiming, with the Word of God, the love of the Father. Is it possible to neglect such a duty where the children are concerned?"[16]

The family is the domestic Church, and the parents' love shows the children the love of God towards men. Yet the parents' love should not stop at the level of the family, but must spread outwards to other persons outside the family as well and must show itself in the form of acceptance and helpfulness to all. Parents are witnesses and teachers by their calling. By their own sexuality, the parents must show the children that physical sex, which is the means of biological generation, is both an image of personal relationship as well as of the divine covenant with the whole of mankind. It has no meaning when it is divorced from its relational aspects which are the vehicles of that divine love. Sex, they must tell their children, is a gift, an invitation to open ourselves to the truth and to descend with it towards the depths, the secret place of our being in which truth wishes to accomplish her work with us.

2   *Christian Attitudes to Sex*
Man is not dual; he is one. It is theologically wrong, therefore, to separate sex from human existence.

In a dualist existence, relations between sexuality and person are lived out in the objective mode: measure, law, mastery of need, equilibrium between enjoyment and generation. But in a genuine experience of incarnation within the creative design of the world, the whole person exists in each of his tasks, in labour, leisure, drinking, eating, and making love: each of these fully express my truth. There are no longer two parts, one left to sexuality and the other to the spirit; the spirit inhabits sexuality, which is one of the modes of its incarnation, carrying out an obedience in its twofold end—and in celibacy itself. I accomplish my sexuality or my celibacy as a vocation, something I do not dispose of according to my own discretion, which is given to me, and whose ultimate meaning belongs to God.[17]

Disdain of physical love or a negation of sexuality are aberrations which must be courageously fought against. Christian doctrine teaches that there is only one love for God and for man, one of whose manifestations is sexuality. But love itself goes considerably beyond sexuality. Even, or rather especially, the calling of celibacy is not a renunciation of sexuality. It is a turning of oneself completely, with all that being human implies, towards God. As Lanza del Vasto said: "Continence is worth only as much as the love which sustains it."

The work of the mystics is to encounter God in their body, sustained by a sexuality to which they refuse any other object. They have been explicit enough on this point to confound any prudishness. Better than a renunciation, it is the substitution of objectives, an attempt which Socrates had already pursued, when he extolled "the fecundity of the soul, as even greater than that of the body". Of this eternal lesson, essential for our time, Christianity is the heir, and brightens it with a new light. But we go nowhere without our body, not even to our death. It is our necessary avenue of communication. To vilify it by disdain, to cover it with mud so as to condemn it as dirty, is to mutilate it and to unleash destructive mechanisms which will overtake us and deliver us to the hateful forces of wounded instinct.[18]

Sexuality must be seen in its true theological light. Its dangers, its restlessness, its claims must not be denied; but in its mature form, the love of man and woman is the best expression of happiness shared.[19]

III   Models for Pastoral Action

1   *Christian Parents in Africa*

We have noted that, by and large, African parents expect their children to help them and to care for them in their old age. In the past this was relatively easy because children, even when married, resided with their parents either virilocally or uxorilocally. It therefore gives some parents a feeling of anxiety, loneliness and at times frustration when children today leave home at an early age and go for studies in boarding schools and universities. And for the young couples, the general practice today is to establish a new home of their own away from either of their parents' locality. To those parents who are not prepared to abandon the traditional custom of their children living with them at the same locality, this can be very painful. It is clear, then, that even the parents need the assistance of the Church to help them accept this fact whenever it is unavoidable—as it may be in many cases today. The Church would do well to advise the young men also not to forsake their parents completely wherever they may happen to be living. The children must find time to visit their parents, to write to them now and then and to send them such gifts as they can afford. It cannot be hard for children to see that after all their parents did for them, they deserve in turn some respect and love. However, exposed to different worldviews from their parents, young people may find it hard to communicate with them and their older relatives. This is understandable but it is not impossible to overcome barriers. John Mbiti says in an appeal to the youth on precisely this point:

I realise that some of the ideas and ways of modern life are completely removed from those of the people in villages, making it difficult for the younger generation to communicate with parents who may not have been exposed to the same kind of ideas. But you need not struggle to disseminate all your modern ideas among people in the village, who perhaps live in a different conceptual world. Let them communicate their ideas to you—hoping that you will at least understand them! This will give you a point of contact around which your relationship could profitably be built. Even if you go to your parents merely to listen to them, to hear their problems, to participate in their work and concern, this in itself is most satisfying to them. It gives them a feeling that they matter, and that you have not rejected them. It encourages them in their life's journey.[20]

It may happen, either for genuine motives or out of parental jealousy for having to share their child's love with someone else, that parents will be critical of the marriage of their child. In some extreme cases they may even try to break off the marriage. The young man or woman must be guided to be considerate and to weigh his/her parents' objection. If they feel as a matter of conscience that they cannot agree with their parents, they must follow their own consciences. But they must be careful not to sever relationships with their parents and other elders, or if relationships are momentarily strained, they should take the initiative to normalize things as soon as possible.[21]

Parents, on the other hand, must constantly be helped to realize that adolescence is the time when their children are seeking their self-identity and independence. They are self-assertive and all too often critical of authority. Parents must at this time be careful not to be too domineering and to crush legitimate aspirations in their children. Tactfully, patiently and with genuine love they must help the children to acquire healthy orientations to life.[22] In the early years of the children's life, this task will fall on the mother more than on the father for it is the mother's influence that has a greater impact on the children in infancy—an influence which plays a great part in shaping one's future life. Mothers or future mothers must have the education, cultural and moral, to exert this influence for the good of the children. This influence applies also in matters sexual.

2 Confronting the Sex-Revolution

The sex revolution accompanying urbanization and industrialization in Africa, is breaking up the view of sex as sacred and mysterious. As we said in the previous chapter, this revolution is turning sex into an investment for profit, into a purchasable commodity. In the words of Erich Fromm, man slowly becomes "alienated from himself, from his fellow men and from nature. His main aim is profitable exchange of his skills, knowledge and of himself, his 'personality package' with others who are equally intent on a fair and profitable exchange. Life has no goal except the one to move, no principle except the one of fair charge, no satisfaction except the one to consume."[23] Although Fromm says this in reference to western, industrial, consumer societies, it is true that one can say as much in reference to urban Africa today. The spread of "casual sex" where there is no need to build an enduring relationship, love or friendship is evidence of this. The situation is lamentable. But to lament the situation will not help as a corrective unless the whole development is viewed from within the larger context of social change and the reasons for the prevailing attitudes isolated and analysed.

The removal of the youth too early in life from parental and community authority and control is one factor, as we have seen, which facilitates unhealthy libertine attitudes towards sex. But can young people be prevented from leaving their homes and communities for higher studies and jobs in urban areas? What can be done about formal education itself which emphasizes only the physical part of sex? What about the influence money has on all these attitudes? These are the kind of questions that must be considered in order to situate the problems where they belong.

Today's genuine cultural and theological revolution must aim at correcting both the unbridled sex of modern revolutionists and the inhibited sexuality of the puritans. This is to be achieved through an education for authentic human development of which mature sexuality is an integral part. This kind of education is badly wanting in many African communities today. The youth who have been torn away from traditional sexual education are left in a vacuum. There is nothing so adequate as the training which the young men before them used to get, as an initiation into not only mature sexuality but also into the acceptance of one's position, rights and responsibilities in society. So the youth struggle through adolescence with a curious mixture of back-alley physiology, ethereal ideas about mystical or romantic love picked up here and there from cheap forms of mass-media, superficial theories about pleasure without pain as projected in the Hollywood-type love films, and various compulsive complexes about sex which they may have absorbed when they were still very young from their parents' implicit or explicit attitudes towards their own sexual lives.

Among the major projects of Church and Society in Africa, then, should be the development of an integrated educational programme whose goals are moral sensitivity, healthy sexuality, joyfulness, self-respect, fidelity and creativity. This is what the Church has been exhorting for ages—but only in the realm of theory. The practice of the Church has been quite different. She has for so long satisfied herself with demanding allegiance to certain devotional and ethical propositions. But social and behavioural sciences give her the red light: this attitude is not going to work in the modern outlook on things any longer. The modern mind is critical. It demands something more, some-thing which will show the beauty and purpose of sex: that authentic sexuality and true love are inseparable.

A sound theology of sex and marriage together with an adequate understanding of human psychology and personal development are also necessary components of education for mature sexuality. It cannot be emphasized enough in instructions about human sexuality, that human sexuality is both *relational* and *personal*. It is within itself a craving for the establishment of permanent relationships. And human off-spring, very unlike animal offspring, need the permanent relationship of their parents for the proper development of their psyche. To say it again: the true meaning of sex is to be found in the context of relationships. True sex and true friendship intermingle with each other and reinforce each other in love. Organized and acknowledged ministry and pedagogy to both youth and married people must revolve around this truth.[24]

That many young people are afraid of the rigid demands made by the Church with regard to stability and fidelity in marriage is an open secret. They also have the idea that marriage is routine and boring. Often, too, they do not see the need to be married in Church. All this goes to show how little catechesis of marriage there is in large parts of Africa. In the AMECEA countries (Kenya, Malawi, Tanzania, Uganda and Zambia), for example, surveys have shown that little or nothing is being done by the Churches to get young people together in youth movements and let them discuss their problems under a competent director.[25]

Opportunities must be provided also for longer courtship periods so that the spouses get to know each other well before they enter into marriage. At present this is not the case. In Rhodesia, out of 185 couples interviewed by Sister Aquina[26] seventy-five, that is 41%, knew each other for less than one year before marriage. Forty-six or 25% knew each other for up to two years. Thirty or 16% for up to three years. 71% met each other from once to three times a month, and ninety-eight, that is 53%, met in the boy's home. Surprisingly, only two men and six women had considered Church affiliation before agreeing to a marriage. For the great majority religious affiliation counted for very little in choosing a marriage partner.

3   *Practical Suggestions*
What is to be done in situations like these? The following suggestions proposed by Hubert Bucher seem to call for immediate practical attention.

(a) There exists a real need for young people to receive sound marriage preparation, which should stress the true aims of love between husband and wife and of the sacrament of matrimony.
(b) For those already married, counselling should be available to help them with the many problems which arise from the difficult situation in which they must live. (Bucher adds in a footnote that "The Christian Academy in South Africa started to run a counselling service in Soweto in 1973. The move by another local agency is also of recent date. The Johannesburg Marriage Guidance Society has trained a team of fourteen voluntary marriage counsellors which is headed by a professional educational counsellor. In the course of 1973 the team dealt with altogether forty-four clients.")[27]
(c) The growing number of young people who use newspaper and magazine columns in an attempt to find their "doll" or "guy", would suggest that serious consideration should be given to launching a Christian marriage bureau.

(d) There exists also an urgent need for vocational guidance. Young people frequently ask "Sophie" of the *Weekend World*, for instance, to help them to make the right choice with regard to their future career. Also they often need her encouragement to continue with their studies. Many of "Sophie's" replies quite bluntly tell youngsters that they are still too young for a serious love affair and that they should therefore rather concentrate on their school work.

(e) Many writers to "Sophie" seek correct medical advice. This could be easily provided by a doctor who is well at home in his subject and who is also a committed Christian in his daily life.

(f) The Church and the authorities ought to foster dialogue between young people and their elders. We must especially help the older generation to understand the forces of change which make the people of today seem to them so different from what they imagine they were like in their own younger days. But we must make sure that it will be a genuine *dialogue*. Young people must be able to voice also their own grievances against the older generation. Many of the young people are puzzled by the lack of good example on the part of their elders. Their widespread lack of respect for human dignity is bound to have a detrimental influence on the younger generation and must not, therefore, go unchastised.[28]

In pastoral planning in Africa today, youth work must be high up in the list of priorities. If young people are genuinely made to feel confident enough to discuss their problems, if they are given time to express themselves, and if structures exist for this purpose, then perhaps pastors can help them and lead them to a Christian understanding of sexuality and human dignity.

References: Chapter Five

1 Lamburn, 1975b, p. 1.
2 Hulsen and Mertens, n.d., pp. 18–19.
3 Nambyan women are locally known as experts in giving great sexual pleasure to their partners and for this reason men of other tribes try to make friends with them.
4 Ndebele girls neighbouring the Nambyans have also adopted the custom of tying beads around their waists in order to attract lovers.
5 Aquina, 1975, II, pp. 11–13.
6 Aquina, 1975, II, p. 24. Courtship among the Tonga is longer than among the Nambyans because marriage negotiations begin at a very early age—well before the girl has reached puberty.

7   Aquina, 1975, I, p. 48.
8   *Report of the Annual Conference* (N. Rhodesia Council of Social Service), 1961, pp. 47–8.
9   Compare *Report of the Annual Conference* (N. Rhodesia Council of Social Service), 1961, p. 47, and Bucher, 1974, p. 402.
10 *Lengo*, March 17th, 1974.
11 Hulsen and Mertens, n.d., p. 20.
12 *Ibid.*
13 *Africae Terrarum.*
14 *Africae Terrarum*, no. 34.
15 *Africae Terrarum*, no. 35.
16 Consilium de Laicis, *The Laity Today*, 1974, p. 56.
17 *Cross Currents*, Ricoeur et al., 1964, no. 2, p. 227.
18 *Cross Currents*, Ricoeur et al., 1964, no. 2, p. 268.
19 *Cross Currents*, Ricoeur et al., 1964, no. 2, p. 268. See also pp. 248–57. Here the question of the problems posed for the adolescent by sexuality is discussed and ways for individuals or educators to solve the problems are proposed.
20 Mbiti, 1973, p. 184.
21 Mbiti, 1973, p. 81.
22 Mbiti, 1973, pp. 27–30.
23 Fromm, quoted by Chima, 1975, p. 3.
24 Chima, 1975, pp. 2–6.
25 Consilium de Laicis, *The Laity Today*, 1974, pp. 98–100.
26 Aquina, 1975, II, p. 13.
27 Our research shows no other comparable organization elsewhere in east, central and southern Africa.
28 Bucher, 1974, pp. 407–8.

Chapter 6

Inter-Church and Other "Mixed" Marriages

I Case Material

1 Inter-Church Marriages

The material collected during the course of the project indicates a low degree of inter-marriage of all kinds among the peoples of east, central and southern Africa. The principle of "like marrying like" has been shown to be highly operative and is a dominant factor in the choice of a marriage partner.

In his survey of *Marriage in Nairobi*,[1] James Holway noted that even in a highly heterogenous and diverse population, the ethnic origin still remains by far the strongest influence in marriage. In the Nairobi congregations marriage between partners from the same ethnic group took precedence over the common Church or denominational identity. For instance, inter-marriage between Meru Methodists and Presbyterians is more frequent than marriage between Meru and Kikuyu Presbyterians. Norman Thomas and Daniel Chisanga have found more or less the same pattern in the fast growing Copperbelt town of Kitwe in Zambia.

In Uganda, however, the situation is different and deeply revealing as to what might be underlying the laxity over inter-church marriages. A survey of the Mityana area,[2] with an agri-cultural rural setting, shows that deep seated denominational prejudices and animosities may hinder the formalization of a marriage between members of different Christian confessions. In the Mityana area, a large proportion of Christians who delayed getting their marriages formalized in church gave the reason that they faced fairly strong opposition from their families and church congregations against an inter-church marriage. In a patrilineal society like that of the Baganda, where Mityana is located, inter-church marriages often end in the conversion of the wife to the husband's denomination, due to pressures of various kinds. The patrilineal family is often afraid of the strong influence a mother has over her children in the rural setting, while in the urban areas the father tends to exercise greater influence.

Hastings' conclusion about the few inter-church marriages recorded for Uganda, was later indicated by the Mityana survey: that there are inter-church unions which are never solemnized in church and the partners are permanently excommunicated by their union. It is therefore true that negative attitudes of church authority do not prevent inter-church unions, "but merely force a large number of Christians out of full Church membership".[3]

On the whole inter-church marriages, which are in any case discouraged, appear to be comparatively few, and church or denominational allegiance seems to be a negligible factor in marriage both in Kitwe and in Nairobi urban areas; Sister Aquina noted that local demography, rather than the partner's religious confession, decided one's likely marriage partner in Rhodesia.

2   *Inter-Ethnic Marriages*
We have already noted above that the familiar trend of marriage is homogamous with particular reference to ethnic groups. Holway found that in spite of government effort to create a homogeneous nation out of the multiplicity of ethnic groups in Kenya, the ethnic group of origin has remained one of the strongest influences in the choice of a marriage partner.[4] What reinforces this tendency is language which controls inter-personal communication. In the urban centres of Africa ethnic social solidarity is often preserved, in a mixed population, by the use of the vernacular. Rural ethnic behaviour is simply imitated or duplicated in the urban areas.[5]

Our project findings agree with those of Hastings three years ago that there were still few inter-ethnic marriages, particularly in East Africa. Where these marriages take place, they are often transient unions. In Zambia and South African towns inter-ethnic marriages are on the increase. Perhaps there is a greater sense of belonging to the urban set-up in these towns than is the case in East African urban life.[6]

In the rural areas of Africa, the vast majority of the populations are geographically located according to their ethnic groups. Exceptions to this general rule occur when projects of agriculture, industry, or education are located in the middle of a given ethnic group. The homogeneity of the rural population reinforces what is already a decisive factor in selecting a marriage partner.

In a climate that favours common ethnic activity, including sports, inter-ethnic marriages do attract considerable social problems to which the churches cannot turn a blind eye. Each ethnic group often regards its culture, customs, and traditional ways of life as normative. There is also a sense of ethnic belonging that is nurtured by the family up-bringing, coupled with a strong element of possessiveness on the part of the members of the family and the ethnic group as a whole. "A Luyia man hearing that a Luo has married a Luyia girl, will complain that he is marrying one of our women." Parents of both partners, or close relatives, may be saddened by the commitment of their daughter or son to one with whom they may not effectively communicate, due to the language barrier, and by the prospect of having grandchildren who will not know them well and their way of life. Inter-ethnic marriages must squarely face the differences in customs, taboos and prohibitions governing family life, child-rearing, inter-personal relations, language usage, and many others.

The younger generation is fairly open and idealistic about inter-marriage. A survey made in 1972 showed that young educated people in the city of Nairobi rated ethnic differences very low as a factor determining their choice of a marriage partner. This seems to suggest that although these young people may in the long run marry from within their ethnic groups, those who will contract inter-ethnic marriages will have the support and approval of their contemporaries.

Inter-ethnic marriages have been observed to be few at present. There appears a strong possibility of a gradual increase of these unions. Inter-ethnic marriages have a positive value and a contribution to make in the building and development of modern Africa. Successful marriages of any kind weave the fabric of society together because they create strong links of intimate relationship. Positive values and attitudes are primarily learnt or encouraged in the family situation. If prejudices, and misconceptions about other peoples' cultures and ways of life are to be cured, inter-marriage is one significant treatment. The nations of Africa can reap the benefits of such marriages, not because the partners have deserted their original ethnic group, but rather because the new family loves, belongs to, and yet transcends the limitations of both ethnic groups.

3 Inter-Racial Marriages

With the authority of personal experience, John Mbiti assures us that "apart from cultural considerations, inter-racial marriages do not pose questions or problems different from those of other marriages".[7] At present inter-racial marriages are a legal problem in the racially-segregating countries of southern Africa where they are expressly prohibited by statute. But the wind of change is blowing fast and strongly. Before very long the situation may be like that of Nairobi, Kenya. There is found a relieving "feeling of liberation from earlier racial discrimination", and marriages between Europeans and members of other races do occur though still comparatively few in number.[8] Like inter-ethnic marriages, partners in an inter-racial marriage can bring a wealth and a diversity to make the marriage a success. In turn such a marriage does blur and ridicule racial boundaries and idiosyncratic prejudices that contribute so much to social tension. On the other hand the partners must be ready to tolerate jeering, scorn and ignorant, foolish behaviour from both of the races to which they belong. If they get children, they too, have to live with their mixed colouring, as well as a degree of resentment they may often arouse from the people of the two races to which their parents belong.

4 Inter-Faith Marriages

Our concern in this category of marriages is the contracting of unions between partners that do not share a common faith. In the actual circumstances, the project has come across cases of inter-marriage between the adherents of Christianity and Islam and African Traditionalists; and to a limited but significant extent, Secularists.[9]

Inter-faith marriages can pose serious problems for the people involved, their families as well as their religious communities. Inter-church marriages, involving a common faith in Jesus Christ, present a fair number of problems, and difficulties. Inter-faith marriages present more complicated issues before and after the marriage. Ecumenism has gone a long way to open the gates of inter-church marriages, but the dialogue between peoples of different faiths has still further to go to be able to enhance the prospect of inter-faith marriages. At present most religious leaders would press for the conversion of one partner to their side or else abandon the inter-faith marriage.[10] However, churches, such as the Roman Catholic Church, do sometimes allow the couple freedom in this case for weighty reasons.

Objections to these inter-religious marriages stem from the fact that religious prejudices and convictions are deeply ingrained in the subconscious mind and behaviour of the people so that a marriage across religious systems and traditions that vastly differ in outlook on life is likely to be shipwrecked in the storms that normally test every marriage. Will the Christian find a common religious anchor with his Muslim or Secularist partner during a family crisis? Who is likely to influence the children for the better in their religious upbringing?

The Muslim school of thought predominant in East Africa often uses inter-faith marriage as a means of conversion to Islam because of its adamant insistence on the non-Muslim man becoming a Muslim as a pre-nuptial condition. The children of a Muslim man and a non-Muslim woman must be brought up as Muslims.

The African traditionalist situation may have two sides to it: a couple married under the traditional customary system where one partner is later converted to Christianity, and the other case of a non-Christian young man or woman intending to marry a Christian partner under the traditional, customary provisions.[11] While the latter case can be pastorally discouraged, the former sincerely demands the community's care and sympathy. In *Christian Marriage in Africa*, Adrian Hastings seems to have overlooked this phenomenon: a customary monogamous union where one of the partners becomes a Christian; and yet he reviews the history of the same kind of problem involving polygamous unions.[12] We do well to observe that all marriages involving Africans have, in varying degrees of intensity, an element of the traditional customary beliefs and practices from their ethnic background. A staunch, non-Christian traditionalist could pose as great a problem to the Christian, as a Muslim would in an inter-marriage.

142

II Theological Reflection

1 The Responsibility of the Churches

The churches have a keen interest in inter-marriages in Africa. This interest is vested in the members of the churches that decide to marry, as well as in inter-marriage as an institution of society, the society of God's people.

For too long the individual church denominations have tended to be concerned more with inter-church marriages than the whole question of inter-marriages. Each church clearly wields a measure of responsibility towards her members who seek and intend to marry persons of a different Christian allegiance. But this should not overshadow the same responsibility for members that get married or are already married before their baptism to persons of other religions, or even other ethnic groups. The presence of the Christian Church in Africa is justified and strengthened by the proclamation and realization of the Good News for the people of the continent. In practice the Church's benefits are realized and enjoyed by her own—the faithful believers. And yet the infectious message can never be confined to the circle of faith alone.

Marriage is one means by which, and through which, God continues to reveal and make his salvation available[13] to Africa and the world. The family that is formed through the married state is the primary social unit and the basis of society. It is needless to emphasize that God's saving, reconciling, liberating, and rehabilitating love should be the foundation stone of a marriage. This love is entrusted to the Church through Christ, so that it may be cast abroad for the healing of the people, and the whole world; a world that is being wooed back into the creator's master-plan through the voice of the Gospel of Jesus Christ.

Have the churches in Africa, and indeed in the whole world, realized that theirs is the apostolate of loving a whore, like Hosea of old? Or have the ancient canons and the traditional theology and understanding got the upper hand? A church that insists on her will, her ways and theology often exhibits little faith and trust in God who "moves in mysterious ways his wonders to perform". As representatives and spokesmen of Christ, our Churches must theologize and make canons and pronouncements for the release and salvation of men and women here and now. We must bear this in mind, that the highest achievement in our ministry is to help people to experience the love of Christ which gives a full and joyful life here and hereafter. We do not protect the Church or God's law against men and women. Christ did not spare himself, but he humbled himself and lost his life so that men and women could live. The churches and ourselves in particular, have no choice but to allow everything that will enhance true life in Africa.

This project's case studies have brought to our notice the fact that inter-marriages affect a small proportion of the married population. Religious, ethnic and church or denominational prejudices are the major reason. Residential patterns of land settlement are another factor. With increased mixing through various associations like schooling, working and living together, with increased inter-communication and inter-personal facilities, inter-marriages are expected to increase. The teaching of the churches will undoubtedly influence the trend both for their members and those outside. It is here that the foregoing discussion becomes relevant to the issue of inter-marriages. As more and more young men and women contemplate building a home, must they eliminate from their field of search all who are outside their tribe, their denomination or religious system? Is this the freedom God has given, or that which is defined by a particular, narrow-minded confession? Will church officers just deal with church affairs or with the pre-nuptial enquiry, the party, the parents—the couple's relationships, etc.? Most Churches would refuse to be involved in an inter-ethnic marriage decision. Is it really the business of the Church to help the partners decide?[14] The churches' involvement would seem to be most effective when it can admit responsibility before, during and after the decisive moments of a marriage.

2   *Evolution of the Roman Catholic Position on Inter-Church Marriages*
The Roman Catholic position on inter-church marriages needs some review, as an example of a consistent denominational line of teaching, that has recently begun to respond to changing circumstances under the clear guidance of the Holy Spirit. The Roman Catholic discipline regarding marriage of Christians of different confessions has faced constant challenges from other Christian churches.

The intrinsic value of Roman Catholic insistence on certain conditions being fulfilled before inter-church marriage takes place has been to highlight the doctrinal, pastoral, spiritual and practical problems created by an inter-denominational union. There have been two outstanding concerns of the Roman Catholic Church in the issue of inter-church marriage: in the first place, there is the demand for the marriage to be celebrated according to canonical form, with the "nuptial mass", "the solemn nuptial blessing", and the presence of "an authorized priest or deacon" of the Roman Catholic Church.[15] The second point is the upbringing of the children springing from the inter-marriage. However, there appears to be more profound issues ingrained in these objections which Paschal Okwachi outlined in his paper presented at the Nairobi colloquium.[16] He pointed out that the vocation of marriage is a God-given responsibility in which the partners undertake to live together in love, stability, and partnership, seeking God together and serving Him. Okwachi further noted that as few differences as possible should be brought into this union. Differences in Christian witness were likely to make seeking God together problematic, since the couple may not worship together very easily, encourage each other in their spiritual lives and receive the Lord's Supper at the same altar. The result could be the slackening of one or both of the partners in their religious commitment; or if both insisted on having their way, they might end in separation or even divorce.

A high divorce rate is often revealed by studies on inter-church marriages.[17] In many, if not the majority, of cases inter-church marriages take place because of the religious indifference of the partners; this may help to explain the high degree of incompatibility which eventually leads to divorce.

There are, however, partners with a deep and sincere commitment to their confessions who, in an inter-church marriage situation, are deeply concerned about the divided Christian witness within their family.

Faced with a potential case of inter-church marriage, there is an obvious temptation to oblige one of the partners involved to change his or her religious allegiance. Such a change under pressure is an abuse of personal freedom and integrity and should be avoided at any cost. This is, however, not to deny the possibility of a genuine well weighed decision to change in freedom of conscience.

The Roman Catholic discipline, we noted earlier, has long been challenged by other Christian churches on the contro-versial issues of the canonical form of marriage and the religious nurture of the children. Roman Catholic authorities have, too readily perhaps, encouraged the religious transfer of allegiance in their favour.[18] Canonical legislation in the Roman Catholic Church prohibited "mixed marriages", as they were called. But there was the possibility of being granted special permission to have the impediment of "mixed religion" over-looked by the Church because of "just and grave reasons". When this was the case, the non-Catholic partner had to pledge, along with his Catholic partner, that all the children of their union would be surrendered to be baptized and educated in the Roman Catholic tradition alone. The permission to have "a mixed marriage" was conditional upon the firm guarantee that the promises would be morally obliging upon the couple. In addition to all these, the validity of the marriage depended on the presence at its celebration of the Roman Catholic local priest or deacon and at least two recognized witnesses. It is a fair comment to state that the Roman Catholic Church has been the most intransigent on this point. However, it would be utterly wrong to imagine or conclude that other Christians are happy or unconcerned about inter-church marriages. All churches and, we dare say, all Christians would prefer to marry within their own church.

Through the growing ecumenical understanding and co-operation among Christians, substantial theological agreement has been reached. Roman Catholic discipline has recently changed, and one happy consequence of the current ecumenical exchange has been the modification of legislation on the subject of inter-church marriages.[19]

In the most recent statement, the *Motu Proprio* of October 1970, inter-church marriages are still prohibited, but the granting of dispensations has been entrusted to the local bishop, instead of referring the cases to Rome with all their details, as was still the case since the instruction, *Matrimonio Sacramentum*, of March 1966. The following conditions are to be considered by the bishop in granting or refusing a dispensation:

1. The existence of a just cause.
2. The readiness of the Roman Catholic partner to avoid the danger of "perversion", making a sincere promise that everything possible will be done to have the children baptized and brought up in the Roman Catholic tradition.
3. The non-Roman Catholic partner is to be informed of the promises and requirements made by the Roman Catholic partner.

4. Both parties are to be instructed in the teaching of the Church regarding the ends of marriage and its essential properties of unity and indissolubility which may not be excluded. Regarding the marriage form, the new legislation empowers local bishops to dispense from the canonical form when grave difficulties hinder its observance.[20]

The most important innovation to be found in the *Motu Proprio* is that the non-Roman Catholic partner is not cajoled into pledges which could rarely be fulfilled. The partner is to be simply informed of the Roman Catholic partner's promises. The right over the nurture and education is no longer renounced by promise but left open for a future decision and the mutual responsibility of the two partners. The non-Catholic partner has the God-given duty to determine equally the religious upbringing of the children with a respect for his conscience.

Although the *Motu Proprio* gives some credit and creative value to inter-church unions as a possible means of helping to re-establish unity among Christians, it leaves a lot to be desired. The document still betrays a lack of trust and faith in the Christian teaching and practice of other churches regarding marriage and the nurture of children. The recognition of unity in Christ through baptism seems to be jeopardized by the scrutiny of Christian credentials of the other churches' members.

In the life of the Church, Christian marriage is taken as the sacrament of Christ's covenant with the Church. The Universal Church is the bride of Christ, Christ is the head or husband of the Church;[21] the unity and love of a true Christian marriage is the prefiguration of Christian unity, harmony and love that are the goals still to be achieved. There is a demand to recognize that the other churches are genuine churches, carrying on the work of Christ, that social changes have created a vast increase in the number of inter-church marriages, and that these inter-marriages may be an important, positive contribution to the life of the Church of Christ as a whole. The logical conclusion is the courageous step that all the churches should take, and this is the recognition and acceptance of the validity of each other's marriage form.

This step will form the springboard of all the pastoral care which we go on to propose below in the next section. But it would be naïve to imagine that all will go well after this openness

147

to each other as churches. Inter-church difficulties will still beset the marriages; the difference, however, is likely to give way to friendly co-operation and eagerness to help the storm-tossed partners instead of blaming it all on the gross mistake of inter-church marriage. The churches involved will ecumenically and jointly support and confirm both partners and their children as they seek and serve God together, emphasizing the richness of their unity in diversity. The difference should be comple-mentary, and never allowed to become contradictory. If the churches have a real commitment to the unity that Christ wished his followers to have in his prayer in John 17, the state of inter-church marriage could be an ecumenical ideal to be exploited to the full for the body of Christ, the Church Universal.

3   The Churches and Inter-Ethnic Marriages

Should the churches encourage or discourage inter-ethnic marriages? Or is it more prudent to ignore the issue and let chance be the driving force? This question should not, and cannot, be answered in isolation from the total role and mission of the Church in moulding and influencing society and her institutions. The Church is expected to be, and should be, at the forefront as innovator.[22] She should spearhead and initiate what she considers to be good for society. Our churches have a theological mandate to make things happen, rather than wait for relief action on what has already been made to happen. Christianity knows God as Creator; the Creator has invited men and women, as his obedient servants and children, to co-create with Him.

There has been no attempt to survey the general position of the churches on inter-ethnic marriages. Individual church officials or pastors take varying attitudes; the influence of these attitudes should not be underestimated. It is not unusual, for instance, for a rural parish pastor to frown at an intended inter-ethnic marriage while his urban counterpart may be neutral, or even positively encouraging to the intending couple.[23]

Christian unity as found in the Bible is proclaimed not only as bridging inter-church differences, but also as embracing the people of another ethnic group, language, race, caste, class, continent, and even those of another religious system. Marriage is, of course, different from social unity; but whenever and wherever men and women are brought together in successful

148

marriage in Africa the bond of unity between the partners, their families and relatives is created. A community of love, understanding, mutual respect and peaceful relationships is called into existence. These are no doubt God-given Christian values that are redeeming, liberating and generally humanizing. The churches stand to gain, rather than lose, if this is the result of a happy inter-ethnic marriage of Christians. In Christ the barriers of race, ethnic group, and language are of no account.[24] The ecumenical concept is inclusive rather than exclusive with reference to ethnic, racial, linguistic and ideological differences; the tendency has been to focus on inter-church unity, overlooking these other vital differences. It is not a surprise to find a church united in her administration but paradoxically being torn apart by racial prejudices, linguistic barriers or ideological persuasions. True and real ecumenism must aim at the total liberation of humanity. Inter-ethnic tensions may be as dangerous as, if not more dangerous than, inter-church quarrels. The ecumenical spirit and movement in the nations of Africa need to come to grips with the formidability of ethnic disharmony.

In the light of these observations inter-ethnic marriages seem to be part of what the churches as innovators should support through doctrine, pastoral care and counselling. Since the ethnic prejudices have been discovered (by James Holway and Sister Aquina in their case studies) to go far deeper than inter-church differences, our churches must take cautious steps, weighing words and situations. Boldness, courage and love must be used in the case of intending inter-ethnic and inter-racial partners, and their families.

4   *The Problem of Inter-Faith Marriages*

Coming to inter-faith marriages, as churches our bias is very strong. The basic problem here is the difference of understanding between Christianity and the other religious systems on the vital purpose of marriage. If we believe that through marriage people seek and serve God, who has been revealed to mankind fully and completely in the life, death and resurrection of Jesus Christ, and calls all creatures to worship and acknowledge him through the same Christ who is the Way, the Truth and the Life for ever, then other religious systems pose a stumbling block where marriage is concerned.

· Would an inter-faith marriage be seriously considered by a

149

deeply committed Christian, or is it often the indifferent believer or backslider to whom the Christian religion is as good as any other religious belief who accepts it? The latter is more likely than the former.

The problem of religious prejudice against another faith is a social one. Theologically we have the possibility of an inter-faith marriage eventually ending in a conversion; this is both our fear and hope. The Christian partner is likely to be won over to the other partner's faith, and we cannot as a responsible Church let our own get lost. The Christian hope (and Christians hope a great deal) is that the Christian partner will be used by God for the eventual salvation of the non-Christian partner. St. Paul on this ground encouraged Corinthian Christians not to desert their non-Christian partners.[25] However, this seems tolerable for the first generation of Christians in a particular place; can the same lenience apply to a young couple intending to marry, or is it merely limited to those already married as non-Christians, one of whom has become converted to Christianity? While community and pastoral care and love may lead to the conversion of the non-Christian partner, where marriage existed before one partner became Christian, the same care and love may be less successful with a young couple that openly walks into an inter-faith marriage. Both cases have tremendous missionary opportunities, with the latter case more complicated than the former. Under rare circumstances a happy religious atmosphere can be created where dialogue and mutual respect could result.and where the partners share a basic understanding of the sacramentality of married love. Such understanding, co-operation and relationship would go beyond the two partners and establish bridges across the religious systems and traditions.[26]

III   Models for Pastoral Action

1   *Marriage and Ecumenism*
The greatest and most compelling model of Christian Action, has been, and still is the *Churches Research on Marriage in Africa* —CROMIA. Through this continental project the churches have been brought together to exchange their teaching, and their differences, and to discover common problems that threaten their missionary and evangelistic activities in the

region of marriage and family life in Africa. Through research, study, and meetings that always included common worship, discussions and informal dialogue, this report is now in your hands. What you have before you is an inter-church "marriage" of ideas of people who belong to different races, continents and ethnic groups!

Inter-church marriages are a testing ground for ecumenical sincerity and commitment for the church leaders and the congregations. Serious and tireless effort is urgently demanded by the ecumenical milieu, in which we live and work, to surmount the difficulties that arise, redirecting them towards the enrichment of faith, hope, love and unity, always "looking to Jesus the pioneer and perfector of our faith". No "ready-made" or "instant" type of answers are suggested here, but we have to emphasize strongly that FAITH and LOVE must be at the root of pastoral care and counselling. The oneness of Christians proclaimed in baptism is the starting point. As a responsible pastor or Christian (member of Christ), the positive constructive approach answers the needs of today for our churches instead of negative over-emphasis on divisive elements that are applied to prevent inter-church marriages. The following factors particularly call for a radical change in approach:

(a) There is today a sincere recognition that other churches are genuinely carrying on the work of Christ.
(b) Social changes have led to vast numbers of mixed marriages of various kinds.
(c) The fact that, after all, inter-church marriages make an important contribution to the life of the churches by emphasizing and realizing an ideal to which the Christians all over the world are committed, unity in Christ regardless of church denomination.

After a strong, disparaging warning against mixed marriages, the All Africa Seminar on the Christian Home and Family Life in 1963 criticized Church legislation which, it was believed by the seminar, would achieve no positive good of itself. Instead, it was recommended that the Church create "such an active fellowship within itself that it may expect its young men and women to find partners there: there where they have grown up together 'in the Lord' and heard together a clear, positive and essentially Christian doctrine and interpretation of marriage. Within this fellowship it can help the partners to face their

151

problems together, and so to make the right decisions." And most important for this part of our project report, the Seminar concluded the discussion on "mixed marriage" by stating that, "For this task it needs pastors who can teach and counsel with love and understanding."[27]

Even at this time when ecumenical thinking within the churches of Africa was only being awakened, the Seminar could see the vital role of the right kind of pastor in marriage and family life. The spirit of oneness in Christ into which the churches in Africa are growing was not as well pronounced thirteen years ago as the oneness we today are privileged to enjoy. Animosities against other Christian denominations were still so prevalent that the Seminar agreed that inter-church marriage was among the "All things (are) lawful for me" and as yet "not expedient". Discouragement was recommended rather than encouragement.

The thrust of the evidence accumulated by this project indicates that we should neither discourage nor encourage inter-church marriages. There are several and sufficient reasons that have been advanced for either side. The resulting position taken at the conclusion of this project is a pertinent request and appeal for MUTUAL CO-OPERATION, UNDERSTANDING, AND LOVE in a UNITED pastoral and congregational Christian action by the churches. In this spirit the following suggestions are being presented to the churches in Africa with the sincere hope that they will be of practical consequence in dealing with inter-church, inter-ethnic and inter-faith marriages. Where the word "pastoral" is used, it often has the wider meaning that includes all Christians rather than the narrow sense of what an ordained person does.

2   *The Churches and Courtship*

All marriages are mixed to some extent. The two persons, the husband and the wife, are very different from each other. They come from homes and families that are different even though they may be from the same ethnic group, district, Christian denomination, or religious system.

In deciding to marry, the two people have, for various motives, been attracted to each other so that they will become one body, one flesh, clinging to each other throughout their lives. This is what we are called to assist in our pastoral action.

Pastoral Christian action must avoid, at all costs, taking the role of the "Fire Brigade" or the "Police", always being called in with a "999 ring" at the last, critical hour of a marriage situation. Our churches must be on the spot from the beginning, even from the first moments of courtship. We can only reiterate the All Africa Seminar's appeal quoted earlier on[28] that the Church should have an active fellowship of young men and women who will meet each other, discover each other as suitable partners for marriage from within the Christian fellowship. It is here that they will have learnt, one hopes, to be frank and open to each other, to face problems and make decisions together, to play and joke with each other, even about their differences. A Church Fellowship of this kind should be open in outlook and generally accommodating and tolerant enough for others that may otherwise be shy or unwelcome.

The provision of a fellowship for young people is not granting Christian independence of the young from the old folk. The ideal fellowship is for the enrichment of the whole Christian community in the area. "Separate development" on the basis of age would be a sad impoverishment to the Church. The elders of the Christian community should make a special effort to be available, and acceptable to the fellowship of the young men and women, not "lording it over them", to impose their old, often outmoded ideals, but to be convincing advisers who seek to win the confidence of the young.

This is hard, admittedly. It precipitates the tug of war between the young and the old, the revolutionary and the conservative forces. Is it worth the risk and trouble involved? Yes, it is. The truth of this can, however, only be vindicated by trying it to see whether it has any positive results. The young desperately need the old folk, just as the old need the young, in whom they are well pleased, especially in the African context.[29] The role of the basic community, which is increasingly becoming Christian rather than traditional in outlook, will be dealt with in another section of this book. Our main point is to call Christian action out of lethargy into lively active presence and involvement in influencing the decisions of young people before problems come.

How can Christian LOVE be experienced by likely marriage partners in a parish, institution, town or village? Different people have different ways of expressing their Christian love, depending on their circumstances and background. What is certain is that people can never mistake sincere love. The cords of love are often invisibly so binding that they can transcend, or work miracles on, any situation. Shall we sing the Hymn of Love according to St. Paul—(I Cor. 13)? Make love your aim as a community or as an individual member of the Church. If love is lavished on all members of all the churches, they will seek help and guidance from the right people before things are too difficult to disentangle.

There are no bounds or limitations to Christian love. This is the Gospel that Christianity brings to every corner of the known world. The most staggering teaching of Jesus Christ throughout the centuries has been on this subject:

But I say to you, love your enemies and pray for those who persecute you. . . . For if you love those who love you, what reward have you? . . . And if you salute only your brethren, what more are you doing than others? (Mt. 5:43–48).

Christian love is involving and sympathetic: to love anybody is to share his or her hopes, achievements and failures. As a Christian you know the consequences of love because of the symbol of God's love, the cross. Therefore a loving church is one that cannot escape bearing the burdens of the beloved. The love of Christ entrusted to the Church in Africa will be broadcast only as it is experienced by individuals who are desperately in need of it, in our local church and situation whether they belong to our particular group or not. We know best how to show this love in practice in our situation. Let us earnestly make love our aim.

3   *Leadership and Community*

We noted above that the CROMIA project is a model of action which our churches could easily emulate in their own local situation. The leaders, from the lowest to the top, have to give the lead. We must repeat, it is the leaders of the people and not necessarily the pastors, ministers or priests. They are only part of the leadership of the community, and may, in certain cases, be of lesser influence in the Christian communities of Africa. The churches of Africa still rely to a great extent on lay cate-chists, church teachers or evangelists who wield considerable influence on the course and degree of Christian action in our churches. Along with these are the lay leaders of the congrega-tions, normally not employed by the churches, who are an important Christian force to be reckoned with in considering any innovation in the basic church community.

To this leadership, ordained or lay, we have something to recommend here. Inter-church cross-engagement should start immediately. We should not accentuate differences; we should start discussing what we have in common in order to lay the foundation. For instance, we have the Bible, hymns and a rich tradition of over sixteen centuries of a united Christendom, and a great deal more that has been shared even after the creation of the unhappy divisions. Today we face so much together that is a common experience, why lay stress on differences? These are secondary.

Every country, or region, will have its own programme of ecumenical activity. What we recommend must be fitted into this structure. The various levels of our churches' administrative set-up will need to co-operate bilaterally with other churches; for instance diocese with diocese or equivalent unit, and parish with parish. The leadership at these levels will then be able to inspire the spirit of unity by word as well as by practical demonstration. Whoever has attempted the practical working together with members of other churches, will bear witness to the most surprising results, and to an experience very close to what Christ wished in his prayer: that we should be one. Those involved in joint Bible translations, and other ecumenical programmes have had a foretaste of Christian unity and co-operation. We must make the move now.

The example given by leaders will need to seep through to the congregation or local community. Marriage is a social institution which involves, and needs, more than the two married partners. The community, therefore, has an important role to play, and a significant contribution to make towards marriage, much more so towards an inter-church, inter-ethnic or inter-faith marriage. A marriage can survive without the sanction and support of the basic religious or ethnic community, but it will survive precariously. Should a crisis face the family, like the sudden death of one of the partners or sudden unemployment of the family breadwinner, there will be great suffering. In African traditional society to cut oneself off from one's community is to commit suicide; and "a victim of suicide gets few mourners".[30]

The Christian community should embrace the couple which has a mixed marriage; the couple, too, should not break loose from the community by activities or by talk that alienates them.

The historic churches that work in Africa created the unhappy impression that pastoral care and concern belongs to the pastor, minister or perhaps rarely to the lay catechist or church teacher. The pastoral care of Christians for each other has still to be learnt. Church members need to be given confidence that they are part of the healing or curing ministry of Christ, not only when they serve in medical centres and hospitals as nursing sisters and physicians, but as sincere members of the Christian community. The pastor should be regarded as the consultant, and Christians can play their part with or without him. When the community is trained and given the chance to play its pastoral role, great things can happen. The minister or pastor in the community should be the enabler, who aids the Church in the area to be the Church in mission and ministry. At present pastors treat most church members as parents often like to treat their children. They try to do everything, and allow little independent activity while they are there. Most Christians are so conditioned that they will not say or lead a prayer in the presence of a bishop or priest under any circumstances. Are we prepared to give responsibility to our local community and help it to use it for its own good? Inter-church marriages will be one aspect that the community can be helped to cope with; other issues big and small may arise. We must be genuine and sincere and avoid using Christians as problem-solving machines. We must start with problems that they can solve, simple issues, before introducing them to the tough issues. Some parishes, towns or institutions will have better resources for dealing with an issue or a situation, while others are more or less helpless.

The most important target is to prepare our community, our congregation, to be open, receptive, loving, and eager to help those in difficulties. An inter-church marriage would be happy in an atmosphere where members of different churches are respected and accepted for what they are. The partner that does not belong to one's own particular church should be carefully handled and loved so that he or she will feel a sense of belonging without being pressurized to be converted to that church. Religious prejudice and animosity should be curbed in this way.

4 *The Combat Against Religious Indifferentism*
Research has revealed that many of the people who accept an inter-church or inter-faith marriage are usually indifferent in their faith at the time. This position is most dangerous for the churches involved, both for the partners and for their children

in the future. These have the possibility of gradually being swallowed up by materialistic secularism, or being tossed about by every wind of religious teaching. They belong nowhere.

In other chapters of this book emphasis has been put on the need for Christian marriage education and instruction. Educational institutions, like schools and colleges, would be the starting point, but the churches separately and ecumenically should go further. The deepening of Christian commitment in the young is of vital importance in this educational programme. Indifferent Christians who enter any marriage do more harm than good. Ways of strengthening the faith of the young should be sought so that before they think of marriage they are convinced Christians.

We presented the idea of the young people's fellowship in section 2 above as a way of growing up "in the Lord" within the Christian community. The church fellowship can also be used to mature the young people's faith as well as an opportunity for teaching them about Christian ideals including marriage. Fellowship of this kind can be denominational but open and receptive to others outside that confession.

Other activities for teaching and deepening the Christian faith could include:

(a) *Conferences:* these could be of varying length, from a weekend to a full week or more.
(b) *Half-day gatherings:* may be quite suitable for the rural or urban parish at the church or nearby school.
(c) *Camps:* these often afford much more than conferences. There is the opportunity to be away from routine activities, and often the rare chance of walking and working together.
(d) *Short regular meetings:* can help the development or teaching of a theme.
(e) *Games:* indoor or outdoor.
(f) *Dancing, singing and drama.*

Little or no restriction should be applied, the married and the unmarried can work and meet together.

The content of instruction or teaching should not emphasize the denominational differences. The churches will be concerned to teach about the purpose, reality and responsibility of Christian marriage. The Methodist, Anglican, Pentecostal or Roman Catholic forms could be given as examples of what is practised without doctrinal bias.

In a number of African countries this approach will be familiar because of the common Religious Education School syllabus, which has been adopted with resounding success, for instance in East Africa. The dioceses and parishes of various nations should explore this possibility and compile inter-church materials to be used by those charged with organizing the above mentioned activities for the young.

Young people are the most ecumenically minded force we have in the world today. In schools, youth clubs, colleges and universities, theological colleges and seminaries, the young are impatient with Church denominations and differences. They tend to appreciate what they share in common with others rather than emphasize their differences. Is this a healthy Christian attitude, or is it merely youthful enthusiasm based on theological ignorance and lack of real experience in life?

Ministers, pastors, and elderly Christians are warned of the possibility of young Christians going faster in demolishing the barriers of division than we may be prepared for. The way the Pentecostal or Charismatic movement has cut across church ghettoes in so many countries has been a great shock to quite a number of church leaders, who are afraid of being swept along by the tide, and desperately hold on to their own with a frantic condemnation of what is really in many parts of the world the reviving work of the Holy Spirit of God.

5   *Inter-Church Marriage Procedures*

The majority of our contributors on the subject of inter-church marriages have been Roman Catholics, but they have approached the subject from a general point of view, as an issue facing all the Churches. What we have noted so far is within the experience of the Roman Catholic Church as governed by the *Motu Proprio* of 1970. Several times, the *Motu Priprio* refers to the need for collaboration with other churches. The church authorities are asked to afford the spouses suitable help; and bishops and priests are asked to assist married couples to foster the unity of their conjugal and family life, based on their baptism into Christ Jesus. This joint pastoral care of inter-marriages emphasized by the *Motu Proprio*, must now be analysed in practical detail, although a fair amount of space has already been devoted to general approaches like fellowships or clubs, parish activities, and leaders' bilateral efforts. With the background of inter-church activity and co-operation outlined above the following suggestions should be reasonably possible to effect:

(a) When an official of any Church is approached by a couple who belong to different churches, the pastors of the church communities involved should be contacted and appropriate steps taken jointly to prepare the two partners for Christian marriage. Often, young people have made up their minds when they approach the church authorities. Trying to dissuade them from the marriage is unlikely to succeed and could undermine their trust and confidence in the Church.

The pastors involved should openly and boldly present the likely disadvantages of such a marriage, giving the couple a chance to reconsider their decision, as well as helping them to accept the difficulties likely to arise if they are convinced about the match. The pastors should also assure the inter-church couple of their support and readiness to help them together or individually.

The congregations and families concerned will have to be involved through information, explanation and appeal for support in constant prayer and visiting.

(b) For the preparation of the couple before marriage an agreed common handbook should be used by the two Churches involved. The two pastors will agree upon the sharing of the instruction. We strongly advise against each pastor giving his church's doctrinal position only; it means that pastors will need to be well-versed in what other churches believe and teach, together with his own church teaching. The pastors should be prepared to learn from each other before instructing the couple. Where no agreed catechetical handbook exists, the pastors should jointly put together the essential emphases of their traditions.

(c) The wedding.

(i) The question of Christians seeking permission to marry from ecclesiastical authorities is certainly awkward unless they are being disciplined by the Church at that time. Churches that insist on this procedure should modify their legislation. However, until this is the case, it should be accepted that permission is granted by both churches.

(ii) The place of the wedding should be selected by the couple with the advice of the pastors. We assume that the joint pastoral care will help the partners to decide to have their wedding ceremony at one of the churches, rather than going in for a civil ceremony. But if the circumstances are such that the civil ceremony may be more harmonious for the inter-church marriage, let the pastors be open and helpful for the good of the couple.

(iii) Like the instruction manual, the order of the church service should be prepared by an ecumenical team, or for the time being by the two pastors. It will be the normal and usual thing to consult higher authority, if in doubt or difficulty over these joint activities. The adoption of elements from either church tradition should produce a peaceful compromise. Sufficient room could be provided for valuable African values and rites as part of the wedding ceremony.[31]

(iv) The couple may need assistance or guidance with a number of other aspects of marriage before or after the wedding. The pastor or pastors should be sensitive to this need, even if it may not be openly stated. The two partners may be shy or unwilling to broach matters to do with inter-ethnic relations, sexual relations or some other question, and the pastor can effect a helpful breakthrough in these areas.

6 *Joint Pastoral Care of Mixed Marriages*

The extent of pastoral care directed to an inter-church marriage will be determined by the care given before the union. Both churches concerned have a joint responsibility for the success and Christian frutitfulness of every inter-church marriage. As before the marriage, the pastors as the official representatives of their churches, must collaborate effectively, in a brotherly spirit, to help the couple, and their children, build up a truly Christian married life together based on a common love, a common faith and a common life of prayer. Where the upbringing of the children is concerned, both parents should decide together about their baptism and Christian nurture. They may decide that all or some of the children should belong to either of the churches. Or they may decide to give them all a Christian upbringing, and allow them to choose either of the churches when they reach maturity.

The pastors and the local congregations of the two churches should show a keen interest in the couple and the marriage. If the couple move from their original situation, efforts to introduce them and visit them in their new place should be made.

Where a number of inter-church marriages are found, an attempt to get the families together occasionally could enable them to discuss the common problems experienced. The pastors' relationship with each other is likely to influence the attitude of the other Christians towards the inter-church marriage. A spirit of mutual understanding and confidence among the pastors of different churches is necessary to facilitate the delicate handling of issues of an inter-church marriage.

Should one of the partners sincerely decide to join the church of the other partner after some years of the marriage,[32] the decision should be received and accepted calmly, without any sense of loss or victory. Pastoral care from both churches should continue unless and until it is not convenient or required.

Inter-ethnic, inter-racial and inter-faith marriages, often call for our Christian care and action. We hope that the programmes suggested above will accommodate people coming from different ethnic groups and different races. Christian commitment, it is believed, transcends our racial and ethnic differences; we expect and pray that this will happen.

Inter-faith marriages appear to present many complicated issues in the theological, spiritual and pastoral areas. Although they should be allowed by the churches as a situation prior to the conversion of the non-Christian partner, as the case has been in missionary situations like Africa, Asia and elsewhere, a young couple intending to marry should normally be discouraged. However, love and open hands should be extended to the couple if they decide to marry against the advice of the churches given to them. The door should be left open, in case the other partner is genuinely converted to Christianity, in which case the Christian marriage could be formalized in the church.

The degree of inter-church action and co-operation cannot be determined in this book. The situation prevailing in a particular place or country, together with the willingness of the churches in that area, under the guidance of the Spirit, will gauge this common approach. The Roman Catholic and Protestant churches in Congo Brazzaville gave an excellent lead in 1975 with their ecumenical agreement on procedures relating to inter-church marriage. May this agreement be a harbinger of deeper and more extensive ecumenical co-operation in this field.[33]

References: Chapter Six

1 Holway, 1974.
2 Shorter, 1973, CROMIA/22.
3 Hastings, 1973, p. 112.

4 Holway, 1974, p. 4.

5 Sister Aquina has noted this attempt to hold on to the traditional ethnic life in her extensive study of *Marriage and Family Life among the African Peoples of Rhodesia*, 1975 (see especially pages 22 and 32–3, vol. I).

6 There is continual interplay between the urban and rural populations of East Africa. Most town dwellers and workers often have a place they call "home" in the rural area. See Holway, 1974, pp. 3 and 4.

7 Mbiti, 1973, p. 86.

8 Holway, 1974, p. 6.

9 Holway, 1973, p. 259.

10 Shorter, Paper presented to the Kampala Ecumenical Study Group, 1975c. Holway (Nairobi Survey) and Mbiti agree on this issue.

11 This form of marriage is legally acceptable in most countries covered by this project. In a number of countries like Uganda and Tanzania, such a marriage would be potentially open to legally recognized polygamy for the man.

12 Hastings, 1973, pp. 5–26.

13 Okwachi, 1974, p. 1 and Lebona in Verryn (ed.), 1975, pp. 134–5.

14 cf. Chap. One, Part III, Section 2.

15 Okwachi, 1974, p. 3.

16 Okwachi, 1974, pp. 1–3.

17 Shorter, Paper presented to Kampala Ecumenical Study Group, 1975c, p. 1.

18 Seventh Day Adventists, African Independent Churches and Muslims exert the same kind of pressure.

19 *Matrimonii Sacramentum*—March 1966; *Motu Proprio*, October 1970, quoted by Whyte in Verryn (ed.), 1975, pp. 141–57.

20 Shorter, 1975c, p. 2.

21 Eph. 5:21–33.

22 cf. Paul Miller: *Equipping for Ministry in East Africa*, Dodoma, 1969.

23 From observation, more inter-ethnic weddings are celebrated or contracted in urban centres than in the rural areas.

24 Gal. 3:23–29.

25 I Cor. 7:12–16.

26 Mbiti, 1973, p. 88.

27 Report of the All Africa Seminar on Christian Home and Family Life. Geneva, 1963, pp. 25–6.

28 cf. above p. 151.

29 The allusion is a reminder about the concept of continuity of vitality through the offspring.

30 Paraphrase of a Rutoro proverb, western Uganda.

31 The Kampala Ecumenical Study Group attempted this in a

suggested *Rite for Marriage* as an appendix to that Group's *Inter-church Marriages* draft proposals, 1975.

32 See Andrew D. Spiegel's paper "Christianity, Marriage and Migrant Labour in Lesotho", p. 445 in Verryn (ed.), 1975.

33 *Ecumenical Press Service*, Geneva, no. 24, 7/88/75, p. 8.

Chapter 7

Population Growth and Responsible Parenthood

I   Case Material

1   *The Churches and Population*

The issue of Population Growth and Responsible Parenthood in Africa has been established beyond doubt as multi-dimensional.[1] In considering the role and position of the family in the total situation, the evidence has widened our terminology from just planned family sizes to the more inclusive term, "Responsible Parenthood". This latter concept appears to sum up most of the discussions at meetings organized by this project and other organizations concerned with this subject. It has been the underlying theme of Family Planning efforts.

The growth of the population and the demand and supply of food should be seen as inter-linked. National and international planners and policy-makers must take into account these corre-lations and integrate them into the development projections that involve population growth rates, human fertility and the availability of resources. The facets of the issue, therefore, are: population, environment, resource allocation and, most important of all, the human factor.

The Church is one of the societal institutions whose religious beliefs and practices, moral evaluations, and theological teaching can influence policy and planning in the constituency of population growth and responsible parenthood. The churches of Africa, in an environment that is often referred to as the "Third World", are duty-bound to contribute to the deliberations that eventually have to affect the peoples of Africa as a whole.

164

At the Yaoundé Consultation in Cameroun, organized by the department on Church, Family and Society of the AACC, the concern of the churches was clearly expressed by participants from fourteen countries of Africa, both English and French speaking. The churches had become aware of the stresses and strains on the African family exerted by the rapid social, economic, political and religious changes sweeping across the continent. One aspect of this consultation was a consideration of the "Trends of Population and Food Demand and Supply in Africa", a paper that was prepared by the Population Programme Centre of the United Nations Economic Commission for Africa. In this fairly technical presentation of data, the view expressed earlier on was the basis of the analysis and projection for the future. In the first place the size of a population that can reasonably live a *qualitative life*, dependent on agricultural products, requires a relative assessment of the agricultural labour force, the stable conditions of weather and marketing, which determine the demand and supply. Secondly, projections often take an optimistic view, forecasting that there will be better land use and utilization of resources that would lead to improvement in productivity. Thirdly, the paper noted, the role played by the type of people involved. "The quality of the population" is seen as the key to the development. This key role has to be recognized so that the agricultural development schemes, in the rural areas in particular, can embrace all the interrelations of population with the different facets of development. This, then, indicates a generalized approach to the improvement of the level of living both in terms of production and of consumption of the individual and the family, which would have to take into account responsible parenthood. In addition, it would have to take into account the adequate care and provision of skills and productivity, together with positive attitudes towards family size in relation to the requirements and the potentials, an undertaking that is often not fully perceived. The paper ends with the encouraging note that this vital integration of the population issue with other aspects of development is being increasingly recognized by African experts and representatives of African governments.

Nearly a year and half after the Yaoundé Consultation, International Educational Development organized a Seminar in Accra, Ghana, sponsored by the United Nations Fund for Population Activities. The theme of this Seminar was "Moral and Religious Issues in Population Dynamics and Development in Africa",[2] broken down into the following objectives:

(a) To increase awareness regarding the complex variables of population dynamics and development.
(b) To contribute to the deepening of reflection on human values, ethical and religious aspects of population dynamics and development.
(c) To bring groups of people together who do not normally dialogue: social scientists, religious philosophers, church leaders, community organizers, demographers and population programme officers.
(d) To stimulate possible subsequent research and action on the part of the participants.

The CROMIA project had been effectively represented at these vital gatherings, with significant contributions made to the proceedings.

2 *Population*

Whereas the Yaoundé Consultation broadly and generally dealt with the Challenges of Family and Marriage Education in the 1970s in Africa, the Accra Seminar concentrated on the different facets of Population and Development in Africa, "the complex variables" involved. The Yaoundé paper from the Economic Commission for Africa, referred to above, had given the broad dimensions in scientific language. The April 1974 Accra Seminar passionately probed the "variables".

Emmanuel Kibirige who represented the project and AMECEA at this seminar in Accra, noted a number of vital points that he shared with us through his report. Some of the contributors had pointed out to the participants that the basis of population theology was God's creation of man as a responsible being, a planner and organizer of creation. Man was imbued with the capacity to act for his own security and peace, taking into account the position of the individual as well as the community, we could add the nation, continent, or even the world. Population and development policy makers had to consider the realities of the situation they were addressing their plans to. The traditional beliefs and behaviour of the people in any country or area still play a significant part in their acceptance or rejection of innovations and new projects. For instance, the traditional ideas about children and childessness are linked with the transmission and continuity of human life.

Caution and tact need to be adopted in introducing anything new, especially to the traditional life of the rural areas. In African traditional society, it was asserted, childlessness or limited fertility were objects of reproach; it was a source of worry that after death the childless person or family would vanish into oblivion with no one to remember or honour them. They would simply perish. The concept of parenthood and marriage was always linked with a strong desire for a numerous progeny. To be a mother, for example, was to aspire to the highest position of respect and esteem, not only from the family members but from society as a whole.

The seminar agreed that the population growth of Africa is not, on the whole, a pressing problem of today; it is, however, the future that has to be seriously considered and planned for now. Care must be exercised at this moment in time so that a satisfactory quality of life can be enjoyed as the population grows. Planned, responsible parenthood was stressed as one way of determining the future quality of the population and life in general.

Some limited ways of planning the family did exist in traditional Africa. The custom of polygamy so widespread over the continent served as a means of birth-control for child-spacing. As a numerous progeny was a blessing, child-spacing was not used to limit the family size. It was a great advantage for mothers to be able to recover well enough before the next pregnancy came. Another practice that helped to limit births were the taboos banning sexual relations with a mother during the lactation period of the child, which could stretch up to between two and five years.

Before we blame or discourage the traditional African viewpoint and attitudes to family size and population, it is important to look at the issue more closely first. We have already noted the importance of child-bearing in traditional Africa. In his Tanzania study, Joinet reported that the married happiness to which young people look forward is basically found in the company of others.[3] The family unit was only the centre of a network of social relationships, and often the social status and influence of the partners depended to a great extent on having a large family. The quality of life was conceived essentially in terms of the warmth generated by the size of the family. There was indeed a warmth of relationships and a sharing of the family means of sustenance.

In a subsistence or consumption economy a large family was likely to be more of an advantage than a disadvantage. The family as a unit had a large measure of autonomy[4] over the work done by its members, labour marketing was limited and even then the work rewards were often for the whole family and not just for the individual who laboured. In these circumstances, procreation was seen as an increase of the family-community, not only as mouths to feed but as hands to help. The family could be defended when trouble approached; the land would be tilled for more food; cattle would be acquired through bridewealth or courageous raids; the dead ancestors would be "brought back" by naming or resemblance, and the family would remain or have a name.

A recent study of rural Tanzania by Kasaka, on marriage and family life in the rural resettlement areas, has suggested that in modern circumstances a large, and even polygamous, family was a distinct advantage to the settler.[5]

This is certainly an exception to the general rule that the changes of urbanization, industrialization and society organization have led to the marketing of labour and skills to others who are not directly related to the needs of the family and that of the individual himself. The family now has needs that can only be satisfied by money earned from those who have work, work that can be done only by a few of the family. The other non-earning members are reduced to the level of "parasites" and kept at a great disadvantage. Whatever values were enshrined in African community life, a decisive blow has been dealt through the modern changes and perhaps new forms and norms will have to be found for the institution to exist longer, if it can.

3 Family Planning

The majority of schemes on population and development have tended to emphasize the use of family planning methods to limit the increase of the population. For Africa the growth rate of the population is threateningly high, compared with the world population growth rate. On a regional basis, the most rapid increase in population is taking place in Africa. The average annual growth rates are 2% or more in forty-three African countries, and twelve of these are experiencing rates of 3% or more! Most countries in Europe (twenty-six out of thirty-four) have a growth rate of less than 1%. As regards population density there are striking differences between the different African countries; the range was as wide as one per square kilometre for Namibia to 127 per square kilometre for Burundi, of the twenty-three African countries surveyed in 1972.[6]

This goes to confirm the conclusion of the Accra Seminar that overpopulation is not an imminent danger for the African continent as a whole, but for some individual countries, it certainly is a pressing problem, and this would justify a continental approach to the problem with particular emphasis on the highly populated areas. How can we evolve suitable acceptable methods of checking population growth rates?

In her Rhodesian study, Sister Aquina has thrown light upon the conditions existing in that country that discourage population control efforts. She noted that the Shona people value the large family and theoretically have no limit to family size. At present family-size limitation through birth-control is viewed with great suspicion and as a political move by the white minority population to reduce the African strength. It is never seen as a means of helping families for their economic betterment. The sanity of the Africans' suspicion is, as Sister Aquina ably illustrates from the Chinese case, proved by the prevalent political climate in Rhodesia.[7]

She also found that people with higher education were more responsive to family planning than the poor and less educated, a fact that has been confirmed by other studies all over the world.[8] The poorer people want large families because, when jobs are scarce, when illness is common and old age is early, children are necessary for protection, security and peace of mind. In poor families children certainly cost little extra money to maintain. They are extra hands to help in the poor people's daily struggle for existence. The children make this struggle worthwhile and bearable. When income levels of the people rise, health care improves, life expectancy increases. When employment opportunities become available and education widespread, and when the status of women rises, the rate of population growth can be more easily limited.

Communist China, for instance, has achieved resounding success in controlling her population growth rate through her ideological commitment backed by economic security. There is a constant insistence by the party that planned parenthood is essential to strengthen the political values of the people. Planned birth is regarded as a direct contribution that every young married couple can make towards nation building. The women have been emancipated and given equal status with men in employment sectors earning the same pay. This freedom of women from purely domestic work and their equality in society have been among the most decisive factors for the Chinese success.[9] Then, in addition, medical services and facilities for family planning methods with experienced trained personnel were made abundant all over the country.

The Chinese example seems to agree with the observation made by the *New Internationalist*, that only a pronounced improvement in the standard of living and economic security of the majority of the people can create a motivation for smaller families and so lead to a significant and sustained slowing down of population growth.[10]

The methods of birth-control are varied, ranging from abstinence from sexual union to abortion. The existence of African traditional herbal contraceptive medicines has been reported by John Kanyikwa,[11] from his survey of Iganga area in eastern Uganda. After two years of field-work among the Kimbu of Tanzania, Aylward Shorter could not substantiate the popular belief that contraceptive practices abounded among the Kimbu people. What was established was the magical contraceptive practice of wearing charms or burying a symbolic root.[12]

Angela Molnos in four comprehensive volumes has put into our hands the socio-cultural research on population studies in East Africa from 1952 to 1972.[13] In volumes II and III she summarizes the major beliefs and practices of a large number of East African peoples, giving cautious and pragmatic indications for the promotion of programmes affecting population, and family planning in particular. Molnos advocates the treatment of family planning in the context of the full knowledge of African traditions which would offer a solid basis for innovations and sound mutual communication. But in apposition, she notes the challenging dynamic context where the rapid socio-economic developments are accompanied by changes in cultural patterns, entrenched attitudes and established customs. In the context of the population issue and family planning, we have here a positive strand that the churches in Africa and society at large may use in introducing new attitudes and norms in family life.

Modern scientific methods of family planning will be considered later. We notice that the weight of evidence of the material collected points to the multi-dimensional approach to the population issue, rather than emphasizing the methods used in controlling conceptions or births.

II Theological Reflection

1 The Population Problem

In presenting the case material on Responsible Parenthood and the Population Growth, it has become clear that CROMIA should, like many current projects and statements, dwell on the issue in its general multi-dimensional perspective. The churches' critique of family planning and methods of birth-control should be one of the dimensions of the wider, complex issue.

The sincere interest of the churches in Africa in the peoples and their well-being is being challenged by the comprehensive question of population treatment. No longer must the churches think mainly of their own adherents, who are a significant part, but still not the majority of the total population of Africa. It is inherent in the nature and mission of the Church to be universal rather than just parochial. The Church as constituted by any parish in Africa is the practical local manifestation of an essentially world-wide body of Christ. No one is too far away from this body to be left out by the embracing love of the Gospel. It would be a failure for the churches if any of their Christian programmes were aimed exclusively at their own members' welfare alone.

Although this does not mean the neglect of a particular attention to their own faithful, it ensures, however, the acceptance of responsibility by the churches. From this point, the churches will launch out, and respond truly and sincerely, in so far as they possess the means and resources, to the demands of society at large.

In this arduous task the Churches have to seek the co-operation of bodies, governmental or voluntary, which are engaged in this field of the population issue, and which have acquired a measure of experience that could be utilized by the churches' own programmes. In co-operating with these various organizations, the churches can speak as a partner, and not as a stranger, in pointing out the religious and ethical aspects that should be given considerable weight in the decision-making processes. Religion is an accepted, vocal and dynamic aspect of African existence, as evidenced by the religious dimensions of birth, puberty, and marriage, and morality. From days past religion has been known to be the cementing factor of a harmonious society.

The churches in Africa need each other. Inter-church bilateral relations are vital in presenting a common witness. The united action of the churches will enable the Church to utilize to the full her enormous potential influence. The Christian Church as "a trans-national actor"[14] is involved in the educational ministry, has a trans-national presence, and pastoral access to the people. The churches of Africa have the potential of influencing both international and national policies, and being able to supervise or follow up specific decisions in the villages of the continent.

The theology of population is inseparably linked with the theology of development. Man who is mythologically portrayed as the pinnacle or centre of all creation, according to Genesis chapters 1–2, has a responsibility for himself, his community and creation as a whole. Mankind has a dual relationship with God, in that it is both the overseer of creation, and yet part of the same creation. St. Paul thinks that the rest of creation inevitably shares in the destiny of man, when he develops the theme of cosmic salvation.[15] The injunction to procreate, so often used to brush family planning aside with what is apparently biblical authority, must be understood in relation to the heavy responsibility entrusted to man for the welfare and fate of God's creation. Man was not created to succumb to the unbridled passions of his creaturely state, nor was he to be his own master. He had to strike a balance, and how often do we discover that creation is a "creation-in-balance".

It is this state of affairs that the Church would like to see continuing. Scientific, statistical data are crying out to us. Human life is threatened, and especially in the so-called Third World, of which Africa is part, by the rapid increase of population. The basic human requirements of food and shelter, not to speak of other needs, will gradually become impossible to supply. A miserable human life will end in starvation and exposure. No one living today would like to see this happen, and this is the reason for the churches' action and involvement in the programme to promote responsible parenthood and limit population growth to avert disaster.

2   Family Planning and Responsible Parenthood

The previous section has prepared us to tackle what we could call the churches' "sore point". Heated discussion has been going on about the methods of family planning, and the practical meaning of responsible parenthood. Is the individual couple, or the community to decide upon what methods *they* consider suitable, or is the Church through its leadership to be the helmsman of all believers on this issue?

In the churches of Africa there is a wide range of opinion. The theological problem is often the conflict between the official doctrinal position of the churches and the conscience of individuals, as well as governmental policies. It is often argued that married couples have the right to exercise their parenthood responsibility as Christians; they should be left to plan their family sizes with the full right to use a workable method for achieving their objectives. The churches' pastoral role remains to assist families where necessary to understand the issues at stake and give any guidance called for, without stipulating standard codes for everybody, since Christian families live in different economic and social environments. The churches' negative stance on certain widely accepted approaches which are deemed immoral has been unfortunate. There has certainly been a practical pluralism according to which Christians have evaded the uncompromising teaching of churches. But this evasion cannot be used to justify a continued negative attitude. The project would like to recommend, in this decade of the total liberation of Africa, that the churches help in liberating the consciences of their members—a liberation which serves an increased sense of responsibility. In many cases church-forbidden methods are secretly used because of their proved usefulness and acceptability. Obviously anything and everything can be justified in the name of conscience. That is not our purpose! The churches have to proclaim an ideal for the ultimate good of the family. Christians will, in conscience, decide how far they can implement this ideal, while keeping the aim firmly before their eyes. Two statements, one by the Southern African Catholic Bishops' Conference, and the other by the Indonesian Bishops' Conference, issued in February and August of 1973 respectively, are relevant here:

We would say that it is for the parents to decide what in their given circumstances is the best or only practical way of serving the welfare of the whole family. In this conflict of duties, their responsible decision, though falling short of th ideal, will be subjectively defensible, since the aim is not the selfish exclusion of pregnancy but the promotion of the common good of the family.[16]

The second quotation is more precise in excluding certain, absolutely unacceptable methods:

There are parents who are troubled because from one side they feel the obligation to regulate births, but from the other they are not able to fulfil this obligation by temporary or absolute sexual abstinence. In these circumstances, they decide responsibly and do not need to feel that they have sinned, if they employ other methods, provided that the human dignity of wife or husband is not diminished, or provided that the means employed do not go against human life (i.e. abortion and permanent sterilization) and provided that the medical responsibility is upheld.[17]

One of the greatest concerns of the churches is the abuse of family planning methods by immoral persons and weak partners in a marriage. Prostitution can easily flourish as a result of contraceptive methods. This is, no doubt, a corruption of what may be basically good. Mankind has the notoriety of contaminating anything good. The fear of encouraging pre-marital and extra-marital sexual relations with the security of no pregnancy resulting, is well founded. Caution has to be exercised in the distribution of contraceptive devices. It is possible for the churches to assist, through their medical apostolate, in teaching methods of birth-regulation and in curbing the indiscriminate use of contraceptives.

The medical security of some methods of birth regulation and family planning is doubted by some who tend to believe popular tales, which may not always be groundless. It is asserted, and there is no evidence to deny it completely, that some medicines and devices are introduced into certain countries of the Third World, where the population issue is acute, to test them before they are used safely anywhere else. If this is the case it is a risk to valuable human life. The Church can easily dispel this fear by ensuring the honest provenance of the means of family planning. But if she continues to "sit on the fence" and merely proclaim the negative and immoral results of contraceptives, the faithful may be tempted to regard the Church as nothing but negative and unconcerned with the totality of their lives.

III Models for Pastoral Action

1 *General Policy*

The nations of Africa derive pride and prestige from their population sizes. How often we hear or read of leaders glorying in a following of "the entire so many million" citizens! The general point of view expressed is that a populous country is, at least potentially, a prosperous one; a high population is a guarantee of strength and security, autonomy and independence. Depopulation or limiting the population growth is a serious and devilish manœuvre to weaken and eventually expose the country to defeat and exploitation by foreigners. In countries of Africa with whites controlling the government this is a common belief held by the black indigenous people.

At the family level, we noted earlier, a numerous progeny was a blessing of God in traditional society. The Mityana survey of the project proved that Christianity, far from discouraging these traditional ideals, did actually enhance them. The survey, which covered a heavily Christianized area in Uganda interviewed 716 Christian married men and 767 women. 88% of the men, and 82% of the women interviewed were of the view that it was a Christian parental duty to have as many children as possible. Among the reasons given were: "What God gives cannot be rejected", "the country needs the children", and "many children mean rising from the dead".[18]

This is the background of our Christian action on population growth and responsible parenthood. We must, to a great extent, dismantle the national, ethnic, and family attitudes to the grandeur of huge populations and big family sizes. And in humility, we, too, have to undo our teaching that is now a danger to our adherents; the duty to multiply and fill the earth has to be countered with the duty to improve the quality of life in our families and nations.

Does the quality of life necessarily imply forgoing the traditional community ideals that included the extended family members? If it does, then the Church in Africa is in a dilemma: either to encourage the quality of family life or to promote the solidarity, generosity and sociability so characteristic of traditional community life. The cry both from within and without the churches of Africa is to preserve the African values of the family community. Will circumstances permit the marriage between the ideal of the family community and the limitation of family size?

Christian families should be helped to face this dilemma. Most married couples today find themselves at the cross-roads with the older members of the family demanding conformity to the more traditional ways, and the couple aspiring to modern ways, supported by the grim realities of the situation. We who represent the Church have the task of reconciling the two positions. We should be prepared to listen to the problems, avoiding paternalism and patronizing attitudes; each case will have to be considered on its own merits, helping the family to weigh their points of view. Of course, any Christian pastoral action assumes the personal trust and confidence of the clients. The churches' concern and involvement in the multi-dimensional problem of population will place them in a trusted position for their pastoral voice to be heard and to receive a positive response.

If we agree that the churches of Africa have a duty and a responsibility in the population issue, we should now go on to explore the ways and means at our disposal for exercising that duty and responsibility. What openings exist for our contribution, influence and innovation? We have all along observed the multi-dimensional character of the population question, and the following subject headings seem to stand out as the most prominent areas of operation: Economic conditions, social attitudes and conditions, education in institutions and elsewhere, medical and health services. Our different churches have already, with varying degrees of emphasis, been involved in all the above-mentioned fields; in many countries of Africa the churches pioneered these services to the people as part of the missionary drive.

2   Economic Conditions

The poorer people have been observed to be less responsive to efforts to limit the size of their families[19] than those enjoying better economic conditions. A church, or a given parish, may launch a project to try to better the conditions of her members; by providing skills, jobs, experimental farms and workshops, co-operative projects and marketing. However, greater achievements would come through eliciting the co-operation of national development and welfare agencies. The efforts or projects of any parish or church should not be limited to her members only. It should be open and for the good and the welfare of all in the area.

For some churches this may mean going into an area regarded as profane and too "this-worldly". This is what the incarnation of Christ means in modern world; for He did not hold on to His divine right of holiness and fellowship with God, He made Himself nothing, becoming like a slave.[20] The salvation of the world is the result of the Holy accepting to be involved with the secular and profane.

3 *Educational Action*

Although there has been a gradual separation of school education from improved socio-economic conditions, and education is no longer the preserve of the wealthy, the expectations and prejudices still persist. Productive education is currently being emphasized, as observed in the preferential treatment given to scientific and technological studies. "Educating people where they are" is recommended as a way of introducing or improving knowledge. It will become increasingly necessary to adopt the concept of education differentiated from schooling and institutionalized learning.

It is in this widened concept of education that the churches now need to plan their pastoral action. An education that will equip people to aspire to a qualitative life, whether they have had extensive institutional education or not. The quality of life, enhanced by such factors as responsible parenthood and better socio-economic, and medical conditions, can be fairly shared without necessarily having had a school experience of many years. The following areas are some of the subjects that could be covered in this broadened view of education for all, and which, we suggest, are within the scope of church programmes:

(a) Rural or urban health, including home lay-out, protection of water supply, etc.
(b) Child and adult nutrition
(c) Literacy
(d) The beginning and growth of human life
(e) Social and economic change, with concomitant factors
(f) Agricultural production and marketing
(g) The use of land and other resources
(h) Home financial management
(i) What makes the quality of life.

These are a few suggestions to indicate to the churches the diverse fields for action in relation to the population issue.

In educational institutions that still respect the Church as a teacher of truth, or in those that are owned by the churches, the same material could be made part of the school, college or seminary programme. At each level of institutional education the course can be adapted to the degree of understanding. Whether it is a Baptism or Confirmation class, a secondary school group or a theological ordinands' class, it is Responsible Parenthood that is to be stressed. An earlier report on this topic described this responsibility as requiring the discipline of every department of life; character, marriage relationships, work, financial expenditure, leisure and spiritual life. "Without the teaching of these, and every help and encouragement in the practice of them, the advocating of family planning as a cure for social and economic difficulties would be but cynical manipulation of people, in the innermost recesses of their lives, for another and inadequate end."[21]

More material for the churches' education action will be found in the following sections on the social and medical models of action. It will require, however, the widening of the Churches' gates to receive, in the Schools, theological colleges and seminaries, in the parishes and village churches, teaching about wider aspects of life than hitherto accommodated. Are we ready for it?

4 *Social Conditions and Attitudes*

Africa is undergoing rapid social change, much faster than has been the case in the so-called developed countries. In the lower-income groups of Africa, the changes often aggravate the problem of population growth because of the people's tendency to have large families. We have already recommended economic action so that the apparent security in a numerous progeny can be minimized. However, we also note that the altered, social status of women in society in Africa is also gradually favouring planned and controlled parenthood. The working mother and her role in society call for special attention, and a reconsideration of the African traditional view of motherhood and of woman. The bid to liberate woman from her long accepted kitchen chores, so that she can play her part in public affairs alongside man, is making great strides in Africa. Bishop John Taylor has described this movement, in another context,[22] as a process of humanization.

Through the education programme, the churches are called upon to acknowledge the evolving status of woman in society, with her tremendous potential for the enrichment of the community and Church. It will be necessary for the leaders of our churches to help men to adjust to this process. The counselling before marriage, and baptism, and the confirmation classes, discussion and seminar groups—and even the pulpit—can be used for this purpose.

Attitudes towards a numerous progeny are gradually giving way in the higher-income group. The Church needs, however, to safeguard the duty of having children which is entrusted to all who marry, and it is therefore recommended (some would say: demanded) that a couple should never intend to have no children at all. To be without children must be viewed as a regrettable, temporary expedient, or misfortune permitted by God. Family planning methods would be abused if they were to be used to stop procreation totally.

5 Medical and Health Services

This last aspect of the churches' Christian action on population growth and responsible parenthood, is the basis of those that have gone before. The churches of Africa are still required to provide and promote adequate health and medical services. Medical and health services have a double purpose in relation to the population question. The services promote the welfare of society as a whole by preventing and curing diseases, and in lengthening the expectation of life. Antenatal and maternity care ensure the safety of pregnancy and the survival of the children who are born. Infant mortality which encourages a large number of births is checked. The second purpose is the link between the medical and health servies on the one hand and the teaching of family planning methods. Family planning clinics, or centres can be associated with these services.

We would like to go on and review what could be done in the area of family-planning methods. It is important to realize that the churches' attitude has been either negative or unconcerned, and still is, in many cases. African governments are not unanimous about the usefulness of controlling population growth. We would like to recommend that the churches weigh the prevailing opinion of both the government and Christians. It is necessary to become involved in, or to open discussions on, family planning methods and their availability to the public. International family planning organizations often ignore the moral implications of their activity. In a recent Population Report,[23] it was asserted that contraceptive distribution was now to be diversified by taking supplies to villages and households, without clinical procedures or the advice of qualified medical personnel. The object of extending family planning services and supplies beyond the clinics is to bring them directly into the daily lives of the people, and to make them easily available to everyone. The report poses the question: Who can safely be entrusted with the supervision of these supplies?

The meetings of CROMIA rejected the indiscriminate distribution of contraceptives because of the possible misuse for pre-marital and extra-marital sexual activity, with the consequent risk of gross immorality and the spread of venereal diseases, but in Pakistan, for example, supplies of contraceptives are made under government auspices and are subsidized and sold in village shops and from door-to-door. "The buyer pays only $2\frac{1}{2}$ cents (US) for a cycle of pills or a dozen condoms."[24] This is the magnitude of the challenge to the churches; if open and cheap "supplies" have not reached our countries, and are not yet indiscriminately distributed, this may be the time to take positive precautions and to get involved in the following ways:

(a) Hold meetings, discussions and seminars on planned parenthood in the parish or church centre.
(b) Include family size, birth control and spacing methods in marriage counselling; and advice or personal presence of a physician could be an added advantage.
(c) Encourage young people, preparing for marriage, to explore and freely discuss reproduction and family life, to help them form positive Christian attitudes towards sex, reproduction and family life.
(d) Seek to influence or control the methods and distribution of contraceptive supplies.
(e) Endeavour to help Christians realize their moral and divine responsibilities in population growth and the exercise of parenthood.

References: Chapter Seven

1 AACC Consultation on "The Challenges of Family Education in Africa in the 70s", 1972, Yaoundé, Part II, p. 60.

2 Kibirige, 1974.

3 Joinet, B., *The Ideal Husband*, Gaba Pastoral Paper No. 11, pp. 4–5.

4 The degree of autonomy has to be qualified because of the African traditional interdependence between relations and neighbours.

5 Kasaka, 1972, CROMIA/14, p. 3.

6 United Nations *Demographic Year Book*, 1974 edition; Population Bureau Inc., *World Population Data Sheet,*, 1972.

7 Aquina, 1975, I, p. 97.

8 Adamson, P., *A Population Policy and a Development Policy, News Sheet of the RCBC*, July 20th, 1974.

9 The same argument is advanced by Carolyn White in her article: "The Politico–Legal Status of Women in Uganda", in *Presence*, Vol. VI, No. 1, 1973, p. 26.

10 *New Internationalist*, September 1974, p. 1.

11 Kanyikwa, 1974.

12 Shorter, 1974a, p. 8.

13 Molnos, A., *Cultural Source Materials for Population Planning in East Africa* (Vols. 1–4), Nairobi 1972.

14 Hehir, J. B., "Church and Population: A strategy", in *Theological Studies*, March 1974, Vol. 35, No. 1, p. 81.

15 Romans 8:18–25.

16 "Pastoral Directive on Family Planning" (February 1973), *AFER*, Vol. XVI, 1974, No. 3, p. 347.

17 *Statement of the Indonesian Bishops' Conference* (August 1973) in *AFER*, Vol. XVI, 1974, No. 3, p. 349.

18 Shorter, 1973b, CROMIA/22, p. 7.

19 Aquina, cf. Shorter, 1975d; CROMIA/31, p. 11 agrees with Shorter, 1974a, p. 7.

20 Adapted from Phillipians 2:7.

21 Report of the *All Africa Seminar on Christian Home and Family Life*, AACC, June 1963, Mindolo/Geneva, p. 29.

22 This was in a debate of the Church of England General Synod on the Ordination of Women to the Priesthood; reported by *Church Times*, July 11th, 1975, London, p. 5.

23 "Population Reports by Family Planning Programmes". Department of Medical and Public Affairs, The George Washington University Medical Center, N.W. Washington, D.C. (Series J, No. 5, July 1975), p. J–69.

24 *Ibid.*, p. J–69.

Chapter 8

Marriage and Community

I Case Material

1 *The Communitarian Character of African Customary Marriage*
There have been various indications in the foregoing chapters that African customary marriage was not a private contract between two individuals but an alliance between two family communities or lineages. Harry Makubire from South Africa quotes an address given by a Zulu pastor to a pair of newly-weds, Paul and Mapule.[1]

Mapule, you should bear in mind that though you are married in church, we Africans, according to our custom and tradition (consider) that you are married not to your husband Paul, but to his family. That means you have to identify completely with all his relatives, look after them, care for them, go out of your way to make them happy. If you do that, you will have no cause for regret. You, Paul, will have to do likewise with Mapule's relatives. Her people are your people and *vice versa*. Both of you will notice that old people in the community will tend to visit you, even for a brief moment, not necessarily to drink tea, but to show their interest in your welfare.

In fact, the family community was the fundamental element of the African, his basic sphere of action, through which he became integrated with the larger, human community. Without necessarily adopting a familistic attitude, he acted always from within the sphere of the family. In marrying his wife, he accepted responsibilities towards another family, and she likewise.

The family community, or lineage, was clearly delineated by a classificatory kinship terminology, by the strict prohibition of incest within a wide circle of kinsfolk, by the rule of exogamy (marrying outside one's family or clan), and by the perpetuation of family and clan names. It was also identified with reference to remembered common ancestors, and both Harry Makubire and Nicodemus Kirima, in their contributions to our discussions, laid heavy stress on the traditional belief that the ancestors formed part of the living community.[2] There being a vital communion between the living and the remembered dead, the latter had to be taken into account on numerous social occasions, not least of all, on the occasion of marriage. Within the family community there was a hierarchy of relationships, privileges and duties. There was, above all, an intense spirit of solidarity, and the individual family member could count on the moral and material support of his family community whenever he was in need. On innumerable social and ritual occasions the family community acted together as a unit, and, even if the households of which it was composed were ordinarily dispersed, its members acted in accordance with rigid principles of co-operation and co-responsibility. It was especially in the vital area of marriage and child-rearing that the family, as a community, exercised its control. These things affected the growth and development of the family and its social relations with other family communities in society as a whole.

Another set of principles existed to regulate the relationships between families joined by a marriage alliance. Social behaviour towards one's in-laws was governed by prohibitions and customs of avoidance designed to minimize hostility and facilitate the integration of two families. Kirima cites Kikuyu (Kenya) rituals of unity and reconciliation, as well as joking relationships which acted as steam-valve for tensions and ambiguities.[3]

Marriage preparation was another community interest. As John Mutiso Mbinda of Kenya points out, citing the example of the Akamba people, marriage was of such importance to society as a whole that the whole local community participated in preparing young people for marriage.[4] Not only were there specially designated categories of elder relatives within the family community itself, grandparents, aunts and the like, who prepared candidates for marriage both remotely and proxi-mately, but puberty and initiation rites were often organized for either or both sexes by the whole local community. Initiation very often took the form of a collective exercise in which instruction was given to large groups of young people from different families and the whole community took part in the collective rituals. The sponsoring families, however, were often more closely involved than other members of the community. In some ethnic groups initiation held marriage explicitly in view and the main purpose of the instructions, physical operation or manipulation, and rituals was to initiate the youngsters into the life of married people. However, even when the process had a more general purpose of initiating young people into adult membership of the tribe, marriage was an important aspect of it. In some cases puberty rituals were less of an initiation or rite of passage from a state of childhood to a state of maturity, than a medical and/or magical procedure to ensure the health and fertility of those about to be married. This was the case, Patrick Whooley assures us, of the girls' initiation among the Xhosa of South Africa.[5] For Xhosa boys, initiation was an important social event, bringing about a profound change in the conduct of the initiates. For girls the change occurred within the first years of marriage itself, rather than in the puberty rituals. In any case, however it was effected, boys and girls were initiated into community life and responsibilities, both those of the family community and of the wider, local community.

The whole community celebrated the marriage rituals, and these, in varying ways, reflected the communitarian character of customary marriage at family and local community level. Customary marriage was effected by a ritual process, lasting weeks, months and even years. It took the form of a series of rites, negotiations, feasts and gift exchanges. Very important in patrilineal societies was the payment of bridewealth, a specified amount of livestock or other goods collected on a community basis within the family of the bridegroom and distributed on a community basis within the family of the bride. In many pastoralist societies, where large herds of animals were kept, the collection and distribution of bridewealth overlapped the confines of the family communities involved in the marriage and so ensured an even wider interest in the alliance. The payment of bridewealth had many functions, social, religious and economic, but, where it operated in its traditional form, unaffected by the exigencies and abuses of a money economy, it certainly enhanced the communitarian character of marriage. There was even a symbolic community value in keeping large herds of cattle, since these were seen as a kind of symbolic, "parallel family", the prosperity and size of which reflected the human family's own prosperity and prospects.

Numerous rituals and exchanges accompanied the marriage negotiations, and, as Kirima points out, in some cases the prospective marriage partners were scarcely involved in the arrangements, meeting face to face only at a comparatively late stage in the process.[6] In some cases, the symbolic capture of the bride or a mock battle between members of the two families emphasized the boundaries and even the potential hostility between them. These symbolic actions were an indication of the finality of the alliance and of the bride's exchange of one family for another. In other societies the stress was laid on the character of the bride as gift, the most precious gift one family could give to another—the gift of a potential mother of their children. The bride was handed over by her brother or other relatives to her new husband. Great attention was paid to the ritual washing, anointing and adornment of the bride, as well as to symbols of her virginity and fertility. The veiling and ceremonial unveiling of the bride were also sometimes related to these ideas.

In some marriage rites the aspect of transition was emphasized, especially the transition of the bride, in a patrilineal situation, from one family to another. There might have been a procession in which the bride was carried or led step by step to the bridegroom's house, the bridegroom being confronted with obstacles, or being made to pay forfeits on the way. In other societies the merging of the two family communities was enacted, for example by the members of both families sitting on each other's knees.[7] Ritual objects carried or worn by the partners, or their relatives, such as spears, arrows, shells or different kinds of fruit symbolized the sex organs, sexual activity and the birth of many children. Then there was the formal instruction and advice offered to both partners and their initiation into their new duties. The latter were often dramatized.

The consummation of the marriage, or first coming together of the man and woman as husband and wife was also often ritualized. In some tribes a temporary hut of grass was built for the first marital act, and the couple slept there for some weeks. In other cases the couple slept together in the sleeping chamber of an ordinary dwelling hut. Often it was necessary to have a witness, if not in the actual sleeping chamber itself, at least in the next room. The witness, usually an older woman, would then testify that the act had been completed. In some traditions there was a ceremonial "encounter" beforehand between the bride and bridegroom, and the formal introduction of the partners to the members of each other's families. Dancing was also an important element in the ceremonial of marriage and the dances and their accompanying songs expressed the expectations of the community in respect of the marriage. Wedding dances were joyous and uninhibited, sometimes miming love-making and copulation.

Feasting, drinking and the exchange of gifts were ubiquitous in marriage celebrations; and also frequent was the offering of sacrifice to the ancestors of the lineage who were deemed to share in the joy of the feast, and to witness the event that was taking place. Often there was a whole succession of feasts, of visits and return visits by members of the two families and the newly-weds, themselves. Then, in some ethnic groups, there would be bride-service, according to which the bridegroom would work, build, hunt or cultivate for the parents of his bride for months or even years after the marriage.

It is difficult in a few pages to do justice to the complexity and variety of African customary marriage celebrations. Each ethnic group had its own traditions and its own symbolism, although many beliefs, values and practices concerning marriage were remarkably widespread, and the same or similar themes recur in many different places. As an example of one set of marriage rites, we give the description by Nicodemus Kirima of the way the Kikuyu (Gikuyu) of Kenya celebrate marriage.

Among the Gikuyu the individual was left free to choose his or her marriage partner. The individual (boy) began by discussing his secret decision to marry a girl with his friends. These friends would then accompany the boy to the girl's home to make their suggestion to the girl.

The next step is taken by the parents of the boy. These come officially to visit the parents of the girl with their son's proposal. Then more people are called in. These are friends of the two families. All take part in a short ceremony of prayer for the future unity and prosperity of the two families. When this is done the boy's parents collect the bridewealth which is contributed by the whole extended family. When enough bridewealth has been given to the girl's family, a ceremony of official engagement takes place. At this ceremony a goat is killed, and the pouring of the "blood of unity" takes place. All the relatives gather at the girl's homestead, and there is eating, drinking and merry-making.

All of this announces to the community that the girl is now officially engaged. Parents and relatives of both sides have a chance now to meet one another and get to know each other. It also marks the agreement on how much bridewealth must be paid. From then on, the interests of the two families and clans are closely associated.

The next ceremony is the obtaining of the official consent of the girl. A goat is killed and many people come to participate in the ceremony and the feasting and dancing. This means that the girl is blessed and is given away to the boy's clan by her parents in the company, and with the agreement, of the whole clan.

Finally, the boy, having prepared a home for his bride, informs his family which meets in council. On an agreed date, the female members of the family go and look for the girl and bring her with them to the boy's new home amid a scene of staged abduction and a mock fight between female relatives of both boy and girl. The girl's agemates also come to express their sorrow at having lost a companion. The new bride is anointed with lamb's fat to mark her adoption into the new clan. She is now a full member of her husband's family.[8]

The local community of neighbourhood and village participated at every stage of the marriage process. Not only did they share in the feasts and the dances, but they gave public testimony to what was going on. By their participation they gave their assent to the marriage, and expressed their expectations concerning it. They were far from passive witnesses. Together with the family, they joined in admonishing and instructing the newly-weds, in blessing and anointing them, in shouting their approval at the speeches of others, in remembering details of the rites to be performed and making sure that all was done as it should be. As Mutiso Mbinda points out, community interest in the marriage was not restricted to the marriage rites them-selves.[9] Even after the wedding, women in the village kept an eye on the young couple, especially to see if the wife became pregnant. Older members of the community visited them and offered advice, and their approval or disapproval exerted considerable moral and social pressure on them. There can be no doubt at all that the stability of marriage institutions in traditional Africa depended on the interest and support of the community and on the control which the community exercised over its members.

2   African Customary Marriage in Social Change

Traditional African society was unitary and homogeneous. The language, culture, beliefs, values and social institutions of the ethnic group were reduplicated in innumerable local, village communities. The basic unit of these communities was the family. Most local communities engaged in settled or shifting cultivation, and mobility between communities was at a minimum. These communities were largely self-sufficient, and the individual was wholly absorbed by them. The community catered for every aspect and department of the individual's life, without much need for rationalization or planning. Alternative courses of action were not available and the community was virtually ignorant of everything except its own socio-cultural inheritance. In these circumstances, there was no room for a change, let alone a reversal of social roles.

Modern Africa is witnessing a violent and far-reaching process of social change. The structures of the old society are being changed, but changed in such a way that there is an enlargement of scale in social relationships. Individuals are no longer tied down to self-sufficient, homogeneous village communities. Education, trade, economics, travel have forced them to broaden their horizons. African society is no longer unitary and homogeneous, but pluralistic. It is not the primary group that is important, but the interaction between groups. Differing cultures, beliefs and value-systems jostle one another and influence one another in this modern, changing situation. People associate in a more transient way, at a more superficial level, and secondary groupings which absorb only a segment of the individual's life have begun to appear. The individual is faced with alternative courses of action, even contradictions, and he is tempted to see his life as a purely functional and transient experience.

This process, of course, affects primarily the individuals who manage, through education or economic opportunity, to rise above their own traditional environment, but those who do not have these resources are also influenced by what is going on. The structures of traditional society are not only weakened in themselves, but are now interacting with larger-scale structures. They no longer have the strength and cohesion they had in the past, and they are no longer guarantees of social stability. Formerly, village society, and the family communities of which it was composed, were not just simply the individual's point of integration with the world at large; they *were* the individual's "world". Now the traditional institutions of village and family appear woefully inadequate to help the individual cope with modern problems of transience, mobility and pluralism. Those who still rely exclusively upon them are in danger of forming a marginal stratum of society. They are disorientated—at a loss in the modern world.

We have already noted in the first chapter that marriage by elopment, or "self-contracted marriage", as Thomas and Chisanga call it, is increasingly replacing marriage by negotiation. Although there are some rural areas where the kinship system, initiation rites and celebration of marriage remain virtually unchanged from the past, there are very few places where marriage customs are not affected in some way by social change. Patrick Whooley describes a rural area of southern Africa which has apparently undergone little change. Yet even here the influence of urban culture can be seen in those communities which are within easier access of the towns. There the traditional system is weakening, if it is not entirely disrupted.[10]

Urban culture is not the only, or even the main, factor in the break-up of the old system, and the character of rural society has changed largely for other reasons. Not only is there an ideological gap between the generations, there are also the problems of geographical distance and economic disparity. Njelu Kasaka describes the tensions that exist in the *ujamaa* villages and resettlement areas of Tanzania where the settlers live and work far away from their homeland and lineage, and who dispose of considerably more monied wealth, as well as of a wider knowledge of affairs, than their parents at home.[11] In this situation it is difficult for the lineage to perform its functions and to exercise control over the marriages of its members. Furthermore, there is the conflict between the family community at home and the newly adopted community of the settler. Sister Aquina noted that on the tea-estates in eastern Rhodesia marriage by elopement had increased sharply since the 1960s, and that even in some of the tribal trustlands marriages by elopement were outnumbering negotiated marriages in spite of the pressure of both church and state in favour of the latter type of marriage.[12]

The growth of a money economy and the need for cash have also interfered with the rights and obligations of the family community. When bridewealth is demanded in cash, it becomes more difficult to collect, as well as more difficult to distribute. More and more it becomes a burden placed on the shoulders of the bridegroom alone, and the prerequisite of the bride's father alone. Moreover, economic inflation affects societies with a traditionally high bridewealth, making an early marriage more difficult and causing the negotiations to be long and protracted. It is tempting for young people to bypass the negotiations, or to force them to a conclusion by elopement.

Mutual support and family solidarity are also jeopardized by modern economic conditions. The late Michel Kayoya, the Burundi poet, describes their effects:

Then the happy and care-free relationships of yesterday become a burden—
On the one hand, a man cannot stop living like an African,
He cannot prevent his brother entering his house and eating his food,
He cannot close his house to those good neighbours, so full of laughter and gay conversation which is a sign of life, neighbours who share their drink together, a necessary accompaniment of conversation.
He cannot fix a time for those innumerable cousins and uncles who know nothing of working hours. . . .[13]

In modern circumstances customary marriage ceremonies, when they are performed, are often conducted in an impoverished and attenuated fashion. If the couple are migrants, away from home, there is the added problem of choosing between the family community and the new work-community. Often both have to be satisfied with separate celebrations. Thomas and Chisanga offer examples from Kitwe town in Zambia.[14] Although kinship ties are resilient in Kitwe and people turn to their relatives in and out of town for choosing partners and arranging marriages, it remains difficult to fulfil the customary obligations. The traditional girls' initiation rite of the Bemba tribe—the most numerous ethnic group in Kitwe—was called *chisungu*. It consisted of various rituals to ensure the girl's fertility, beauty and purification, as well as in instruction in the conduct of a married woman. When marriage was finally arranged the bridegroom was obliged to pay a *chisungu* payment for the right to marry a virgin. In Kitwe today, the *chisugu* payment is made upon the girl's first marriage, but there are no tests to see whether she is a virgin or not. Since many marriages take place without the consent of the girl's parents, instruction is frequently omitted. When it is given, instead of a training period that includes a seclusion lasting from one week to three months, a concentrated instruction is given just before the legal marriage ceremony in church, court or office. Sometimes bride and groom sleep together before the official ceremony and selected elders give instruction afterwards. The problem of housing in Kitwe is acute, and houses are only allocated to families by the Council or the Mine when the couple can prove that they both consent to the marriage and that certain relatives of the female have given their consent. Traditionally, consent was given by the maternal uncle, but nowadays the father or another relative may give the required consent. It is interesting that couples who have contracted marriage in town tend to be more assiduous about visits to the homeland, than couples who married at home and then moved to the town. Thomas and Chisanga suggest that those who marry in town feel a greater need to reassure their relatives of their loyalty to the family community.[15]

The city of Nairobi in Kenya presents a comparable picture in many ways. James Holway discusses the dilemma faced by the town dwellers in deciding where to celebrate their marriage.[16] Whether the actual wedding ceremony is performed in the city or the country, there will probably be a reception in Nairobi and another at home, and if the bride and groom come from different villages, there may be three receptions in all. It is interesting to note that with the decline in parental participation in the choice of marriage partners, parents tend to compensate by taking a more active part in the arrangements for the reception.

Hans Boerakker, in his study of marriage in eastern Uganda, believes that with the passing of control over marriage from the parental to the younger generation, a fundamental change has taken place in the nature of African customary marriage.[17] He argues that in the past the processual aspect of customary marriage applied mainly to proximate marriage preparation, and that the whole series of events led up to a clear stage at which these preparations culminated in a definitive contract which could not be dissolved. Today, as a result of self-contracted or elopement marriages, the preparation is curtailed, if it exists at all, and it is the contract or central moment of the marriage which is drawn out or indefinitely postponed. This development has had the effect of obscuring the true nature and central moment of customary marriage. It must be added, however, that Boerakker is not pessimistic about the situation. He is unwilling to say whether customary marriage in the past was better than it is now. To say that marriages were more stable in the past is not to say that they were accompanied by a greater freedom and love, and, as he drily remarks, a stable marriage in which husband and wife live in daily hatred is not the Christian ideal. Boerakker is convinced that customary marriage is slowly becoming better equipped to deal with modern life, and that it has enough resilience to cope with the forces of modern change. Just as many traditional African rituals have become streamlined to fit a modern, urban context and have been given new and wider areas of application, so the traditional celebration of marriage may also adapt itself to the demands of modern living. The tensions which we now observe are not just symptoms of the break-up of an old social order, they are the birth-pangs of a new, more complex and more sophisticated social order. The question that we must now ask is: What role are the churches playing in the development of this new social order and in the strengthening of the human institution of marriage?

3   *The Irrelevance of Church Marriage*
In some areas the churches took up a hostile attitude to African customary marriage and fought a long and unsuccessful battle against it. An example of this is provided by the area of southern African studied by Patrick Whooley.[18] There, the question at issue was that of the bride's free consent, a strong preoccupation of white missionaries and legislators. In view of this missionary antagonism it is not surprising that only a tiny percentage of Christians get married in church in the first instance, and that most church marriages are a *post factum* "patching up".

In other areas the churches tolerated customary marriage celebrations while insisting on the performance of church marriage. An example of such a situation is the area of eastern Uganda studied by Hans Boerakker.[19] There, the two forms of marriage were uneasy bedfellows until customary marriage itself entered into a decline in about 1940. We have already discussed the reluctance of African couples in many areas to get married in church, but there is plenty of evidence that when they do agree to a church marriage, whatever the church's attitude to customary marriage, the ceremony in church holds very little meaning for those who take part. The real celebration of marriage is the social celebration in the community itself, not the ritual conducted by the priest or pastor in the church building. The church ceremony is conducted in unimpressive circumstances before a handful of people, and it apparently bears no relation to the customary celebration which follows it. Quite clearly, the majority of African Christians regard the church marriage ceremony as a meaningless preliminary which must be gone through in order not to incur the displeasure of the church authorities. One of the authors well remembers officiating at the wedding of a Nigerian couple in Britain. After the church ceremony, the uncle of the bride, who had travelled from West Africa to be present at the ceremony, declared at the reception that the church ceremony was valid because the couple had previously gone through a customary ceremony in his hotel room, and all the traditional requirements of the tribe had been fulfilled!

The contrast between church ceremony and customary celebration is striking. Nobody in the local community is likely to miss a customary marriage. Relatives and friends travel immense distances in order to be present. Large amounts of refreshments are provided and drinking and dancing go on until late in the night. There can be no doubt whatever of the social importance which people attach to a customary wedding.

Even in town where church weddings are more common than in the rural areas the church ceremony is insignificant beside the social trappings that surround and follow it. In Kampala City, Uganda, town weddings achieve a degree of sophistication rarely found elsewhere. A white wedding with a number of bridesmaids and pages in specially designed costumes is the height of fashion. Before the church ceremony, the wedding party usually gathers at the photographer's shop to pose for the group photograph which will appear in the national and local newspapers. They then proceed in hired or borrowed cars to the church. Although weddings usually take place on a Saturday afternoon, relatively few people manage to be present in church and there is little or no active participation by the congregation in what is going on. In the Roman Catholic Nuptial Mass practically nobody except the bride and bridegroom receives Communion. Outside the church there is confetti, and a long time is spent taking group photographs. Then a procession of cars forms for the journey to the reception hall. Sometimes there is a veritable motorcade of twenty or thirty cars, with the bridal car adorned with flowers and streamers and sometimes flanked by motor-cycle outriders.

The reception at a Kampala wedding may be held at a hotel, in one of the University halls of residence, in the hall of a school or institute or in the City's indoor stadium. The observer forms the impression that the reception is the central moment of the wedding celebrations. Crowds of people gather for it, and some members of the families involved are busy all day at the place of the reception and do not have an opportunity to attend the church ceremony. A dance band from one of the city's night clubs is usually in attendance, and to the strains of "Here comes the bride" and to the plaudits of the crowd, the bridal couple enter the reception hall with a solemnity far exceeding their entry into the church an hour or so before. The families of bride and bridegroom are usually seated in two blocks of chairs facing one another in the centre of the hall. The two groups are tenuously connected by a table in the centre, at which are seated the bride and bridegroom, the best man, the master of ceremonies and the chief bridesmaid. A great many speeches are made and eating, drinking and dancing continue into the evening. An important highlight of the proceedings is the cutting of the wedding cake. If he is present, the priest or pastor who officiated at the church wedding may be called upon to bless the cake with a prayer before it is cut and distributed. Another important moment is when the bridal couple themselves take to the dance floor. Everything that happens in the reception has an air of stiffness and formality, and one has the impression that one is taking part in a solemn ritual feast, in which the trappings of a western wedding have been magnified and endowed with a new symbolic significance deriving from African, rather than western, traditions. The formal reception is followed usually by a less formal gathering at the bridegroom's house where the drinking of local beer and the performance of traditional dances continue far into the night. As in the case of the Soweto wedding described by Martin Peskin and cited in the first chapter, the church ceremony is only one element in a whole complex of events and rituals which cater for different levels or aspects of urban social life in Africa.

In the Copperbelt town of Kitwe, Zambia, Thomas and Chisanga found that, even among active church members, there were very few public marriages in church.[20] One large United Church of Zambia congregation of about 500 members had had only seven church weddings in the past nine years. This was in spite of the fact that a large proportion of respondents claimed full membership of their respective churches and even a regular weekly attendance at church. Kitwe clearly possesses active church congregations among which a majority of members enjoy stable marriages characterized by fidelity and devotedness. Yet the fact remains; church marriages are the exception rather than the rule. Church weddings in Kitwe can be as expensive as in Kampala, and yet expense did not loom large in the minds of those opposed to church marriage. The impression conveyed by the replies which Thomas and Chisanga have cited is that Christians simply do not appreciate the relevance of church marriage to the Christian life. As a young woman in the Evangelical church remarked: "Christianity does not mean marrying in church". For most people there is nothing particularly Christian about the white dress, the bridesmaids, bands and expensive clothes. The church ceremony itself has been swallowed up in social paraphernalia that are merely a modernized version of the customary social celebration. For most Christians in Kitwe, this form of marriage celebration, besides being too expensive, is still regarded as something foreign, and the authors of the Kitwe study disagree strongly with Adrian Hastings' equation of church wedding and Christian marriage. In their eyes this equation is simply "folly".

James Holway, writing about Nairobi City, Kenya, makes the point that African townsmen may be attracted to a church community because the churches offer an experience of welcome familiarity.[21] This is particularly the case where the mission activity of a church was restricted to a particular ethnic group and where religious affiliation and ethnicity coincide. Yet, in spite of this feeling of "being at home" in the urban church congregation, it does not seem that the various churches (apart from some African Independent churches) have succeeded in building up a spirit of community that can replace the local community of the traditional rural village. In Chapter Two we already noted the relative inability of the churches to cope with the tensions and problems of married people. Although the inner core of the church congregation exercises an influence upon active members, and marriage instruction and guidance is offered through such bodies as church women's groups, Thomas and Chisanga found in Kitwe that opportunities for lay leadership in the church communities were few. They also noted that the success or failure of the churches in coping with the problems of Christian marriage depended to a large extent on the personal insight and spirit of understanding of church leaders.[22] In the opinion of Holway, the clergy of Nairobi (Kenya) compare unfavourably with trained welfare workers. Ecclesiastical training and resources cannot cope with all the problems raised by marriage and family life in the city, and what is more, Christianity itself is divided into a "multiplicity of non-co-operating denominations". A rapidly growing population keeps Nairobi churches full and keeps priests and pastors busy without their needing to look for more work. Yet the churches' pastoral work in Nairobi is basically passive and the initiative lies, not with church leaders, but with the needy individual who approaches his pastor on an *ad hoc* basis.[23] While the towns obviously pose a more difficult pastoral problem than the rural areas, it must not be thought that the churches are very much more successful in influencing marriage institutions through community-building in the country than in the town. As Marie-France Perrin-Jassy has observed, most churches have a vertical or hierarchical organization that is both unfamiliar and inflexible in the local community situation, and western marriage liturgy—as it now stands—is, in her opinion, completely incompatible with the celebration of customary marriage.[24]

Part of the problem is undoubtedly concerned with the place of the Christian celebration—the church building. Our discussions revealed a very widespread reluctance on the part of pastors to take the marriage ceremony out of the church building, and this possibly has something to do with the African's appreciation of sacred space. A marriage is hallowed in the eyes of many African pastors by the fact that it is celebrated in a consecrated building. On the other hand, it has already been demonstrated that this idea is not widely shared by members of their congregations, and it is, in any case, of doubtful theological value. Unfortunately, even where pastors and church authorities are prepared to celebrate a Christian wedding elsewhere than in the church building, e.g. at the home of the bridegroom, Civil Law places obstacles in the way. Brendan Conway notes that in most of the countries studied the place of marriage celebration must be licensed or there is a legal restriction of the statutory celebration to recognized places of worship.[25] This is true of South Africa, Zambia, Malawi, Kenya, Uganda and Tanzania. It is only in Rhodesia where the marriage officer may use his own discretion as to the place of celebration. This is yet another price that the churches have had to pay for the linkage of church marriage and statutory legislation. It would appear, then, that the churches are not at present playing a very positive role in the strengthening of marriage as a human institution, and the remainder of this chapter must be devoted to suggesting possible courses of action, having, as usual, first established a theological basis for the suggestions that are being made.

II Theological Reflection

1 *The Contemporary Re-emphasis on Community*

Possibly because of the challenges posed by sweeping social change, the Christian churches in the second half of the twentieth century have experienced a rediscovery of human values. Human values—particularly community values—are threatened by a bewildering pluralism and by the transience and superficiality of everyday relationships in a world that lives at a faster pace and on a wider scale. The emphasis has been away from the religious practice of the individual and towards his experience of God in interpersonal relationships; away from the so-called "crowd church" and towards the small Christian community in which the individual Christian can find greater personal fulfilment and relate with others at a deeper and more human level. The Second Vatican Council, and even more so the Fourth Assembly of the World Council of Churches at Uppsala, placed heavy stress on human culture and development. It was recognized that man is, in his innermost nature, a social being, and that, unless he relates to others, he cannot live or develop. Human life is essentially something shared with others.

More important still, Christian revelation is being presented as a phenomenon essentially communitarian. The God, in whose image and likeness mankind has been created, reveals himself as a Trinitarian Community of abiding love. His purpose for mankind, revealed and effected through the life and death of Jesus Christ, is the reconciliation of all men and all things in himself, and the "great commandment" bequeathed by Christ to his followers is the commandment of brotherly love. It is essentially in the local church community that God's loving presence manifests itself and that the Christian participates in the great movement of reconciliation launched

197

by Christ. The local church community is not seen today as simply a cell or subdivision of a larger worldwide communion. Rather, the primary reality of the Church is experienced first and foremost in the local church community, and the starting point for the sharing and interaction that takes place in the worldwide communion is found there.

Closely related to the theology of the community and of reconciliation is that of dialogue. Dialogue presupposes a pluralistic situation, but it also assumes an optimistic outcome for the interaction that takes place between differing views and values. Dialogue starts from the premise that no one and no community possesses a monopoly of the truth. All of mankind, even those who see the world in the light of the Christian revelation, are on a pilgrimage towards an ever greater understanding of the truth. Diaolgue is not the attitude of one who says: "To know the truth you must become like me!" It is the more humble attitude of the one who says: "Let us see how we can help one another to acquire a greater and deeper understanding of the truth!" Dialogue, however, demands a process of self-identification, a clarification of one's own position as a pre-condition for communicating with others. The activity of dialogue is basically a reciprocal communication of meanings in the attempt to see things as others see them, so that all may grow towards a common horizon of truth.

The processes of change which the contemporary world is experiencing must not all be seen in a negative or pessimistic light. There are positive aspects in the situation which are the hopeful foundations of a new social order. These aspects can be reduced to three essential ones: interdependence, congruence and incorporation. Interdependence refers simply to the fact that in the pluralistic, large-scale society of today, there is a greater measure of specialization by individuals and groups, resulting in a greater degree of mutual dependence. Congruence implies that there is an area of concord or agreement between different value-systems, an area that usually expands through interaction and communication. Finally, incorporation means that, although individuals and groups have differing viewpoints and value-systems, there is a degree to which they influence one another and come to accept each other's ideas.

The fruits of dialogue really correspond to those three positive aspects of organizational change. In the sphere of interdependence men come to realize that they are functionally dependent on each other, even though they hold opposing or contradictory views. In the sphere of congruence, they seek always to enlarge the area of their agreement. In the sphere of incorporation, they learn new interests from one another. Dialogue is therefore an act of faith in the possiblity of convergence. The individual who engages in dialogue necessarily does so from within a community, for his own identity depends to a great extent on his membership of, and his personal growth in tension with, a community. However, this has to be a new kind of community. It is no longer possible to be satisfied with a homogeneous, closed community, like the family and village communities of the past. Such a community runs the risk of becoming "privatist" or "particularist"—a "drop-out" community that is irrelevant in the modern world and cut off from the processes of change which are affecting everyone else. The new type of community must be open to, and in dialogue with, all the other communities with which, in the modern situation, it interacts. It must be reconciled to variety and to continual self-renewal. It must be fundamentally flexible, without sacrificing its basic identity. It should not be a barrier to communication, but be itself a category of meaningful interaction. The only other courses open to individuals in the modern world are disorientation and withdrawal, and both are fatal for the Christian Church. Christian evangelization today means the rediscovery or reconstitution of the small community as a means of integration with, and impact on, the world at large.

2   *The Meaning of Christian Community*
The focal point of the Christian Revelation is the "paschal mystery"—the mystery of the passion, death and resurrection of Jesus Christ. A Christian community is necessarily one which, in its daily existence, participates in the mystery of Christ. It has to share in the sacrificial death of Jesus Christ and in the love which inspired it. It must share also in the certainty and joy of the resurrection. How does it do these things? It shares in Christ's handing of himself over into the hands of men by another "handing over" in love. True Christian love consists in the Christian handing himself over in fraternal service of his fellow man. It shares in the joy of the resurrection through an optimism founded on faith and hope in redeemed humanity on

its pilgrimage towards fulfilment in the "Whole Christ". It believes that all its efforts in listening to others and in communicating its own vision to others are worthwhile, that all of this leads to fulfilment in Christ, and that the victory over human failure and malice rests ultimately with him.

The Christian, therefore, does not seek to create a "parallel community" or an "alternative society". His aim, like that of his Master, is incarnation in the natural society in which he lives, the world in which he finds himself. He does not carve out of his experience a "sacred sphere" to which his Christian principles apply, leaving the rest aside as a neutral or secular common denominator that he shares with the rest of men. On the contrary, to the Christian everything is sacred. Every department of his experience and every aspect of his daily life can be seen in the light of the death and resurrection of Christ. The truly Christian community does not cut itself off from society; it acts as an agent of reconciliation among men, a healer of social divisions.

The Christian community draws its strength and impulse from the celebration in its midst of the paschal mystery of Christ. Through word and sacrament Christians take part in Christ's once-for-all, redemptive self-offering and express this worship in their "lives for others". Roman Catholics and Protestants alike have been rediscovering in recent years the centrality of the Eucharist in their worshipping communities. Christian communities are essentially "Eucharistic Communities". This should provide food for thought in African countries where the shortage of ordained ministers makes the celebration of the Eucharist an infrequent occurrence, and where so many Christians in irregular marriage situations are excluded from sharing in the Eucharist.

Finally, the Christian community gives expression to the richness and diversity of the Spirit of Christ, through the varied gifts of its members and through the freedom and initiative that they are encouraged to exercise. Another fact which the churches are coming more and more to realize is that the "vertical" or institutional church does not monopolize all the gifts of the Spirit, and that church order exists to foster these gifts in ordinary church members. Christians must be able to grow in the exercise of their gifts and to feel that they are making a real contribution to the mission of the Church to serve the world—their world.[26]

3 Marriage as a Christian Community of Love

Mankind was created male and female, and one of the lessons of the first chapters of Genesis is that the companionship of man and woman creates the primary form of interpersonal communion, the fundamental community of love. Marriage, and the family that it becomes, is a communion of life and love. It brings the community into being, not only through the procreation of members and through building up alliances within and between human groups, but also through its own life and witness to the paschal mystery of Christ. The family, as we saw in Chapter One, is the "domestic church". The Christian's first experience of community, as well as his first opportunity to contribute to community, are found in the family. But marriage is primarily a secular reality and is the property of the natural, human community. Just as the Church should not seek to create an artificial "parallel" community, but should try to identify itself with what it conceives to be the best interests of the natural community, so it must not seek to create a Christian marriage that is an artificial institution of its own. Marriage is first of all human. It becomes Christian through a deepening of its human reality in reference to the mystery of Jesus Christ. An obvious conclusion to be drawn from this consideration is that church marriage and customary marriage in Africa should not exclude one another, still less be opposed to one another. The task of the churches is to strengthen and develop the institution of marriage as it is found in contemporary African society. Does that mean that Christians can simply extend church recognition to customary marriages? The Roman Catholic Bishop of Eldoret (Kenya), Bishop John Njenga, believes that the regulations of his church "are more and more moving towards the recognition of customary marriages".[27] However, he proposes that certain tests be applied to safeguard the quality of the marriage covenant and to ensure social approval. It has to be admitted that, in view of the threat which modern social change holds for the institutions of customary marriage, it would be unwise for Christians to canonize them without a very thorough investigation and without the explicit assurance that the parties have a genuine understanding of, and commitment to, the ideal of marriage held by Christians. There would also have to be explicit reference to the paschal mystery of Jesus Christ, so that the marriage covenant could be viewed and developed in the light of the faith which the partners share as baptized people.

That being said, the principle must be accepted, of bringing customary and church marriage together, but it must not stop there. The Christian community must act as an animator of the natural community. It must help it to fulfil those functions with regard to marriage and the family which are slipping from its grasp. It must promote community care and support for the marriages which take place in its midst. It must not be content with a celebration only.

Some Christian writers on marriage in Africa have assumed far too readily that Christian marriage is incompatible with the communitarian approach to the family which was traditional in Africa.[28] The assumption was that Christian marriage was identifiable with the western, social model of the autonomous, nuclear family, with neolocal residence; and, of course, the equation made between Christian and statutory marriage encouraged the assumption. It was also frequently suggested that the rights of Christian spouses and parents were infringed by the older members of the family community who took the decisions about the education of the children and the choice of marriage partners. Apart from the question of arranging marriages, the conjugal rights of those who were already married were seldom infringed by other members of the family. The education of children, however, was very much a communal responsibility within the family and children stayed with different categories of relatives at different stages of their upbringing, the result being that they were educated by a community for a community.

Western theologians have often grounded the rights of the parents with regard to the education of their children in the fact of physical generation. The parents have given life to their child, therefore they have the prior right to educate the child for membership of society. It is difficult, however, to object to the traditional African system of communal upbringing without also objecting, for example, to such hallowed institutions as the boarding school in Europe and the West. Parents have the right to delegate their responsibilities where the education of their children is concerned, and it is, in any case, unusual—even in Africa—for decisions regarding the rearing of children to be taken without reference to the children's own parents. It remains a fact that the relatively large family community has the effect of making its members more community conscious in general than does the small, nuclear household. Pope Paul VI went out of his way in 1967 to praise the African sense of family and the moral and religious value of African attachment to the family,[29] and it is surely no accident that the experience of the family community has been made the starting point for a political programme in Tanzania, involving the setting up of village co-operatives—the ideology of *ujamaa* or familyhood. The disappearance of the family community has frequently been predicted by observers of modern Africa, but although it has undergone severe strain, the family community still continues to operate in one way or another. The churches have to recognize its continued existence and to work with it, especially in the area of marriage preparation where the future spouses must be taken for what they are, members of a lineage or family community, and not isolated individuals.

III Models for Pastoral Action

1 *Adapted Marriage Rites*

Those who are reluctant to perform the marriage ceremony anywhere but in the church building are faced with the well-nigh impossible task of focusing a united, customary-cum-Christian celebration on this building. Elements from the customary ceremony would have to be incorporated in the Christian service to such an extent that people recognized the rituals as their own, and accepted the church celebration in lieu of what would normally take place at home. Perhaps the magnitude of the task has daunted the liturgists, for it is a fact that the suggestions for an adapted marriage rite have been extremely half-hearted. Boniface Luykx, in his survey of African liturgical initiatives since the Second Vatican Council, has a diminutive paragraph on the celebration of marriage.[30] He recommends inserting a marriage ceremony into the liturgy of the Easter Vigil, after the adult baptisms have taken place. Essentially it would consist of a verbal exchange of consent, followed by the exchange of rings "or some other, more African symbol" while the faithful sing a song about love to the accompaniment of drums. It is difficult to imagine what African symbol the bride and bridegroom could exchange, but Laurent Mpongo of Zaïre has made the somewhat unimaginative suggestion that European rings be replaced by African bangles.[31] This is just the kind of artificiality one would wish to avoid, for it considers only the materiality of the symbol and not its meaning, and it comes no nearer to communicating this meaning to the African.

A considerably more ambitious suggestion was made as long ago as 1959 by Ben van Amelsvoort.[32] This involved the use of the veil, crown and oil for anointing, important symbols in the southern Nyamwezi and Kimbu area of Tanzania. The parents take part in an interrogation at the church door, but a more important role is played by the bride's paternal aunt and the bridegroom's own witness. The oil is blessed and the priest anoints both bride and bridegroom, after which, with the help of the aunt, the bride is veiled and crowned. The author of this adapted rite did not, unfortunately, feel able at the time of writing to propose that it should replace the regular Christian ritual. He therefore followed it up with the usual ceremony involving exchange of consent and rings. Another suggestion for an adapted marriage rite was published at Gaba, Uganda, in 1975 and slightly modified by Brian Hearne to make it suitable for inter-church marriage celebrations. It formed part of a draft proposal on inter-church marriages presented to the Uganda Joint Christian Council.[33] In this suggested rite the bride's father and bridegroom's father each interrogate their own child to elicit his or her consent to the marriage, after which the bride's father hands his daughter over to the bridegroom. The ring, however, again makes its appearance, since the bridegroom is expected to slip a ring on the finger of the bride after she has been handed over. The ceremony ends with a blessing in which the pastors of the two communions both take part.

Marie-France Perrin-Jassy has pointed out that those African Independent Churches which have stuck to the liturgical formulas of their parent mission churches have had no more success in the area of marriage celebrations than the mission churches themselves.[34] However, Harold Turner gives a fine example of an adapted marriage rite from a West African independent church which manages to dispense with the otherwise ubiquitous ring.[35] The church in question is the Aladura Church, found in several West African countries, notably Nigeria. In the Aladura marriage rite, the ring is replaced by the Bible and the formula "With this ring I thee wed . . ." is altered to the following, as the bridegroom gives the book to the bride:

With this Holy Bible, which is the Word of God and the Spirit written with the prophets of old, the man weds this woman, and with it makes her a covenant in the presence of God and of man today, that he will not divorce her, neither give her place to any other, provided she remains in this word of God. Those whom God has joined together, let no one put asunder.

The idea of the biblical covenant, with, preferably, a further reference to the New Testament, and perhaps even some elements from traditional African covenants, such as the blood-pact, is certainly one worth pursuing in the search for an adapted African marriage rite.

Perhaps the simplest expedients are the most effective in the long run. In the former kingdom of Buganda (Uganda), the custom is for the brother of the bride to give his sister away, and this handing-over of the bride is what constitutes the marriage. The ceremony either takes place at the home of the bride-groom, or, in the case of a church marriage, on the steps of the church building when the marriage service is over. In the Roman Catholic Church in Buganda it is now becoming increasingly common for this handing-over ceremony to take place during the Christian service itself. After the preliminary dialogue before the altar, the brother of the bride steps forward and hands over his sister to the bridegroom using words of his own choosing. When this is done, the bridal couple proceed to exchange consent before the priest and to place rings on each other's fingers.

Marie-France Perrin-Jassy describes the way in which some African Independent Churches in northern Tanzania and southern Kenya have succeeded in Christianizing customary marriage itself and integrating it into the religious and social life of their church community.[36] Clearly, in the last analysis, this is the only realistic way to bring Christian and customary marriage rites together. In the Roho Church the faithful gather in the house of the young man and pray. When a sufficient amount of the bridewealth has been paid, the elders of the church accompany the father of the young man to seek the young woman at her father's homestead and conduct her to her husband's house. Similarly in the Nomiya Church, when the first instalment of bridewealth has been paid, the faithful gather in the chapel to pray before going themselves to find the young woman and bring her to her husband's home. In the Pentecostal Assemblies, on the day set for the marriage, the young woman is customarily carried off by the young man and his friends and brought, not to his house, but to the church first of all, where the marriage is consecrated by the elders and community. These offer interesting solutions to the problem of using the church building in an integrated marriage ceremony. The church building is a stopping-place, either on the way to the bride's house, or on the way to the bridegroom's house.

It is becoming an increasingly common practice in the Roman Catholic Church in some parts of Africa to celebrate a Requiem Mass for the dead at the house of the deceased, and for a priest or catechist to preside at the burial in the family compound. This practice absolves the bereaved family from the tiresome requirement of carrying the body to a distant church and of performing the burial in a cemetery that is untidy and ill-kept. This accommodation to traditional custom in the case of funerals might form a precedent for the celebration of marriage. If Christian marriage was to be celebrated in this way, at the home of the bridegroom, for example, then care would have to be taken to integrate the Christian element into the existing ritual structure, and not attempt to commandeer the whole celebration by imposing a Christian framework on the entire proceedings. The pastor could, for example, take his turn among the relatives and distinguished participants to deliver his speech or homily and elicit a formal Christian response from the bride and bridegroom. If the Christian celebration of marriage is to be a celebration of the whole community, then something on these lines will have to be adopted.

2 *Marriage and Community in the African Independent Churches*
There is no doubt whatever that some African Independent Churches offer their members a more intense experience of community than do the older mission churches. The remark quoted by David Beckmann from a member of the Eden Revival Church in Ghana is, perhaps, typical: "Edenians love their church. They treat each other like blood relatives. There are so many Catholics, you don't even know who they are. But Edenians greet each other on the street like brothers and sisters."[37] Marie-France Perrin-Jassy, who has carried out research among the independent churches of the Luo tribe in northern Tanzania and southern Kenya, argues that these churches offer their members a new experience of community which substitutes for the older lineage or family community,

now no longer equipped to integrate the individual into wider society.

Marie-France makes use of the concept "basic community", a concept which has also been used by the theologian, Karl Rahner.[38] Not every community, not even the local community, is necessarily a basic community. Basic community is defined as the community which provides the point at which the individual is integrated into general society. The bonds between its members are of a personal nature, and act as a kind of hinge between the individual and the world at large. A person's lineage or family is ordinarily his initial basic community. As he grows up he adopts other, successive basic communities. It may be a school class, a peer-group, a work-gang, an office-department, a housing location and so forth. Marie-France demonstrates convincingly that the African Independent Church takes the place of the old basic community, the lineage, for people who find the lineage system inadequate and yet who cannot rise above their own environment. The church community compensates for the frustrations of life in a period of rapid social change and offers a form of ideological brotherhood which performs many of the functions of the traditional family community. It offers a system of mutual help in health and sickness, help both spiritual and material. It relates to every aspect of human existence, and offers solutions that are familiar and acceptable to people who are used to living in small communities. On the one hand, the traditional lineage is not flexible enough to cater for changed modern conditions; on the other, the big, hierarchical organizations of the mission churches appear largely unfamiliar and unadapted to the needs of people at that level.

Two factors ensure the success of the African Independent Churches. One is the size of their communities. They are at their most effective when they number about fifty persons. If they are much bigger, the number of non-active individuals in the community also increases. If they are much smaller, community action is weak, and the group is too small to contain all the elements necessary for survival and growth. The second factor is the community's totalitarian character, its character of "wholeness". It offers the individual a totally new conception of the world, but at the same time holds out the possibility of total community involvement. In other words these churches are creating a "parallel society", a world within a world. The individual must give himself totally to this new world. He or she must constantly wear the religious uniform of the church and must witness at all times through other modes of behaviour to the church's ideals.

Although, as has been pointed out, many of these independent churches have had their difficulties with regard to marriage and family life, some have achieved considerable success. It is often said that these churches owe their success to their tolerant attitude towards polygamy. Marie-France, however, points out that, in reality, they have had a limiting influence on it. The ideal is very definitely that of monogamous, life-long marriage, and social pressure to obtain the realization of this ideal is more easily exercised in a small group than in a large, anonymous one. The church community is able effectively to oppose the family in any conflict of ideal or practice. Moreover, the participation of the community in every stage of preparation for, and celebration of, marriage guarantees respect for the institution of marriage and confers prestige on monogamy and indissolubility. The basic communities of the African Independent Churches offer a lesson in the way the institution of marriage can be strengthened and Christianized through real church-community action.

3 *Christian Basic Community and the Future of Marriage in Africa*
The African Independent Churches are exemplary in several ways, but their major drawback is precisely that they constitute a "parallel society", catering for marginal people. They run the risk of what we earlier termed "privatism" or "particularism". There is no true dialogue between them and other ideologies or value-systems, even though they seem to cater for the changed needs of individuals in the modern world. What they have done really is to re-create the homogeneous community—more flexible, more up to date than the traditional community, it is true, but still homogeneous and unitary. Although independent churches have had brilliant insights in some fields, in most others they remain conservative, unsophisticated, even closed. This is evidenced by their biblical fundamentalism and literalism, their opposition to hospital medicines, their clinging to esoteric liturgical usages and many other characteristics. One fact which Marie-France does not fail to notice in her study of African Independent Churches is their neglect of the Eucharist. Celebration of the Eucharist plays an insignificant

part in their community life and worship. Many reasons can be advanced for this. One is the unfamiliarity of the Eucharist among the mission churches themselves, due to a shortage of ordained ministers. For many ordinary Christians in African out-stations, celebration of the Eucharist is still a rare occurrence. Another reason is the unfamiliarity and unavailability of the Eucharistic materials, bread and wine. Yet another reason is the Old Testament emphasis in so many of the independent churches, an emphasis which finds an echo in the lives of their members, with their family loyalties and their closeness to nature. The absence, or at least the relative insignificance, of the Eucharist in the independent churches means that in practice the centrality of the paschal mystery of Christ may be threatened. Instead of faith which sees every aspect of life in the light of the death and resurrection of Jesus Christ, the church member cultivates a totalitarian allegiance to his or her church community, an allegiance expressed in rigorous, material and social forms, such as the continuous wearing of a religious costume.

The churches must avoid setting up "parallel communities", but they need to exploit the notion of basic community. This does not mean creating a substitute basic community artificially. What it means is searching out and identifying the real basic communities in which people live and through which they integrate into the contemporary, pluralistic society. It means a sub-division of our administrative "police-station" parishes and sub-parishes (to borrow a colourful image from Rahner!).[39] It means recognizing a multiplicity of small groups, possessing the cohesion and the capacity for community action. These must be worshipping communities, with a prayer life of their own, and ultimately they must be Eucharistic communities. A great many problems will have to be worked out. The administration of these basic communities will raise all kinds of difficulties, and there is the basic question of reshaping the minstry to cater for their catechetical and sacramental needs. But it does not seem that there is any other alternative to creating this new type of community if we are really to meet the challenge of the world in which we live.

In the rural areas it may well be that basic community can be identified in the new village co-operatives that are coming into existence. It was highly significant that the World Assembly of Christian Family Movements chose Tanzania as its venue in

1974 and conveyed all the participants to *ujamaa* villages, to share the life of these communities for three days.[40] The concept of *ujamaa*, or the extension of family-community principles to a whole village community was highly appreciated by the Assembly both as an initiative deriving from the family itself, and as an environment in which the family could integrate with the wider community. Christian faith would come to strengthen and deepen this ideology.

What should unite the basic community, whatever shape or form it takes, is not the externals of religious dress or public manifestation, but inner faith. Its unifying principle is the experience of Jesus Christ, the Risen Lord, in their community —Jesus Christ experienced through common meditation on Scripture, through the sharing of prayer, and through sacramental celebration. This encounter with Christ, if it is genuine, will make them sensitive to the wider community and attentive to other voices around them. It will enable a process of dialogue to begin in which the basic Christian community becomes a healing and reconciling agent in society.

It is against the background of the basic Christian community that we must see the development of structures for the strengthening and stabilizing of human marriage institutions. In the basic community the right climate will be created for fostering Christian ideals and obtaining their realization through community action. Sex-education for the young and preparation for marriage could also be organized on a community basis; and so, with the necessary expert help, could marriage counselling and facing up to the difficulties and tensions of married people. One thing is abundantly clear: the fundamental ingredient of the basic Christian community must be the community of love that exists between husband and wife, parents and children. This must be true, whatever the basis of community may be, whether it is neighbourhood, work situation or any other principle. It is also obvious that the basic Christian community cannot be a source of division in the wider community. In its character of reconciling agent, it must help to strengthen the bonds of society through dialogue, and it must strengthen equally the values of the traditional family community and the ethnic group, for as long as these remain social realities with which the individual must reckon.

The problems which beset the churches in Africa in the field of marriage and family morality cannot be effectively tackled in isolation. They must form part of the general reconsideration of the churches' role in society which is at present taking place. Undoubtedly, the future of Christian marriage and the Christian family in Africa depends on the shape of the Church to come. The shape of this future Church must give full scope to the family as a creative force for the improvement of the quality of human life, and for the realization of the Church's own mission of reconciliation and unity in the world.

References: Chapter Eight

1 Makubire, 1974.
2 Makubire, 1974 and Kirima, 1974.
3 Kirima, 1974.
4 Mutiso Mbinda, 1974.
5 Whooley in Verryn, 1975b, p. 259.
6 Kirima, 1974.
7 This is the case among the Kimbu of Tanzania. Aylward Shorter participated in a number of Kimbu customary marriage celebrations in 1965–7. The bride herself sat on the knees of the bridegroom's mother and a girl of the bride's family sat on the knees of another woman from the bridegroom's family, while a boy from the bridegroom's family sat on the knees of a woman from the bride's family.
8 Kirima, 1974.
9 Mutiso Mbinda, 1974.
10 Whooley in Verryn, 1975b, *passim*.
11 Kasaka, 1972, CROMIA/14, and Kasaka, 1976.
12 Aquina, 1975, I, pp. 45–6.
13 Kayoya, Michel, 1970, *Entre Deux Mondes*, Bujumbura, p. 126 (tr. Shorter). Aylward Shorter and Wandera Chagenda are currently working on an English translation of this book.
14 Thomas and Chisanga, 1976, pp. 12–13.
15 *Ibid.*, p. 19.
16 Holway, 1974, p. 9.
17 Boerakker, 1975, p. 45.
18 Whooley in Verryn, 1975b, pp. 245–378.
19 Boerakker, 1975.
20 Thomas and Chisanga, 1976, pp. 34–6.
21 Holway, 1974, p. 7.
22 Thomas and Chisanga, 1976, p. 38.
23 Holway, 1974, pp. 13–14.
24 Perrin-Jassy (Marie-France), 1973, p. 159.

25 Conway, 1975, *passim*.
26 Much of this section is based on lectures at the AMECEA Pastoral Institute by Brian Hearne.
27 Njenga, 1974, p. 121.
28 An example is that of John M. Robinson, 1964, *Family Apostolate and Africa*, Dublin; another is Adu, A. K., 1967, "Christian Marriage and Family life in Ghana" in *Christians in Ghanaian Life*, Accra, p. 38.
29 *Africae Terrarum*, Message to Africa, 1967, no. 9.
30 Luykx, 1974, p. 144.
31 Mpongo, 1968.
32 van Amelsvoort, 1959, pp. 111–15.
33 Hearne, B. and Lucas, D. C. (eds.), 1975, *Celebration*, Gaba Pastoral Paper No. 39; and Draft Proposal on Inter-Church Marriage by Kampala Ecumenical Study Group 1975 (mimeographed).
34 Perrin-Jassy, 1973, pp. 160–1.
35 Turner, 1967, II, p. 239.
36 Perrin-Jassy, 1973, pp. 188–9.
37 Beckmann, 1975, p. 86.
38 Rahner, 1974, *The Shape of the Church to Come*, London, Chap. 3; Perrin-Jassy, 1973, pp. 246–7.
39 Rahner, 1974.
40 cf. Lubowa, 1974 (CROMIA/28).

Appendix I

Table 1:

CROMIA Steering Committee

Chairman:	Rev. Ralph Hatendi (Anglican, Zambia).
Executive Secretary:	Rev. Aylward Shorter (Roman Catholic, Uganda).
	Rev. Sr. Mary Aquina (Roman Catholic, Rhodesia).
	Rev. Dr. David Barrett (Anglican, Kenya).
	Rev. Stephen Kauta-Msiska (Presbyterian, Malawi).
	Rev. Pastor (later Rt. Rev. Bishop) Eliewaha Mshana (Lutheran, Tanzania).
	Rev. Joseph O'Doy (Roman Catholic, Uganda).
	Rev. Canon Trevor Verryn (Anglican, South Africa).
	Rev. Professor Tjaard Hommes (Congregationalist, U.S.A.).

Table 2:

CROMIA Panel of Consultants

Rev. Adrian Hastings (Roman Catholic, England).

Rt. Rev. Bishop Donald Jacobs (Mennonite, Kenya).

Rt. Rev. Bishop Patrick Kalilombe (Roman Catholic, Malawi).

Rt. Rev. Bishop Josiah Kibira (Lutheran, Tanzania).

Mrs. Bernadette Kunambi (Roman Catholic, Tanzania).

Rev. George Mambo (Special representative of the All Africa Conference of Churches, Kenya).

Rev. Canon Professor John Mbiti (Anglican, Switzerland).

Rt. Rev. Bishop Raphael Ndingi (Roman Catholic, Kenya).

Rev. Hans Staub (Lutheran, Tanzania—replaced at a later stage by Rev. Edward Mwangosi).

Rev. Patrick Whooley (Roman Catholic, South Africa).

Appendix II

CROMIA Circulars

CROMIA No.	Date	Writer	Title
1	January 1971	Shorter, A.	"Short History of events Leading to the Convening of the Planning Meeting".
2	January 1971	Shorter, A.	"Some First Very Tentative Hypotheses".
8	April 1971	Shorter, A.	"Report on the Planning Meeting" (Gaba).
9	June 1971	Kataza, E.	"Minutes of the Planning Meeting" (Gaba).
10	August 1971	Kataza, E.	"Information Bulletin No. 1".
11	October 1971	Shorter, A.	"Notes on Traditional and Christian Marriage in Africa".
12	November 1971	Shorter, A.	"Progress Report, for Information of the Uganda Joint Christian Council".
13	February 1972a	Shorter, A.	"Information Bulletin".
14	February 1972	Kasaka, N.	"Patterns of Marriage in Rural Re-Settlement Areas of Tanzania".
15	February 1972	Boivin, M.	"The Specificity of Christian Ethics, With Particular Reference to the Ethics of Marriage".
16	March 1972	Ulbrich, H. and Driessche, J. van	"Some Elements for a Possible Solution of the

16	March 1972—*cont.*		Crisis in Christian Marriage Life in Africa and Especially in Rhodesia".
17	March 1972	Ssennyonga, J.	"Christianity as a Factor in African Marriage Patterns".
18	April 1972b	Shorter, A.	"Progress Report to the Uganda Christian Council".
19	May 1972	Kataza, E.	"Bibliography".
20	December 1972	Nomenyo, S.	"Sexuality, Marriage, Family".
21	April 1973a	Shorter, A.	"Report of the First Executive Committee Meeting" (Blantyre).
22	June 1973b	Shorter, A.	"Marriage and Attitudes to Marriage Among Christians in Rural Uganda".
23	July 1973c	Shorter, A.	"Information Bulletin".
24	July 1973	Hart, R.	"Attitudes on Marriage in Nassa Tanzania".
25	January 1974b	Shorter, A.	"Progress Report".
26	May 1974	Holway, J. D.	"Marriage in Nairobi" (Summary of Area Study).
27	August 1974c	Shorter, A.	"Progress Report".
28	August 1974	Lubowa, F. A.	"Report on the World Assembly: Familia '74 in Dar-es-Salaam".
29	December 1974d	Shorter, A.	"Final Information Bulletin 1974".
30	December 1974e	Shorter, A.	"Report of the East African Colloquium on the Theology of Marriage" (Nairobi).
31	June 1975d	Shorter, A.	"Report on the Final Executive Committee Meeting and Central African Colloquium on the Theology of Marriage" (Chilema).

Appendix III

Area Studies commissioned by CROMIA

Aquina, Sister, 1975, "African Marriage and Family Life in Rhodesia", Part I, Eastern Rhodesia.

Aquina, Sister, 1975, "African Marriage and Family Life in Rhodesia" Part II, Nambya and Tongaland.

Boerakker, Hans, 1975, "Church Marriage in Eastern Uganda".

Conway, Brendan, 1975, "A Survey of Marriage Laws in East, Central and Southern Africa".

Holway, James D., 1974, "Marriage in Nairobi".

Kauta S., Welshman H., and Gastonguay D., 1975, "Malawi Marriage Research".

Kasaka, Njelu M., 1976, "Factors Affecting Christian Marriage in Rural Re-Settlement Areas—Tabora, Moshi and Chunya".

Peskin, Martin, 1975, "Christianity and Marriage in Soweto".

Shorter, Aylward, 1975b, "All-Africa Survey".

Spiegel, Andrew, 1975, "Christianity, Marriage and Migrant Labour in Lesotho".

Thomas, Norman and Chisanga, Daniel, 1976, "Marriage Patterns in Kitwe" (Zambia).[1]

Whooley, Patrick, 1975b, "Marriage in Africa—Ciskei" (South Africa).

[1] In 1973 Dr. Wim van Binsbergen commenced a study of Marriage Patterns in Lusaka (Zambia) for CROMIA. This study was abandoned because of ill-health, but Dr. van Binsbergen kindly allowed Dr. Norman Thomas to adapt his interview schedule for use in Kitwe.

Appendix IV

Theological Papers commissioned by CROMIA

Arden, Archbishop, Donald, 1975, "Divorce, Remarriage and Nullity".

Ashby, Godfrey, W., 1974, "Sex Revolution".

Berglund, Axel-Ivar, 1975, "The Biblical Concepts of Man/Woman Relations".

Blum, William G. 1974, "Childlessness and Christian Marriage".

Chima, Alex, 1975, "The Sex Revolution".

Dwane, Sigquibo, 1975, "Polygamy".

Edwards, Felicity, 1975, "Designing a Theology of Sexuality".

Gaybba, Brian, 1975, "The Remarriage of Divorced Persons".

Kakokota, P. Stephen, 1975, "Remarriage of Divorced Persons".

Kalanda, Paul, 1974, "Christian Marriage and Widow Inheritance in Africa".

Kanyikwa, John L., 1974, "Family Planning".

Kirima, Nicodemus, 1974, "Community Interest in African Marriage".

Lamburn, Robin, 1974a, "Polygamy".

Lamburn, Robin, 1974b, "Matriliny".

Lebona, Evelyn A., 1975, "Reality of Marriage".

Mahara, Maqalaka, 1975, "Equality in Marriage".

Makubire, Harry, 1975, "Community Interest in African Marriage".

Mutiso-Mbinda, John S., 1974, "Community Interest in African Marriage".

Ncozana, Silas, 1975, "Problem of Matriliny".

Nkaisule, J. A., 1974a, "Equality in Marriage".

Nkaisule, J. A., 1974b, "Sex Revolution".

O'Flynn, Anthony, 1975, "Divorce and Remarriage".

Okwachi, Paschal, 1974, "Inter-Church Marriages".

Peters, Louis, 1975, "Sacramentality in General and Marriage".

Pretorius, Hennie, 1975, "Childlessness'.

Tau, John, 1975, "Pastoral and Catechetical Approaches to Marriage".

Taylor, Gerald, 1974, "Recent Developments in Canonical Legislation, Jurisprudence and Church Practice. Declaration of Nullity and Dissolution Cases".

Whooley, Patrick, 1975a, "Equality in Marriage".

Whooley, Patrick, 1974, "Childlessness—Some Comments".

Whyte, Stephen, 1975, "Inter-Church Marriage".

Whyte, Stephen, 1974, "Remarriage of Divorced Persons— Some Comments".

N.B. The date of those papers included in Verryn (ed.) is given as 1975, although they were presented in 1974.

Appendix V

Other Books and Articles relating to CROMIA or cited in the text

All Africa Conference of Churches, 1972, "Consultation on the Challenges of Family Education in Africa in the 70's", November–December 1972 (mimeographed), Yaoundé, Cameroun, 2 vols.

All Africa Conference of Churches in Collaboration with the World Council of Churches, 1963, *Report of the All Africa Seminar on the Christian Home and Family Life*, Mindolo/Geneva.

Amelsvoort, Ben van, 1959, "Suggestion for an adapted Marriage Ceremony", in *AFER*, Vol. I, No. 2, pp. 111–15.

Barrett, David B, 1968, *Schism and Renewal in Africa*, Nairobi.

Beckmann, David M., 1975, *Eden Revival: Spiritual Churches in Ghana*, St. Louis, Mo.

Blum, William G., 1972, *The Unity of Christian Marriage Considered in Relation to the Polygynous Cultures of Uganda*. (Dissertation presented to the Alfonsian Academy.) Kisubi, Uganda.

Boerakker, Hans, 1972, "The Influence of the Catholic Church on Marriage in Padhola" (mimeographed). Sociology working paper No. 126, Makerere, Uganda.

Bucher, Hubert, 1974, "Youth's Love Problems Tackled by a Columnist—an Analysis of the 'Dear Sophie' column in *The World*", *AFER*, Vol. XVI, No. 4, pp. 401–8.

Catholic Priests' Association of Kenya (CPAK), 1975, "Seminar on Marriage" (typescript).

Colson, Elizabeth, 1960, *The Social Organization of the Gwembe Tonga*, Manchester.

Commission on the Christian Doctrine of Marriage, 1971, *Marriage, Divorce and the Church*, London.

Consilium de Laicis, 1974, "Marriage and the Family", *The Laity Today*. Nos. 17–18.

Deniel, Raymond, 1975, *Religions Dans La Ville* (INADES), Abidjan.

Doucette, Melvin, 1972, "A Marriage Catechumenate", *AFER*, Vol. XIV, No. 2, pp. 108–18.

Douglas, Mary, 1969, "Is Matriliny Doomed in Africa?" in Douglas M. and Kaberry P.M. (eds.) *Man in Africa*, London, pp. 121–36.

Enderley, Gladys, 1972, "Factors Contributing to Marital Harmony and Disharmony", *AACC: Consultation on Challenges to Family Education in the 1970s*, Yaoundé, Cameroun, II, pp. 26–36.

Family Planning Programmes, 1975, *Population Reports*, Department of Medical and Public Affairs, The George Washington University Medical Center, Washington D.C.

Gachuhi, Mugo J., "Marriage and Prostitution: a Theoretical Consideration", Working Paper No. 6, Institute for Development Studies, University of Nairobi (mimeographed).

Häring, Bernard, 1975, 'Notes on Lectures at Gaba Pastoral Institute, 19th–20th August 1975".

Hastings, Adrian, 1973, *Christian Marriage in Africa*, London.

Hearne, Brian, 1975, "The Sacramentality of Marriage", CPAK (typescript—see Catholic Priests' Association of Kenya).

Hearne, Brian, 1976, "Theology, Basic Course", AMECEA Pastoral Institute Eldoret, 1976, p. 30 (mimeographed).

Holway, James D., 1973, "Marriage as a Factor Affecting the Transfer of Religious Allegiance in Kenya" (typescript, thesis presented to University of Nairobi).

Hillman, Eugene, 1975, *Polygamy Reconsidered*, New York.

Hochstenbach, Gerard, 1968, "Towards a True Christianization of Marriage and Family Life in the Lower Shire Valley of Malawi". Essay submitted for the Diploma of Pastoral Studies, Pastoral Institute of Eastern Africa, Gaba.

Huber, Hugo, 1973, *Marriage and the Family in Rural Kenya*, Friburg.

Huet, Edmund van, 1975, "The Marriage Catechumenate", Catechetics Course, Gaba Pastoral Institute.

Hulsen, C., and Mertens, F., *Survey of the Church in Ghana*, Chapter Eight: "Marriage and Family".

International Justice and Peace Commission of the Episcopal Conference of England and Wales, 1974, *The Population Problem and the Church*, London.

Kibirige, Emmanuel, 1974, "Summary Report on the Seminar on Moral and Religious Issues in Population Dynamics and Development in Africa", Accra (typescript).

Kirwen, Michael C., 1974, "The Christian Prohibition of the African Leviratic Custom" (typescript, Dissertation for Degree of Ph.D. presented to University of Toronto).

Kofon, Engelbert N., 1974, "Polygyny in Pre-Christian Bafut and New Moral Theological Perspectives" (mimeographed: Thesis presented to Alfonsian Academy).

Lamburn, Robin, 1975, "Report on Discussions at St. Cyprian's College, Lindi" (typescript).

Lewis, I. M., 1962, *Marriage and Family in Northern Somaliland*, London.

Lufuluabo, François-Marie, 1969, *Mariage Coutumier et Mariage Chrétien Indissoluble*, Kinshasa.

Luykx, Boniface, 1974, *Culte Chrétien en Afrique après Vatican II*, Fribourg.

Mayala, A., and Balina, A., 1970, "Traditional Marriage in Tanzania Today" (mimeographed: Kipalapala).

Mbiti, John S., 1973, *Love and Marriage in Africa*, London.

Mitchell, J. Clyde, 1956, *The Yao Village*, Manchester.

Molnos, Angela, 1973, *Cultural Source Materials for Population Planning in East Africa*, 4 vols., Nairobi.

Mpongo, Laurent, 1968, *Pour une Anthropologie Chrétienne du Mariage au Congo*, Kinshasa.

Murray, Francis, 1969, "Trends in Church Membership from 1957–1967 in Tanzania as Evidenced in Catholic Statistical Returns" (mimeographed).

Njenga, Bishop John, 1974, *Customary African Marriage, AFER*, Vol. XVI, Nos. 1 and 2, pp. 115–22.

Northern Rhodesia Council of Social Service, 1961, *Marriage and the Family Report of the Annual Conference*, Lusaka.

Paul VI, Pope, 1967, *Africae Terrarum: Message to Africa*, St. Paul Editions, Kampala.

Perlman, Melvin L., 1963, "Toro Marriage" (thesis presented to Oxford University for degree of Ph.D., mimeographed).

Perrin-Jassy (Rot), Marie-France, 1973, *Basic Community in the African Churches*, New York.

Rahner, Karl, 1974, *The Shape of the Church to Come*, London, tr. Edward Quinn.

Rhodesia Catholic Bishops' Conference, 1973, "Interdiocesan African Marriage Commission". Report and Recommendations (mimeographed).

Richards, Audrey, 1940, *Bemba Marriage and Present Economic Conditions*, Rhodes Livingstone Paper No. 4, Manchester.

Ricoeur, Paul et al., 1964, "Sexuality and the Modern World", A symposium, *Cross Currents*, Vol. XIV, No. 2, Spring, pp. 129–269.

Rooyackers, Marinus, "Statements on *Humanae Vitae* by the Bishops of Different Countries" (mimeographed).

Sarpong, Peter Kwasi, Bishop, 1967, "African Values and Catechetics—The Matrilineal Father", *Teaching All Nations*, Vol. IV, No. 1, pp. 162–173.

Shorter, Aylward, 1969, "Christian and Traditional African Ideals of Marriage and Family Life", in *Essays in Pastoral Anthropology*, Gaba Pastoral Paper No. 5, pp. 12–22.

Shorter, Aylward, 1927c, "Trends Being Revealed by the Churches' Research on Marriage in Africa". Paper presented to AACC "Consultation on Challenges to Family Education in the '70s" (mimeographed), Yaoundé, Cameroun, Vol. II, pp. 11–25.

—— 1974a, "Parental Ideals and Family Institutions in Africa: Factors of Relevance for Population and Development". Paper presented to the IED "Seminar, Accra, on Moral and Religious Issues in Population Dynamics and Development in Africa" (typescript).

—— 1974f, "What's Wrong with Marriage and Family Life in Africa Today", *Sharing*, June, Vol. 6, No. 3, pp. 6–8.

—— 1975a, "The Pastoral Problem of the Falling Christian Marriage Rate in Uganda", Paper presented to Association of East African Theological Colleges' Meeting, 1975 (mimeographed).

—— 1975c, 'Inter-Church and Inter-faith Marriages", Paper presented to the Kampala Ecumenical Study group (mimeographed).

Shorter, Aylward and Kataza, Eugene, 1972d, "The Churches' Research on Marriage in Africa" (CROMIA), *AFER*, Vol. XIV, No. 2, pp. 145–9.

Southern African Bishops' Conference, 1974, "Pastoral Directive on Family Planning from the South African Bishops' Conference", *AFER*, Vol. XVI, 3, pp. 345–8.

Spiegel, Andrew David, 1975, "Christian Marriage and Migrant Labour in a Lesotho Village", Dissertation submitted for the degree of Bachelor of Arts (Honours) in Social Anthropology. University of Cape Town (mimeographed).

Swantz, Lloyd, 1970, "The Migrant and the Church", *Sharing*, II, No. 6, August, pp. 5–6.

Trobisch, Walter, 1968, *I Married You*, London.

Turner, Victor W., 1957, "Schism and Continuity in an African —*Church of the Lord*, Oxford, 2 vols.

Turner, Victor W., 1957, "Schism and Continuity in African Society", A study of Ndembu village life, Manchester University Press.

Verryn, Trevor D. (ed), 1975, *Church and Marriage in Modern Africa*, Johannesburg. (Contains the Southern African Area studies and most of the Laverna Theological Papers.)

White, Carolyn, 1973, "The Politico–Legal Status of Women in Uganda", *Presence*, Vol. VI, No. 1, pp. 23–7.

Yeld, R. E., 1966, "Marriage Patterns Among the Kiga of Kigezi" (South West Uganda). EASSC (mimeographed).

Zwarthoed, J. N., 1973, "Note on Marriage in the Apostolic Vicariate of Jimma" (mimeographed).

Appendix VI

Glossary of Terms

affinity relationship through marriage of oneself or one's blood relatives.

"agape" self-giving love.

androcentricity man-centredness, male dominance.

avoidance social customs regulating relationships between "in-laws".

basic community group of persons through which the individual is integrated in general society.

bestiality coition of a human being with an animal.

bride-service work done by the bridegroom for his bride's parents.

bridewealth payment of cattle or other stock, goods or money by the bridegroom's family to the bride's family (cf. "dowry", "bride-price", and other terms used).

care of widows When a widow's sexual, procreative and material needs are looked after by a male relative of her husband, with or without a form of marriage (see: levirate).

church marriage rate number of church marriages per 1,000 of church population per year.

clan social category based on putative kinship and descent, with common nomenclature, totems, taboos, ritual areas, etc.

clandestine polygamy husband with more than one wife, each of whom is ignorant of his other marriages.

communitarian marriage/family family or marriage in which a community of relatives is involved or interested; also, in many cases, the wider community.

concubinage cohabitation for a length of time of a couple without formal marriage.

consanguinity blood relationship.

crude polygamy rate number of married women for each married man in a given population.

diriment impediment impediment which invalidates a marriage (see: impediment).

elopement marriage marriage which begins with elopement and without parental consent, or negotation between the families (see: self-contracted marriage and "U.D.I." marriage).

endogamy marriage within a given social group.

ethnic group See: tribe.

exogamy Marriage with a partner who does not belong to one's social group.

extended family See: family community.

family community community of blood relatives, descended from a common ancestor alive or dead, co-operating and sharing responsibilities between households for family affairs (see: extended family, lineages).

familism when the interests of the individual are sacrificed to those of the family.

fertility-orientated marriage when a marriage partner is valued mainly or solely for his/her ability to sire or bear children.

homogamy the principle of persons marrying those with similar characteristics as themselves.

homosexuality attraction to, and/or carnal relationships with, a person of the same sex.

impediment external circumstance that renders a marriage invalid or unlawful.

inter-church marriage   marriage between persons who belong to different churches.

inter-ethnic marriage   marriage between persons who belong to different tribes or ethnic groups.

inter-faith marriage   marriage between a Christian and a non-Christian.

inter-racial marriage   marriage between persons who belong to different races.

joking-relationships   custom of formal obscenity, intimacy, buffoonery between relatives who are usually first generation descendants in families united by marriage. It is usually cross-sexual.

levirate, leviratic custom   when a man takes his brother's widow and begets children by her to be the dead man's heirs (see related concept: care of widows).

lineage   See: family community, extended family.

marriage by capture   when marriage is begun by the physical abduction of the bride (see: *thwala*).

marriage catechumenate   catechetical preparation for marriage; or social, psychological and sexual initiation to marriage for couples seriously intending marriage (see: marriage in stages).

marriage in stages   See: marriage catechumenate.

matriarchy   political/social dominance of women.

matriliny   descent system according to which name, status, property, etc., are inherited from one's mother's family.

monogamy   marriage of one man and one woman.

mono-polygamy   situation of a monogamously married man obliging his wife through threats of desertion to permit him to have a concubine.

negotiated marriages   marriages which begin through negotiations between the two families.

neolocality   when the newly married couple takes up residence in a new place, not the homestead of either family.

nominal reincarnation custom of bestowing names of grandparents on grandchildren, and belief that there is a spiritual relationship between the ancestor and his/her namesake.

nuclear family/household relating to the basic unit of husband, wife and their own children.

nullity judicial decision that there never was a legal marriage in a given case.

Nuptial Mass Eucharist celebrated on the occasion of a Roman Catholic wedding and incorporating the solemn or Nuptial blessing.

"oikonomia" power claimed by the Eastern Churches from Christ to find pastoral solutions in individual (marriage) cases which the general law cannot solve.

"patria potestas" See: patriarchy.

patriarchy political/social rule of men in a patrilineal system, male domination.

Pauline Privilege exception based on I Cor. 7:12–15, according to which a marriage between a baptized person and a non-Christian can be dissolved if the latter deserts the Christian partner or refuses to live with him/her without serious danger to faith or morals.

person-orientated marriage marriage which has primarily the good of persons themselves in view, spouses, children, and relationships in the family community.

Petrine Privilege various extensions and applications of the Pauline Privilege by Popes to cover cases of polygamy and separation over great distances.

polyandry marriage of one woman to several men.

polygamy generic name for polyandry and polygyny; or synonym for polygyny.

polygyny (polygamy) marriage of one man to several women.

radical healing See: *sanatio in radice*

Requiem Mass Roman Catholic Eucharistic Celebration on the occasion of a funeral or service for the dead.

sacramentality effective sign value of created things, particularly of human relationships.

"sanatio in radice" a fiction of law according to which a marriage is validated after an impediment has ceased or been dispensed with, and without the need for a renewal of consent.

self-contracted marriage See: elopement marriage and "U.D.I." marriage.

serial monogamy See: successive polygamy.

sex-ratio the comparative numbers of men and women in a given population.

simultaneous polygamy See: polygamy, polygyny—having more than one wife at the same time.

successive polygamy taking a second wife without formal divorce or separation from the first; marriage to second wife after effectively deserting the first.

"thwala" See: marriage by capture; Xhosa word for the custom.

trial marriage marriage that is conditional upon compatibility and fertility.

tribe social grouping, formerly self-subsisting, and politically autonomous, with its own language, culture and institutions.

"U.D.I." marriage See: elopement marriage and self-contracted marriage. "U.D.I."=Unilateral declaration of independence.

"ujamaa" "familyhood", socio-political ideology of Tanzania advocating the setting up of village co-operatives or block-farms.

uxorilocality when the married couple live at the homestead of the wife's family.

virilocality when the married couple live at the homestead of the husband's family.

Appendix VII

Abbreviations

AACC   All Africa Conference of Churches.
AFER   African Ecclesiastical Review.
AMECEA   Association of Episcopal Conferences in Eastern Africa.
CPAK   Catholic Priests' Association of Kenya.
CROMIA   Churches' Research on Marriage in Africa.
EASSC   East African Social Sciences Conference.
IED   International Education Development Inc.
MISSIO   Pontifical Mission Aid Societies of Germany.
SPCK   Society for Promoting Christian Knowledge.
WCC   World Council of Churches.

NOTE

At the time of going to press it has been announced in Kenya that a new marriage bill will be debated in Parliament. The intention of this bill is to give effect to the recommendations of the Commission of the Law of Marriage and Divorce of 1968 (otherwise known as the Spry Commission). As we note in this book, the Tanzanian Law of Marriage at 1971 follows the provisions of the Spry Commission very closely. The Kenyan marriage bill departs from the Spry Commission's recommendations on one or two points. The most controversial clause, No. 150, imposes a maximum penalty of six months' imprisonment on married persons who have sexual intercourse with persons other than their spouse. The Spry Commission recommended compensatory damages for adultery, not punitive measures. This is more in line with African tradition, and it is doubtful if a prison sentence will be at all helpful in restoring good relations between spouses after an act of adultery.

Index